MOTHERS IN ACADEMIA

Mothers in Academia

Edited by
Mari Castañeda and Kirsten Isgro

COLUMBIA UNIVERSITY PRESS NEW YORK

Columbia University Press
Publishers Since 1893
New York   Chichester, West Sussex
cup.columbia.edu

Library of Congress Cataloging-in-Publication Data
  Mothers in academia / edited by Mari Castañeda and Kirsten Isgro.
       p.   cm.
  Includes bibliographical references and index.
  ISBN 978-0-231-16004-9 (cloth : alk. paper) — ISBN 978-0-231-16005-6 (pbk. : alk. paper) —
  ISBN 978-0-231-53458-1 (e-book)
  1. Women in higher education—United States 2. Working mothers—United States. 3. Work
  and family—United States. 4. Work-life balance—United States. I. Castañeda, Mari II. Isgro,
  Kirsten Lynn, 1965–

LC1567.M68 2013
378.0082—dc23
                                                            2012033019

Columbia University Press books are printed on permanent and durable acid-free paper.

Printed in the United States of America

Cover design and image: Martin Hinze

CONTENTS

ACKNOWLEDGMENTS

FIRST AND FOREMOST, we thank our immediate and extended families, without whose love and support this project and our lives as mothers in academia would not be possible. In addition, we thank the many feminist activists-scholars who have paved the way for us to produce scholarship, teach classes, and theorize motherhood in the flesh. Without the work of these women—many of whom are cited in the forthcoming chapters—the very concepts of mothering as a political, emotional, and personal act would be decidedly undertheorized. We are grateful to be part of a growing body of literature that has collectively generated and informed how we think and rethink our roles as parents, teachers, citizens, and intellectuals. We thank the amazing contributors to this volume for their thoughtful efforts to make their personal stories public as part of that legacy. We also thank the numerous other women who shared their stories as mothers in the academy, but who were not able to be part of this final publication due to limited space.

As with any edited anthology, there is a long list of people who made this book possible. We thank the peer reviewers, staff, and editors (Jennifer Perillo and Stephen Wesley) at Columbia University Press for their insightful and productive feedback; Annie Barva for the copyediting; the University of Massachusetts–Amherst and Five Colleges community, especially the Department of Communication; the Department of Communication at the State University of New York–Plattsburgh, especially Shakuntala Rao; Bohyeong Kim for research assistance; the National Association for Chicana and Chicano Studies and the Mujeres Activas en Letras y Cambios Social for accepting conference presentations on the topic; and a large network of extended family and friends who provided feedback and support throughout the process of editing the book.

In addition, Kirsten owes an enormous debt of gratitude to Mari for asking her to be part of this project at a time when such pursuits were crucial to her emotional and professional well-being. As a recent graduate and a new mom with sixteen-month-old twins, Kirsten had just found out that one of her daughters had a rare and fatal degenerative disease. Specific staff members, faculty, and students at the Weismann Center for Leadership at Mount Holyoke College were instrumental in helping her transition to parenthood within academia under extremely trying circumstances; thanks also to Dr. Lois Brown, Michelle Deal, Kim Parent, Janet Lansberry, Patricia Scigliano, Jennifer Curran, and many fabulous students from the Speaking, Arguing, and Writing Program. Lori Walters-Kramer gave a careful reading of previous versions of this manuscript, and Eric Ronnis offered thoughtful conversation about being a parent in academia. Much appreciation and love to the Elson-Patch family, who provided necessary respite and haven in some very beautiful places as we planned, wrote, and organized this book project. Kirsten has tremendous love for and gratitude to her partner, Tom Schicker, who for more than twenty years has been a source of companionship, encouragement, frustration, laughs, and unconditional support. Without his constant care and attention to their daughters, Sylvie and Uma, this book may never have come to fruition.

Mari thanks Kirsten for her compassionate engagement in the process of writing and editing this volume as well as for embodying a truly feminist demeanor of heartfelt collegiality and friendship. She also thanks Las Profes Online Writing Group (Mérida Rúa, Lorena Garcia, Amanda Lewis, Martha Fuentes-Bautista, and Jillian Baez) for their encouragement throughout this life-changing endeavor, the UMass Post-ISHA women's group (especially Betsy Krause), and Susan Davis for planting the seed for this project long ago in her doctoral communication course at the University of California–San Diego. Mari is also grateful to her family: her mother, Guadalupe Hernandez, who reared her and her four siblings (Veronica Jiménez, Andrés Castañeda, Margarita Luna, Joaquín Castañeda) under difficult circumstances but persevered with boundless love and a fierce commitment to continuing en la lucha, as well as her siblings, her in-laws (Chris Jiménez, Vanessa Castañeda, Orlando Luna), and her nieces and nephews (Devina and Alma Jiménez; Tessa, Sienna, and Andrés Castañeda; Emilio and Elias Luna), who provided her with an enormous amount of joy and reprieve from academic life. Last but not least, Mari is full of gratitude to and love for her husband, Joseph Krupczynski, a co-conspirator in life and in social justice struggles inside and outside academia, and her teenage son, Miguel Angel Paredes. Mijo, you went to grad school with me, moved three thousand miles so I could begin my professorial career, and have seen the joys and challenges of academic life. Your love has sustained me all these years, y sin tí, este libro no sería posible. Te quiero mucho.

    Mil gracias to all!

Mari Castañeda, Amherst, Massachusetts
Kirsten Isgro, Plattsburgh, New York

MOTHERS IN ACADEMIA

INTRODUCTION

Speaking Truth to Power to Change the Ivory Tower

Mari Castañeda and Kirsten Isgro

WE MET in the autumn of 2000 in western Massachusetts, when both of us were embarking on new academic journeys: Mari was beginning her first professorial job fresh out of graduate school (a Chicana from the University of California–San Diego), with a five-year-old son in tow, and Kirsten was returning to her doctoral studies after a decade-long hiatus from graduate school. Mari relocated her family from Los Angeles, and Kirsten relocated from Vermont with her partner of five years and her aging dog. Both of us became parents while in graduate school, albeit with a fifteen-year age gap and at different points of our lives. Like most of us who become parents, we did not fully anticipate the delight, exhaustion, intense love, ambivalence, and distress that come with raising a child.

It is not coincidental that this project was spawned at a time when notions of motherhood were once again being contested at the turn of the twenty-first century. In 2004, Susan Douglas and Meredith Michaels's witty and controversial book *The Mommy Myth* came out, quickly becoming a best-seller. As communication scholars, we found this book incredibly useful in its critical assessment of the cultural representations of mothers in the media. This "new momism," as Douglas and Michaels call it, "is a set of ideals, norms, and practices, most frequently and powerfully represented in the media, that seem on the surface to celebrate motherhood, but which in reality promulgate standards of perfection that are beyond your reach" (5). How does this momism affect women professionally, especially those of us who have chosen careers in higher education? For many of the authors who contributed to this anthology, life as a parent and as an employee in institutes of higher education—in various positions—is complicated, with both productive and contradictory tensions.

This "new momism" closely followed the media-fueled "mommy wars" between stay-at-home mothers and mothers who work outside of the home. Women compose 47 percent of the total U.S. labor force, 73 percent (approximately 66 million women) of whom are working full-time (U.S. Department of Labor 2010). Moreover, the participation of mothers in the labor force has risen over the past twenty-five years. As of 2008, more than 60 percent of mothers are working outside the home for paid wages (U.S. Congress Joint Economic Committee 2010). In U.S. academia more specifically, women compose nearly 50 percent of the workforce, and of that population it is estimated that more than 65 percent are working mothers. In other words, many women working at colleges and universities across the country are also parenting. These percentages not surprisingly correspond with the shifting demographics in higher-education institutions, where female students compose almost 60 percent of all students in the United States and 47 percent worldwide (United Nations Educational, Scientific and Cultural Organization 2002). Indeed, the emerging workforce changes anticipated for the twenty-first century inspired the publication of several books aimed at addressing the ongoing struggle of work–life balance for women. As more women graduated with college degrees, the challenge of becoming a supermom and superemployee has dominated the literary conversation since 2000 and has since become a central theme especially for women with professional white-collar careers (A. Crittenden 2001; Hewlett 2002; Mason and Ekman 2007; Stone 2007a, 2007b).

The ideal of the supermom-employee-student is especially poignant in academia, where the existence of flexible schedules as well as extended winter and summer breaks creates the misinformed assumption that the demands of the academy are compatible with the demands of parenting. However, the bureaucratic, hierarchal, and swelling expectations that characterize so many institutions of higher learning make it difficult to maintain a forty-hour work schedule, even in the summer. Academics and professional university/college staff often work overtime week after week. In addition, the different institutional structures and gradations of faculty/staff positions place uneven and inequitable burdens on workers, which are increasingly evident in the blogosphere discussions about working conditions in academia. There are vast differentiations between two-year, four-year, and doctoral public and private colleges and universities that impact the rising standards for faculty members employed as adjuncts, lecturers, instructors, assistant professors, associate professors, full professors, and administrators. For full-time, tenure-track, and tenured faculty, excellence is expected in three areas—research, teaching, and service, although scholarly output is often considered the most important, particularly at Research I institutions and increasingly at historically "teaching-oriented" four-year colleges. A forty-hour work week is simply not enough to produce excellent scholarship, engage in master teaching, and cultivate service an outreach partnerships. Staff and students are also not immune to these rising standards. Pressure is increasingly put upon graduate students to achieve excellence in their student, research, teaching, and service years before becoming professors. This very real pressure is deeply influencing female scholars in their decisions to become mothers and remain in the realm of higher education.

As a consequence, academia as a collegiate and professional work environment and its impact on mothers have become an important site of analysis. Andrea O'Reilly, for instance, established the Association for Research on Mothering and promoted research on mothering, including how to be a mother and negotiate an academic career. From this association emerged a number of projects, conferences, and essays that address motherhood in all of its configurations, including the Motherhood Initiative for Research and Community Involvement. O'Reilly also helped spur a new area of interdisciplinary feminist scholarship on motherhood, called "motherhood studies," which is concerned with mothering not only as an institution, experience, or identity, but also as an important site for empowerment (see O'Reilly 2010a, 2010b). As O'Reilly reminds us, feminists such as Adrienne Rich and a long list of others have been grappling with the distinction between mothering and motherhood for decades. Motherhood is "not naturally, necessarily, inevitably oppressive"; reproduction and child rearing need not be perceived as a private, nonpolitical undertaking limited to specific patriarchal nuclear family structures (O'Reilly 2010b, 18).

THE NEED FOR INCLUSIVE ACADEMIC CULTURES IN NEOLIBERAL TIMES

The publication of *Parenting and Professing* (Bassett 2005), *Motherhood, the Elephant in the Laboratory* (Monosson 2008), *Mama Ph.D.* (Evans and Grant 2009), and other such books in the past five years remind us that there is still much to do in terms of challenging the cultural notion that the ideal intellectual worker in the academia is male gendered. As is made clear in a report issued by the American Federation of Teachers (AFT, 2011), the academy as a whole continues to wane as a welcoming place for women. The report offers recommendations for making positive changes, such as correcting inequities in compensation, expanding family-friendly policies on campus, clarifying and providing more flexibility in hiring and promotion policies, and ensuring that women have a voice in their workplace. A 2003 scholarly analysis of the *Chronicle of Higher Education* over the past decade clearly indicates that issues related to family and work are "on the mind and conscience of academicians" (Wolf-Wendel and Ward 2003, 112). Our own search yielded more than seventy-five articles on work and family published in the *Chronicle* between 2004 and 2011. In addition, the pool of graduate students and junior faculty no longer consists predominately of young men with stay-at-home wives; there is instead a generation of intellectual workers who envision dual-career couples sharing in child care (Mason 2009a). Yet the newer generation is operating within not only a cultural norm, but an increasingly neoliberal framework that requires unrelenting work hours in higher education with little room for a gratifying family life (Mason and Goulden 2002, 2004b; Mason 2009a). The *Chronicle* runs an advice column called "The Balancing Act" that addresses work–family concerns, and it often features heated debates regarding the accommodations academe should offer to professors who are parents.

See, for example, the barrage of comments in response to Mary Ann Mason's recent article in the *Chronicle* on "the pyramid problem," where she addresses the fact that women continue to heavily populate the lower faculty ranks: "There are far fewer women than men at the top of the academic hierarchy; those women are paid somewhat less than men, and they are much less likely than men to have had children" (2011, para. 2). The nearly all-male executive administrative team at Mari Castañeda's university, for instance, demonstrates this point. Mason argues that this pyramid of gender inequity is unlikely to change its shape unless serious structural shifts take place in higher education. Interestingly, the comments page for Mason's article showed that in fact many (male and/or nonparent) readers had an aversion to such changes. Yet mothers learning and working in academia are experiencing a reality that deserves to be acknowledged and taken into account. Mary Ann Mason's scholarship is particularly informative on the state of women and mothers in academia. More than 50 percent of recent Ph.D.s awarded by American universities are now granted to women, with women accounting for 38 percent of faculty members overall (American

Association of University Professors [AAUP] 2006; AFT 2011; Mason 2011). However, there continue to be marked gender disparities in terms of faculty positions, pay, and family formation between men and women in academia. Women are best represented in less-prestigious teaching institutions (e.g., community colleges) and in less-secure positions (e.g., adjunct/part-time instructors or lecturer positions) (Wolf-Wendel and Ward 2006; Mason 2011). In addition, full-time women faculty members tend to earn less than their male colleagues at each of the professorial ranks (AAUP 2010; College and University Professional Association for Human Resources 2011). Women in academe are also far less likely to become biological or adoptive parents than other professional women or their male counterparts and are more likely to remain single for the purpose of achieving career success (Mason and Goulden 2002, 2004a, 2004b; Drago and Colbeck 2004). Moreover, the professoriate as a highly male-dominated occupation creates a "chilly climate" for women faculty. As Cheryl Maranto and Andrea Griffin (2011) examine, the reality and even the perception of exclusion, devaluation, and marginalization in academia serve as major impediments to women faculty members' achievements.

Some exemplary reviews have been made of the status of women in academia (Hornig 2003; Ropers-Huilman 2003a; Philipsen 2008), but more telling are the personal narratives that describe college and university climates. As the volume editor of *Gendered Futures in Higher Education* notes in her introduction, "Higher education is one of the primary institutions that shape culture. While those of us who participate in that institution cannot take the blame, credit, or responsibility for current gender relations, we can insist that gender discrimination will not be perpetuated in the very institutions that hold promise for developing both knowledge and people—a development that is certainly stymied by gender discrimination" (Ropers-Huilman 2003b, 9).

The personal narratives expressed in Ropers-Huilman's anthology and a variety of others illuminate the challenges that researchers, writers, teachers, and students face as women in academia—challenges that are often exacerbated for them if they are also mothers (Coiner and George 1998; Evans and Grant 2008; Monosson 2008). For example, having a child with any type of disability—chronic or not—adds to the long list of potential barriers for mothers in academia. There are indications that those individuals who are parenting children with disabilities may forego job changes that involve geographic relocation (something quite common in the academic job market) and experience a higher rate of marital disruption (Mailick

Seltzer et al. 2001; Yantzi and Rosenberg 2008). In their study of mothers of young children who are on the tenure track, Lisa Wolf-Wendel and Kelly Ward (2006) found that there is great diversity in how women experience academic life across disciplines and institutional types. Women faculty members with children are often encouraged to pursue their careers at lower-tier institutions (e.g., community colleges, four-year programs). This push has the potential to steer talented women away from pursuing faculty careers at Research I and II institutions based on the implicit assumption that the roles of scholar and mother are incompatible. Furthermore, even if women (with children or not) are granted tenure, fewer of them are promoted to full professor, which is often the result of poor mentoring and networking once women achieve tenure and the lack of standardized policies across departments (Stout, Staiger, and Jennings 2007). Such circumstances affect not only tenure and promotion, but also the future of leadership development and capacity building in all academic fields (Castañeda and Hames-García forthcoming).

Moreover, the "chilly climate" for mothers in higher education is compounded for women of color (Williams et al. 2005; González 2007; Flores and Garcia 2009). Although faculty positions have almost doubled in the past two decades, most faculty of color (except Asians and Asian Americans) remain underrepresented in higher education, and minority women—especially Latina, African American, and Indigenous women—are far less likely than their male counterparts to be on tenure-track lines (Tuitt et al. 2009; Cotera 2010; AFT 2011). Numerous scholars have written about the problematic climate for students, faculty, and administrators of color in higher education, noting the Anglo-centric paradigm that shapes the culture of many colleges and universities (Padilla and Chávez 1993; Valverde and Castenell 1998; Brown-Glaude 2009). Other collections have pointed to the particular challenges all women of color face due to the structural and personal racism and sexism on college campuses (Benjamin 1997; Johnson and Harris 2010). Despite some gains in position in the ivory tower for female students and faculty as a whole, many women of color who are both scholars and mothers find they continue to be blocked in their progress by sex and racial prejudice and biases.

Since 2008, *Inside Higher Ed* has hosted the "Mama Ph.D." blog, in which various women with or working toward doctorates share almost daily their efforts in balancing parenthood with academics. Many women describe the productive intersections of such balancing acts as well the challenges, some of which are made more difficult by institutional bureaucracy. Despite the growing body of blogs, literature, research, and media commentary on motherhood—as both an institution and an experience—the topic is far from exhausted. If truth be told, the issues facing mothers in the twenty-first century are perhaps more complex than in previous decades, thus making mothering and motherhood continual compelling topics for exploration (O'Reilly 2010a).

In attempts to navigate the less-than-hospitable culture of academia, many women (regardless of motherhood) have found particular strategies to (re)balance work–life priorities and stressors. For many, the degree of occupational stress in higher education is clearly gendered, where women experience heavier workloads and significant stress in managing multiple roles, juggling the work–home interface, and negotiating in a sometimes nonsupportive organizational climate (Michailidis 2008). The occupational stress of higher education often inhibits women's (and men's) ability to maintain life-affirming and health-promoting lifestyles. As some scholars have found, academic mothers sometimes engage in negative stress-management behaviors such as smoking, drinking, overeating, and maintaining a sedentary lifestyle (Michailidis 2008; Vancour and Sherman 2010). For other academics, self-care and stress management mean seeking out peer mentors that affirm one's work and create a more collegial work environment (McGuire and Reger 2003; Goeke et al. 2011). These individual efforts are only a few of the ways to deal with the hypertransformation of higher education that is fueled by neoliberal practices and the increasingly commercialization of academia.

Katherine Romack argues in her commentary on the corporatization of the academy that, given the "negligible impact of education on the wage gap, women's continued legal and civic privatization within globalization, and their declining economic status, it is reasonably certain that women will continue to be second-class citizens of the corporate academy" (2011, 245). Over the past thirty years, state funding for higher education has been dramatically reduced, and, as a consequence, an inversion of the academic labor force has occurred wherein almost 75 percent of today's instructional workforce is employed on a contingent basis (AFT 2011). This move to a contingent model of employment for higher-education professionals also coincides with the increased numbers of women entering the instructional workforce, especially as the roles of community colleges expand, and there is an increased preponderance toward online teaching in order to raise more revenue by serving "student customers" in and outside the United

States. These changes affect female contingent labor disproportionately and more so those who are mothers because of the impression that there is flexibility in part-time (online) appointments. Higher education at the administrative level is simultaneously being touted as primarily a tool for securing economic achievement in a global marketplace as many progressive people on campuses argue for global citizenship (Gildersleeve et al. 2010).

In order to deal with the social inequalities that are deeply ingrained in higher education and the larger contemporary society, a fundamental shift needs to be made in how resources and power are managed. The AAUP's "Statement of Principles on Family Responsibilities and Academic Work" argues that the "development and implementation of institutional policies that enable the healthy integration of work responsibilities with family life in academe require renewed attention" (2001, 216). At the time this influential AAUP document was published, it gave new life and attention to the struggles mothers in academe face and offered instrumental principles and guidelines for academic institutions to construct appropriate policies and practices regarding family leave. It suggests family-friendly policies that include the creation of modified-duty policies to allow faculty to obtain relief from some teaching or service obligations while remaining in active-service status; provisions for child, elder, and other family care; and ability to craft flexible work policies and schedules. Yet even when family-friendly policies exist, faculty members may not know about or take advantage of them. The AFT revisits the negative impact that the lack of family-friendly policies has on the hiring process, retention, and women's prospects for career advancement. This national organization takes the position that "effectuating a diverse faculty and staff [is] an essential element in achieving a greater measure of economic and social justice in America" (2011, 6). Both the AAUP and the AFT documents highlight the double bind women faculty members with children may find themselves in because they are bearing and raising children at the same time that they are building their careers. These organizations point to the ways in which the creation and support of family-friendly policies may lead to the retention and promotion of women in higher education. Although the broader goal may be to change the sociocultural landscape of colleges and universities, it is undeniable that achieving success in changing the institutional policies is an important step toward shifting structural and cultural efforts. As a consequence, this book is an attempt to make transparent how mothers' voices about their lives in academia are critical for inspiring policy and cultural shifts.

IMPORTANCE OF *TESTIMONIOS*

Despite emerging changes, many mothers continue to struggle for a voice in an academic landscape that privileges Western, competitive masculine frameworks for learning, teaching, and research. In 2008, Mari first conceived of this project as discussion circles where academic women would share their stories about mothering. From these discussions, developed with the help of a mentoring grant from the University of Massachusetts–Amherst Graduate School, it was apparent that women have many thoughts and feelings on the topic of parenting in the academy. The very act of telling personal narratives reveals how the self is constructed, disclosed, and implicated in a society that has mixed messages about women, mothers, and parenting. Informed by feminist researchers and activists who have theorized the relationship between self and culture, the narratives included in this volume expose the "political–social dimension of motherwork" (O'Reilly 2010a, 14), thus giving agency to the women who are mothering in all sorts of circumstances. As is evident in the essays included here, several family structures are represented in academia: single, blended, traditional, and same-sex families. We are concerned with how mothers in academic settings have been represented and valued (or not) in the multiple forms of work we do in higher education. We are convinced that personal narratives have the potential to serve as a critical intervention in the social, political, and cultural life of academia. Patricia Hill Collins is but one of many feminists who assert that one's lived experience can serve as a criterion for making meaning and producing knowledge. She argues that in the United States a scholar "making a knowledge claim typically must convince a scholarly community controlled by elite White avowedly heterosexual men holding U.S. citizenship that a given claim is justified" (2000, 253).

Inspired by the Latina Feminist Group's process of collaborating, we approached this project with a commitment to creating knowledge and theory through our personal experiences as mothers in academe. This writing collective "arrived at the importance of *testimonio* as a crucial means of bearing witness and inscribing into history those lived realities that would otherwise succumb to the alchemy of erasure" (Latina Feminist Group 2001, 2). The result is a volume that provides a "polyphonic *testimonio*"—accounts by different women who have studied, worked, and taught at the college and university level (Beverley 2005, 549). We firmly believe in the importance and value of women's autoethnography and oral history, and, as a result, our own volume gives voice to women who are or have been mothers as undergraduates, graduate students, administrators, staff, and professors of various ranks in order to bear witness to their lived experiences of mothering and motherhood while learning/working in academia. These narratives often coincide with Patricia Stout, Janet Stagier, and Nancy Jennings's (2007) findings that female faculty, students, and staff feel demoralized based on their experiences in higher education, often as a result of believing that they have no voice or agency. The act of writing our testimonials is an attempt for us to maintain a level of agency in our birthing/parenting experiences, in all of their configurations, while collaborating with community and producing intellectual work. Each of the stories perceives mothering in a slightly different way, thus shedding light on how power and domination have uneven effects of those of us working in academe.

Carolyn Ellis and Arthur Bochner suggest that personal narratives serve as a mode of inquiry; the stating of one's own experiences "offer lessons for further conversation rather than undebatable conclusions" (2000, 744). Some scholars argue that, borne out of the desire for solidarity, personal and testimonial narrative is fundamentally a democratic and egalitarian form that affirms the authority of personal experience (Beverley 2005). This description is particularly relevant to those whose voices have been marginalized, such as, in our case, women who are mothers in higher education. As Ellis and Bochner explain, testimonials raise questions such as: "'What are the consequences my story produces? What kind of person does it shape me into? What new possibilities does it introduce for living my life?' The crucial issues are what narratives do, what consequences they have, to what uses they can be put. . . . Often our accounts of ourselves are unflattering and imperfect, but human and believable. The text is used, then, as an agent of self-understanding and ethical discussion" (2000, 746, 748).

We share these *testimonios* as a way to illustrate what much of the feminist and higher-education scholarship has pointed to over the past twenty years: there is much to be grateful for, but there is also much work yet to be done within the walls of the ivory tower. The *testimonios* also illustrate how the complex contingencies of race, ethnicity, socioeconomic class, age, sexuality, and ability are intertwined into these women's lived experiences in higher education. Many of the authors included in this anthology have specifically drawn on the work of Patricia Hill Collins and her discussions of the importance of dialogue, an ethics of caring, and the significance of black women as agents of knowledge. For scholars such as Collins, the use of an intersectional paradigm examines mutual systems of oppression in social organizations, with the potential to stimulate new interpretations of women's experiences.

Many of the authors in this volume also echo what Juliann Emmons Allison describes as "psychological adjustments" (2007, 26) — contradictions that repeatedly surface for women engaged within academic settings who are balancing dual roles as mothers and scholars. Although many academic institutions have made considerable progress in accommodating academic parents' pragmatic concerns, there is still a systematic failure to recognize the ways that motherhood can alter a female academic's career in profound ways (Mason and Goulden 2002, 2004a; Allison 2007; Mason 2011). This anthology confronts these biases and reveals the strategies we as mothers may engage in so as to not jeopardize our academic lives. Our collection aims to offer counterstories as to who constitutes a viable and reliable colleague, scholar, and student, which follows in the tradition of Chicana/Latina scholarship on counterstorytelling while also adding to the voices of women who are in academia (Yosso 2006; Chávez 2012).

Many of the essays in this volume push us to consider how parenting is gendered in the contexts of interlocking systems such as colonialism, racism, sexism, ethnocentrism, ageism, and heterosexism. They are in conversation with each other, revealing the often stark differences in how people experience the academy. What we expose are structurally informed disparities between ranks of women working in academia. The authors in this volume embody a variety of academic positions, working as administrators, professors of all ranks, graduate students, and academic support staff. As editors of this volume, we imagine the following pages as a forum where we can not only see the nuanced differences between mothers in the academy but also understand our commonalities. As a consequence, several authors in this collection discuss their experiences in academia as scholars and mothers of color — experiences that include a lack of valuable networks of mentors, the presence of tokenism, and the constant need to prove their academic qualifications. The women of color contributing their voices to our project bear witness to and also share their insights regarding what policies and cultural changes need to happen for more scholars of color to feel welcomed and taken seriously in academe.

In addition to the testimonial accounts, which lay bare women's lives as mothers in academia at various stages, the book also includes chapters that discuss theoretically and empirically the material and labor conditions of mothers learning and working in increasingly inaccessible sites of higher education. As the political economy of academic institutions shifts toward corporate-based models of teaching in both blatant and subtle ways, it is critical to ascertain how women's lives in the academy and by extension their families will be affected by these structural–cultural changes. Gaye Tuchman describes in *Wannabe U* the growing organizational cultures in higher education that prioritize institutional branding and marketing, diminishing resources, increasing workloads, and a structural ambivalence toward diversity in all its forms. The global competition to become elite institutions is deepening the efforts by universities and colleges to "promote the transformation of knowledge into capital" (2009, 59). There is also the pressure to brand oneself as a professor—in short, to become known for a specific (scholarly) "product." Although personal branding allows each individual to be more marketable, the consequence is a lack of participation in or decreased service to his or her present institution.

The capitalist approach to academia inherently assumes an approach to the life–work balance that is unfortunately in fact imbalanced because revenue generation through research and teaching can occur only through longer work hours. Such hours disproportionately affect mothers, often negatively, and in the status-conscious consumer culture of the higher-education industry it is becoming progressively more difficult for all parents to keep up with the academic life. In the new transformed environment where universities and colleges are also struggling with the tension of education as a public good and commodity, it is more important than ever to reveal "emerging aspects of American life" and to bear witness to how mothers in academia are situated personally, culturally, and structurally "in the context of contemporary American higher education" (Tuchman 2009, 21). Through such bold acts, we are making visible what is often invisible and in the process shifting the conversation so that mothers' experiences are on the radar for university officials. Taking women's issues into account is vital if any institution of higher education wants to be successful in the twenty-first century, and motherhood is in the top ten of those issues.

BEARING WITNESS IN THREE PARTS

This volume is divided into three parts that are interrelated but distinct in particular ways. Each part features short testimonial chapters from mothers who are students, administrators, and faculty, demonstrating the often tricky balance between home and work life. The collection also includes several lengthier research-based chapters. Part I, "Working/Learning in the Academy While Working/Learning as a Mom," offers readers a larger political, social, and economic context of what women working in academia are facing. Part II, "Unexpected Challenges and Momentous Revelations," discusses some of the serious unexpected challenges and unanticipated revelations mothers in academia have encountered. These unexpected circumstances include cultural relocation and acculturation, terminal illness and disabilities, and overt and covert forms of heterosexism, racism, sexism, and classism. Part III, "Creating More Parent-Friendly Institutions of Higher Learning," contributes to the larger conversation on how academia can include more family-friendly institutions in order to change the ivory tower.

Our book ultimately demonstrates that *testimonios* are powerful tools for the production of new knowledge and that by focusing on mothers' lives we are contributing to the feminist epistemology about gender, race, sexuality, and class in the twenty-first century. It is tempting to make gestational analogies when discussing a collaborative writing project pertaining to mothers in higher education and including more than thirty authors. Like many pregnancies, this project took on a life of its own. Spurred on by our belief that there is more to be said, this collection of first-person narratives sheds light on the lives of women who parent while learning, working, teaching, and researching in twenty-first-century colleges and universities. We acknowledge that most of the authors in this collection are from the humanities or social sciences. Although our initial call for papers was distributed widely, we did not receive any submissions from female faculty and students in the natural and physical sciences. For those readers interested specifically in the experiences of women in science, technology, engineering, and math (STEM) fields, Emily Monosson's excellent anthology *Motherhood, the Elephant in the Laboratory* (2008) addresses an array of issues for mothers-scientists. Many of the contributors to Monosson's book wrestle with what it means to be a "scientist" and how to reconcile various "career" trajectories that may or may not include mainstream academic or research positions. Clearly there are fewer women in the hard sciences than in the humanities and social sciences, although the percentage of female Ph.D.s in STEM fields has grown since 1958, when the National Science Foundation began keeping track (Burrelli 2008). Nonetheless, STEM female faculty continue to represent a microscopic percentage of all faculty, and, despite increases in the number of awarded doctorates, the wide discrepancy in career paths demonstrates a rampant disregard for women professors, postdoctorates, and students in these particularly male-dominated/male-oriented fields. The *Chronicle of Higher Education*'s coverage of a particular female postdoc's career derailment in physics due to the lack of institutional support during and after her pregnancy points to the "highly competitive nature of academic science, which leaves little time for female scholars to have children. Young scientists who works as postdoctoral researchers are particularly vulnerable because their careers are dependent on the goodwill of a single faculty supervisor," who is often a man (Wilson 2005). Disciplinary differences do exist between the natural and physical sciences on the one side and other fields of study on the other (for instance, the emphasis on laboratory-based research in STEM fields); however, we do believe that many of the larger cultural and structural issues for mothers are similar across academia.

We thus took great pains as editors to make sure that the chapters spoke to these broader realities of how to balance children with an academic career. To do so, we negotiated with and coached the women authors in this book, much as a midwife does with a woman who is in the throes of labor. We also ensured as much as possible that the writing process was humane, transparent, and encouraging, while also being rigorous. While the project was being born, at least three of the contributors literally gave birth to children; other women tended to a sick or dying child or parent, prepared lectures and conference papers, wrestled with research projects, and attended to an array of administrative tasks. At least two of our authors obtained their doctorates as the book developed, and four of the authors were granted tenure and promotion. Thus, some of the stories included here reflect the authors' positionalities prior to obtaining their degrees or tenure. We tell our readers this because it is this type of emotional and physical labor that is often invisible in academia. In the very act of writing, editing, and rewriting our manuscripts, we experienced fluidity between our professional and personal lives as academic mothers. It is our hope that through these narratives, we both reveal and revise the world of higher education as mothers know it.

PART ONE

WORKING/LEARNING IN THE ACADEMY
WHILE WORKING/LEARNING AS A MOM

OVER THE COURSE of her academic career as a renowned sociologist, Arlie Hochschild (1997) made poignant observations about the precarious balance between home and work life. Her work therefore provides us with a vocabulary to describe the second-shift phenomenon where mothers employed outside the home continue to carry the brunt of domestic work once they return home. Hochschild's research also questions how human feelings have become commercialized in the global market place; she questions what emotional labor entails and the ways in which such labor is gendered. In many ways embodied through the chapters in this book, her work offers readers a larger political, social, and economic context for what women working in academia are facing. In this first part, we begin with "How We Learned to Stop Worrying and to Enjoy Having It All," by six academic mothers from four disciplines at the University of Wisconsin–Oshkosh, who investigate the media-generated "mommy wars" and the need for an academic community dedicated to a discussion of the work–life balance as it applies to their lives. Michelle Kuhl, Michelle Mouton, Margaret Hostetler, Druscilla Scribner, Tracy Slagter, and Orlee Hauser question the tone of media portrayals of working women, challenge one another's notions of feminism, confront the virtual absence of discourses on fatherhood and spousal relationships, and investigate their own reactions to stay-at-home motherhood. Larissa M. Mercado-López considers throughout her chapter, "Academia or Bust: Feeding the Hungry Mouths of the University, Babies, and Ourselves," how academia as an institution is not always accepting of mothers and their decision to breastfeed, yet there are structures in place that may enable mothers-professors to mother their children without compromising too much. In addition, she discusses how the physical and political act of breastfeeding works on both the physiological level and the psychological level and should be acknowledged as a way to remain engaged in scholarly work. In "Diverse Academic Support for an Employee, Mother, and Nontraditional Student," Wendy K. Wilde intertwines her experiences as a young student and mother with her status as a female staff member working in the academy for thirty years. Wendy began working full-time at the age of nineteen; she tells her story by showing how conversations and connections with women on campus, regardless of their status, helped her create a balanced life as worker, student, and mother. Wendy's experience is juxtaposed with Kim Powell's story of raising four children, one born prematurely the year before her tenure review and three adopted special-needs children, while she was serving as department head and director of women's studies. She concludes in "Breaking the Glass Ceiling While Being a Mother: Parenting, Teaching, Research, and Administration" that higher-education administration, with its twelve-month contract and eighty-plus-hour weeks, often assumes a life without children, thus creating an institutional loss of talented academic mothers who have excellent skills for academic leadership. Such values are also present in Virginia L. Lewis' story "To Tell or Not to Tell: Single Motherhood and the Academic Job Market," about how she lost tenure over an institutional decision governed by corporate thinking. Thrust back onto the academic job market at age forty as a single mother of three young children, she embarked on a journey that taught her the importance of family as a key academic value. Concluding part I is "Class, Race, and Motherhood: Raising Children of Color in a Space of Privilege." Irene Mata discusses her experiences as a new Chicana professor from a working-class family and the challenges and prejudices she and her children face while living in an affluent and Anglo college suburb. She contributes to the dialogue of what it means to be an academic mother, torn between a job one loves and raising children in a community whose values are often antithetical to one's own.

1

HOW WE LEARNED TO STOP WORRYING AND TO ENJOY HAVING IT ALL

Michelle Kuhl, Michelle Mouton, Margaret Hostetler,
Druscilla Scribner, Tracy Slagter, and Orlee Hauser

IN 2006, six academic mothers from four disciplines at the University of Wisconsin–Oshkosh started a sociable reading group focused on the "mommy wars." According to Toni Zimmerman, and her colleagues (2008), the media derives high ratings by explicitly pitting working moms against stay-at-home moms on TV programs. Many in our group had noticed a growing literature of mainstream articles and books on the subject, such as Lisa Belkin's *New York Times* article "The Opt-Out Revolution" (2003), Linda Hirshman's manifesto *Get to Work* (2006), and Danielle Crittenden's *What Our Mothers Didn't Tell Us* (1999). Women's hallway conversations evolved into a reading group that tapped into a real need for a discussion of the work–life balance as it applied to our immediate academic community. For two consecutive summers, we met monthly to examine common readings. We found we agreed on many issues, mainly the difficulty of juggling work and motherhood, but disagreed on the exact nature of the problem and the best solutions. Our meetings mixed the personal and the political as we debated feminism, swapped personal stories, and lent each other used baby clothes. Most important, we learned to stop worrying about the "mommy wars" and to value our social ties to one another.

We are exactly the target demographic at which current media judgments and exhortations are directed: thirty-five- to forty-five-year-old Generation X women. We are all middle and upper-middle-class professional women with advanced degrees and children. Judith Warner calls us "a generation of control freaks" who have turned inward to focus exclusively on

ourselves and our immediate social and familial circle, causing our motherhood instincts to blossom freakishly into "perfect madness" (2006, 47).
Linda Hirshman calls us "the backlash generation" who deserted the gains
of the second-wave feminist movement (2006, 1). Caitlin Flanagan thinks
we have a "stubborn longing for an earlier way of life" that undercuts our
desire to leave children for work (2006, xxxiii). We fit the generic caricature
of the stressed-out woman stuck in the office racing to meet deadlines as her
child languishes in a never-ending string of day-care and nanny situations.
Depending on which author one reads, we are the generation that is opting
out or opting in, destroying the family or carrying the torch of progress, or
squandering the feminist revolution.

The members of our reading group acknowledge that we are elite. We
recognize that we are more privileged than the majority of women in
America and in the world. We are non-Hispanic white, heterosexual, highly
educated, and relatively affluent, and we have flexible schedules. Not every
woman gets to wring her hands over whether to put her baby in a quality
day care so she can work at an intellectually stimulating job and go home to
share housework with a feminist husband. However, research suggests that
the very flexibility of academic work may make it more difficult to carve out
time to do the intellectual projects required of the job. As Belinda Probert
reports, "Much of what academics do can be done from home, at night or
on weekends. This maybe, however, have [sic] precisely the opposite of its
expected consequences. . . . [T]he flexibility of academic work makes it
more difficult for women to exert the power of absence since there are relatively few hours when they are required to be in the workplace (2005, 69).

The notion of "the power of absence" originated with Alison Morehead's
assertion that the ability to be absent from the household to do paid or meaningful work or both is essential to increasing gender equality in the workplace
(cited in Probert 2005, 69). Our identities as professional women also make
our work flexibility problematic. Although research has shown that working-
class women and middle-class women share values of motherhood and fulfilling work, and both are pulled in different directions by commitments to work
and family, middle-class (defined as professional) women "were unable to resolve their dilemmas in favor of one direction," whereas working-class women
"tended to orient their lives more around their families" (Walker 1990, 313,
314). Professional women felt more commitment toward their jobs for a variety
of reasons, but they used the flexibility of their work to try to resolve the work–
family dilemma—for example, "cut[ting] out lunches rather than stay[ing]
late in the office" (Walker 1990, 314). In many ways, these findings dovetail

with Linda Hirshman's assertion that "educated and privileged women matter" because they influence a wide array of decisions at top levels of society, politics, the economy, and the media, which can have positive effects (2006, 9). After all, if we (privileged women) can't make this work, what chances do women with fewer resources have? And it seems that professional women are using all their resources and working very hard to make it work.

Our plan was simple: we would collectively decide on a book list and meet once a month, rotating living rooms, to discuss the book we read. Unlike all of the other scholarship we are expected to produce, this informal book club was the result of an organic process. We were curious about the "mommy wars," but we did not plan to cover the literature exhaustively or write a paper. The book group started in the summer of 2007 and read Hirshman's *Get to Work* (2006), Caitlin Flanagan's *To Hell with All That* (2006), and Judith Warner's *Perfect Madness* (2006). In the summer of 2008, we read Leslie Bennetts's *The Feminine Mistake* (2007), Amy Richards's *Opting In* (2007), and Allison Pearson's *I Don't Know How She Does It* (2003), and we revisited Betty Friedan's classic *The Feminine Mystique* ([1963] 1997). We also branched out individually and shared choice bits of other relevant works, including Danielle Crittenden's *What Our Mothers Didn't Tell Us* (1999), Neil Gilbert's *A Mother's Work* (2008), Arlie Hochschild's *The Time Bind* (1997), and Pamela Stone's *Opting Out* (2007a).

For each of us, combining motherhood and an academic career is a patchwork, and we all feel compromised in both the work we accomplish and the mothering we do. This chapter interweaves our analysis of the literature on working mothers with reflections from individual group members that bear witness to the personal nature of our struggle. After introducing ourselves, we compare the authors' suggestions to our own experiences. The chapter concludes with a discussion of what we have gained through our participation in this reading group and the subtle impact it has had on our university community.

STRUGGLING ALONE

Among the six group members, we have ten children. Some of our children were born while mom was in graduate school, others while mom was junior faculty; only one was born after tenure. To cope with work and children, we utilized many different strategies that hinged on a host of factors, including job flexibility, spousal participation, and individual children's emotional and physical needs. Most of us used day care, although two fathers stayed at home full-time at least temporarily, and one of us had an au pair. We also discovered how even a good child-care situation can devolve into a problem, forcing readjustment: day-care hours are limited, children become ill, cross-country moves are disruptive, and our stay-at-home fathers also needed time to write. These moments are stressful. And yet we all remained committed to juggling work and motherhood. As one of us put it, "It's not possible to balance it all. . . . It's just possible to tread water and hope not to drown. But I'm happy just to be in the pool—wouldn't trade it for anything." For all of us, this reading group helped us stay "in the pool" as we balanced jobs, children, and our personal lives. Many of us had experiences in graduate school at universities that were hostile to women with children. When we arrived at Oshkosh, there was neither a maternity policy nor a network in place to help working mothers, something not unique to our institution. We started this group to read books and to develop such a network.

The following reflections provide a glimpse of our struggle to balance work and family when we started the group.

"During the first year of my son's life I felt very much like an imposter. I pretended to be a 'real professor,' up to date on my material, up to date on my research. Anyone who managed to look past my clumpy clothing and my raging acne seemed to be fooled, but I was not."

"I am tired all the time (but joyful) and have to compromise on both work and parenting all the time."

"By the time I returned home after a day of teaching and then carting a five-month around, I was too exhausted to do anything else. This meant that the household organization slipped, my quality time with my husband and older son slipped, and my time to work on anything aside from my teaching slipped."

READING TOGETHER

Many of us joined this reading group hoping to discover the secret to living a fulfilling, organized, balanced, guilt-free life that had thus far proven to be elusive. Despite our "flexible" academic schedules, the consensus was that none of us had the time we wanted to devote to our scholarship, our marriages, our children, or ourselves. Our feelings were not unusual. Karen Walker's 1990 sociological study found that mothers in both working-class and professional jobs were tired, felt tension between their roles as mothers and workers, and felt guilt over inadequate time with their children. The following discussion synthesizes our responses to the books we read.

One characteristic of much of this genre of literature is its overt proscriptive nature. Most blatant in this regard is Linda Hirshman's manifesto *Get to Work*. Although we were enamored with Hirshman's contention that women deserve a flourishing life and that it is a societal problem when elite women drop out of professional careers for family, we were surprised to discover how far we were from her model of a successful woman. Hirshman demands that women (1) take financially lucrative jobs, (2) take work seriously and refuse to mommy-track their careers (that is, put their careers on hold as they raise their children), (3) bargain aggressively in their marriages for an equal division of household work, and (4) bear only one child. As professors in the liberal arts, we have failed her first test by not seeking financially rewarding jobs. Hirshman would say that many of us have failed her second test, too, by taking jobs at a comprehensive university and by scaling back scholarship goals. However, we feel that Hirshman misses the mark by defining too narrowly her proscription "take work seriously." Despite our adjustments, none of us has been mommy-tracked; our salaries and responsibilities continue to be in line with our male colleagues; and we all are active scholars in our fields. Although we negotiate responsibilities within our marriages, we disagree widely about what shape this bargaining should take. The most obvious (and least regretted) breach of Hirshman's rules is that four out of six of us have two children.

Hirshman's model is elegant and clean. In contrast, our lives are realistic and messy. Perhaps this explains our positive responses to Allison Pearson's novel *I Don't Know How She Does It*. The main character, Kate, a frantically overstretched mother of two who loves her job in the high-stakes world of international finance, is a witty, overdrawn portrayal of the crisis all working moms suffer. We found it both hilarious and cathartic to read about fictional Kate's attempt to "distress" a store-bought cake and try to pass it off as her own. We related as Kate worked the "third shift," worrying obsessively over every piece of her carefully crafted child-care system and its potentially detrimental long-term impact on her children. However, we hated the ending as Kate concedes defeat, quits her job, and moves away from London. We questioned Alison Pearson's decision to have Kate give up her career rather than seek a less perfectionist strategy to balance work and family.

Our frustration with Kate and our acceptance of the chaos of our own lives explain why Leslie Bennetts's *The Feminine Mistake* resonated the most clearly for us. She argues forcefully that women should continue to work not only for personal fulfillment, but also for economic security, thus rejecting the false dichotomy of work and feminism. Bennetts suggests that the most intense years of mothering are when children are young. Unlike Hirshman, she thinks it is appropriate to be flexible and scale back career ambitions, as she herself did for roughly fifteen years out of a fifty-year career (she calls this period the "fifteen-year paradigm"). Bennetts validates our own life decisions by emphasizing that though it is difficult to balance young children and a career, it is worthwhile both personally and economically.

Our overwhelmingly negative reaction to Caitlin Flanagan's *To Hell with All That* was equally revealing. Challenging the traditional feminist contention that a career is a vital part of a woman's life, Flanagan presents herself as a stay-at-home mother. However, because she has continued to write and has outsourced her duties to housekeepers and nannies, many of us questioned her credentials. Her muddled narrative offers the tempting fantasy that opting out of employment and being a stay-at-home mom would be easier and more fulfilling based on the assumption that financial resources come from a male breadwinner. Flanagan admits to shifting her allegiances from stay-at-home mothers to working mothers depending on the social context. We felt that the real problem lies in the difficulty women face when American culture offers so few positive social identities for working mothers. In addition, the fact is that many mothers have no choice but to work outside of the home for wages.

Judith Warner rejects Flanagan's suggestion that solutions are personal. In her book *Perfect Madness*, she calls for the government to provide more family-friendly programs. Critiquing women's increased devotion to motherhood as status anxiety, Warner claims that women internalize the pressure to perfectly, madly mother their children in an effort to maintain a white middle-class lifestyle in the increasingly high-stakes economy. Warner believes that American individualism and choice feminism have combined to give women the false illusion of free choice. Her argument complements Lynn O'Brien Hallstein's mistaken assertion that second-wave feminism's silence on motherhood and emphasis on choice encouraged the next generation of women to think that they needed experts to guide them (because motherhood was not natural) and that because motherhood was their choice, they alone should shoulder its burdens (2008, 148–149).

Warner ends by encouraging women to band together for "a politics of quality of life" and mobilize in moving the United States toward the western

European model of expanded state "institutions that can help us take care of our children so that we don't have to do everything on our own" (2006, 268). Although we did not agree with Warner's solutions, her assertion that women tend to struggle alone and tend to believe that their choices are theirs alone did hit a raw nerve. We agreed that a state that economically subsidized quality day care and publicly accepted as normal women's use of day care would help us financially and psychologically. We also heard Warner's criticism echo in Pamela Stone's suggestion that the unrelenting demands of both high-powered jobs and modern motherhood are forcing women out of the labor market.

One of our largest critiques of the books we read concerned the virtual nonexistence of fathers in them. Although several authors devoted a chapter to men and marriage or mentioned paternity leave, the work–family balance remained essentially a women's issue according to them. We all agreed that the relative absence of men and partners from the literature is shocking given how integral our spouses have been to our personal solutions. Because fathers' roles, like mothers' roles, are culturally constructed, even men with the best intentions sometimes feel pressured by traditional expectations. Indeed, one member's husband found that fatherhood intensified his sense of financial responsibility and pulled him away from domestic work. Conversely, some women's decisions to stay home reinforce a male breadwinner role. We criticized Flanagan's whining about her husband's absence from home even as she recognized that his high-paying job enabled her to stay home and pay for housekeepers and child-care workers. Flanagan's isolation is a result of a stay-at-home culture that values a father's income more than his parenting. And herein lies the crux of the "mommy wars": the suggestion that those who can afford to stay home with their kids make better parents than those who seek professional fulfillment.

Even though we disagreed with some authors, overall we enjoyed engaging with their ideas and acquiring a language that clarified feelings we previously could not articulate. We loved the snarky term *choice feminism*, coined by Hirshman (and echoed by others) — that is, a woman's choice is not necessarily a feminist choice. We explored the moral high ground that certain economically well-positioned stay-at-home mothers have staked out in the media and mourned the lack of national support for working moms. Hirshman and Bennetts's affirmation of work as valuable hearkened back to Betty Friedan and countered the cultural stereotype that working moms are selfish. One of the most helpful results of our reading was the connection to the larger cultural conversation on the work–life balance. The readings and the conversations made us realize we were not alone in the struggle to balance work and motherhood, as indicated in the following comments by group members:

"It was bracing to hear Hirshman say that my participation in a profession was not just about my individual success but part of maintaining and extending the feminist movement. Aha! My crying kid, my paltry scholarship, my messy house, my attention-deprived husband are not my individual failure, but part of the revolution!"

"As academic mothers we all are trying to get our kids good educations, good medical care, diverse extracurricular stimulation while keeping our marriages intact and getting our work done—all the while at least partially skirting madness."

"I did find my validation . . . that working was a reasonable choice, that it was not selfish, that it is possible to do it well, but that balance is not attainable. . . . Mostly I learned to just stop worrying about achieving the unattainable balance and enjoy the messiness of trying to do it all."

If the books made it easier for us to gain peace of mind as mothers and connected us to a national discussion, the group strengthened our ties to one another and to our wider university community.

REACHING OUT

Social relationships matter because they build networks that help to build social trust, tolerance, and, ultimately, shared values and norms of reciprocity. Norms of reciprocity and social trust are like savings in the bank, a stock of "social capital" that we can collectively draw on to solve social problems. Social capital theorists such as Robert Putnam suggest that "bridging social capital," resulting from social networks of friends and colleagues, widens our awareness of how our individual experiences are similar and interconnected and serves as a way to disperse information and develop shared understanding (2001, 22). We had no such lofty goals in the beginning. At our meetings, we had fun: we socialized, sampled home-baked goods, traded parental and professional advice, and cooed over new babies. The sociologist Karen Walker (1990) has found that professional women were more likely than working-class mothers to socialize less on the job after they had children (as a time-management strategy), but that they missed out on that aspect of their life. We all were excited that the group, ostensibly for academic and social reading, gave us more time to develop friendships. Our experiences confirm what Jocelyn Crowley and Stephanie Curenton assert in their study of mothers groups: "The most frequently cited benefit . . . was social support via networking with adult friends who provided a way to de-stress, to socialize with like-minded women, and to gain information about parenting and educational opportunities" (2011, 10). Yet we also created benefits that diffused beyond the confines of our small group.

One of the first benefits of the group was that we got to know each other well outside of our normal university spaces. Two of us came from political science and two from history; five of us also had connections through the Women's Studies Program. But aside from these "built-in" relationships, this group was composed of casual acquaintances. After a few group meetings, feelings of friendship and professional collegiality were enhanced the more we met, traded emails, and ran into each other in the hallways. We came to see each other not only as working women with children, but as professionals to be trusted in other situations as well. For example, members called upon each other in the course of academic business for advice that was discipline specific.

The benefits of our reading group extended farther than our insulated network. Many pregnant faculty members have had difficulty finding information on whether the university provides any support outside of federally mandated unpaid leave. One member of our reading group, with the guidance of a sympathetic department chair, successfully stopped her tenure clock for one year after having a baby. The news traveled quickly, and it was not long before other members with infants also successfully worked with their department chairs to take advantage of this existing yet unpublicized option to adjust the tenure clock for maternity. After these initial successes, other women at the university who were not associated with the reading group began soliciting group members for advice on the tenure-clock issue. In addition to word-of-mouth information, the group has given three presentations on our experiences—two at our university and one at a statewide women's studies conference. These presentations were well attended and sparked lively discussion. During the question-and-answer portion of the last in-house presentation, an administrator in attendance stood up and assured the audience that the university maintained a commitment to maternity issues and was working on creating a policy.

Women's groups such as ours are sometimes not taken seriously in the social capital literature because they are informal and attached to a single issue (e.g., motherhood, child care). According to Crowley and Curenton, "There is little research on the benefits of formal mothers' organizations as they related to offering maternal social support and the provision of parenting education resources" (2011, 1). Nonetheless, in our group's experience, this dismissal underestimates the capacity of such informal groups to build the kind of relationships that result in social capital. Our group's members have created or strengthened their social and professional relationships to one another, have accrued concrete material advantages from disseminating information, and have encouraged a wider university conversation on the work–life balance among faculty, staff, and administration.

Our reasons for joining the reading group varied: wanting to engage the "mommy wars" literature, looking for advice on the work–life balance, and wanting to build social connections. Many of us have worked together cordially for years, but until we joined the reading group, we had not realized the extent of one another's turmoil and triumphs. Although we did not find clear or easy solutions to our difficulties, at least now our struggles are not as desperately private, and we have a measure of kinship. The woman whom Pearson describes in *I Don't Know How She Does It* is the same woman whom Danielle Crittenden cites as the problem and the same woman who is suffering from perfect madness in Judith Warner's tony suburb. All of the women in the books we read are in part versions of ourselves.

We are professors, researchers, teachers, and moms. We love all these parts of our identity, yet we battle to maintain the whole. The "mommy wars" literature presents these identities as conflicting and subject to correction rather than constrained choices. As Zimmerman and her colleagues state, the "mommy wars" have "deflected attention from the real issues that have had an impact on a family's ability to provide good parenting" (2008, 205). Reading collectively gave us a framework and language to understand these choices. We avoid the "perfect madness" of obsessive motherhood; we defy Hirshman's stringent rules; we do not make the "feminine mistake"; and we are not "opted out." And to hell with Caitlin Flanagan! Instead of measuring ourselves against media abstractions, we see other women in our group facing similar challenges and making similar, reasonable choices. This reading group did not end the struggle, but it did provide a measure of comfort to us in the knowledge that at least now we struggle together.

2

ACADEMIA OR BUST

Feeding the Hungry Mouths of the University, Babies, and Ourselves

Larissa M. Mercado-López

"THEY TINGLE like a good idea, a sprouting poem, a witty paper title. I know she's hungry even though we're separated by concrete buildings, books, and oceans of parking lots. And I know that when we're done, she will be as happy as a couplet, the milk on her chin the end of my body's poem."

Eating is one of the many desires women have been expected to suppress. From the cumbersome belly-hugging clothes we wear to the expansive diet articles in magazines, the desire to enjoy food and fill our hungry *panzers* (bellies) with warmth and nutrition is squelched by social and cultural expectations. Although historically women have been denied bodily pleasures, they have unequivocally been expected to satisfy the physical hunger of others. Many women can recount watching their mothers serve the men in the household much larger portions of food, some can even remember watching their fathers and brothers eat meat while the women received none. Even the act of breastfeeding has been subjected to social control because it has often been considered a racialized, classed, and sexualized practice, as Bernice Hausman explores in *Mother's Milk: Breastfeeding Controversies in American Culture* (2003). Thus, it can be argued that feeding and eating have always been part of the process of gender colonization.

I have always been a hungry girl. I have vivid memories of eating my friends' sandwiches during lunch and feeling anxious on days I forgot to bring snacks for my bus ride home from school. I'd often wonder if my appetite was normal because none of my friends seemed to eat very much, but when I tried to "diet," my parents would question my mental stability because they often used appetite to gauge mental and physical health.

My eating habits during my three pregnancies were no exception. Although I knew the idea of "eating for two" did not mean I needed to double my caloric intake, I allowed myself to indulge in cravings that changed daily. One day I would crave oranges, the next day it was steak, and the next day it was pumpkin pie. I was amused by my in-laws' approving smiles as I happily plopped myself down with my plate of overflowing portions. Given my pregnancies, I was glad that for once I could eat to the point of satisfaction without the scrutiny of others. It was OK to eat so much because I was growing a baby inside me.

Such eating freedom was restrained once my children were born. As I lay in the hospital bed after each delivery, I would wonder why I was given such small meals; I was nursing, after all. After the birth of my third daughter, Yoltzin, I buzzed the nurse so often asking when breakfast was coming that she kindly brought me a piece of Dutch apple pie, the taste of which still lingers on my lips years later. Years of anemia and other maternity-related health complications taught me that if I was going to feed my children, I needed to properly feed myself. However, hungers compete, I quickly learned, and it has been a daily struggle deciding whose mouth to feed first, as my experience nursing my daughter while I was in graduate school has taught me.

In this *testimonio*, I recount my experience breastfeeding my daughter while I was a graduate student and teaching assistant in an English doctoral program in San Antonio, Texas. Through this essay, I reclaim the erotic maternal body as a neocolonial instrument of self-treatment through which breastfeeding mothers in academia can feed their children as they reap the physiological benefits of lactation and also produce scholarly work. The experience of breastfeeding while working within the traditionally patriarchal institution of academia further reminded me that resistance to hegemony many times begins with and in our bodies. As Audre Lorde states, "In order to perpetuate itself, every oppression must corrupt or distort those various sources of power within the culture of the oppressed that can provide energy to change" (1984, 53). I believe, as other women who participate in organizations that promote breastfeeding activism and "lactivism," that breastfeeding is a source of power that can provide the energy for revolutionary change.

I hope that the specificity of my experience will enable readers to recognize the great diversity and complexity among mothers in academia. Even more so, I hope that academic mothers will reconsider the relationship they have with their bodies and recognize the potential for revolution that emerges when they choose to satisfy their own bodily hungers.

SUTURING MY MATERNAL AND ACADEMIC SELVES THROUGH BREASTFEEDING

As a mother in a doctoral program, I have come to understand "hunger" on many levels. Feminists have politicized hunger to assert how poverty disproportionately affects women and children more than men. However, woman of color feminists such as Linda Burnham (1985) have challenged the "feminization of poverty," asserting that for people of color, race plays a more significant role than gender in impoverishment and hunger. In literature, "hunger" is often a trope to explain desire for language, poetry, writing, or reading. Feminist scholars such as Gloria Anzaldúa have clearly illustrated the connections between writing, the body, and the psyche. In her writings, Anzaldúa (1995, 2007) works to destabilize the Cartesian body/consciousness dichotomy that grounds much of the philosophy undergirding traditional areas of study in academia. This dichotomy has sustained as well as imposed apartheids in the academy that have objectified women's bodies, rendering them, their stories, and their needs (e.g., insurance coverage for women's health needs, rooms to pump for nursing mothers, maternity leave, etc.) "messy" and "excessive." It is no coincidence that the terms *mother* and *matter* are of the same Indo-European root, *mater*. The mother's body has historically been the point of origin from where life begins; with the transcendent mind held in opposition to matter or the body, the mother is not the intellectual from a Cartesian worldview.

This dichotomy has significant research method implications as well. As Patricia Hill Collins (2000) has indicated extensively in her work on black feminist thought and epistemology, traditional research methods that value "objectivity" and emotional distance while discouraging self-reflexivity effectively promote a disavowal of the self and render untheorizable the embodied experience of research. In my own research, I read representations of the mestiza maternal experience in Chicana/Latina literature. *Mestiza* refers to a woman of both indigenous and European origins, and *maternity* specifically refers to the bodily experience of pregnancy and lactation. As a mestiza mother researching mestiza maternity, I am both scholar and primary text.

The semester before I began the qualifying exam process to advance to candidacy in my doctoral program, I discovered I was pregnant with my third daughter. Not wanting to delay my advancement, I arranged my qualifying-exam schedule according to my pregnancy. Between months two through five, I would develop reading list rationales. During month six, I would have the reading list approval meeting. Months seven through nine, I would write position papers and have the baby. Finally, after the birth would be the oral exam and prospectus approval. It was an ambitious schedule, my committee acknowledged, and those nine months proved to be the most challenging of my life. In addition to writing, I was also teaching two freshman composition classes. I told my students about my pregnancy right away, and after scheduling the induction of labor with my doctor, I wrote the I had selected into the syllabus. My pregnancy was pleasantly uneventful until my seventh month, when I came down with a cough and severely pulled a stomach muscle. Between writing and researching, I'd lay my head on my desk and cry over the pain that radiated throughout my belly, hips, and lower back. My sympathetic feminist officemates offered pillows, blankets, and the kindest of words. Every pain and discomfort I experienced would somehow turn into learning moments as my colleagues and I theorized the place of women's bodies in academia and discussed the antimaterialism that we knew occurred on other campuses that kept many women from pursuing motherhood for fear of not being hired after graduation or during the tenure process. Not before long, I'd be inspired to work once again. My body evolved during pregnancy, and so did my research as I came to embody the brown maternal body I was attempting to render visible in my qualifying-exam readings of race and maternity. My raced and pregnant body became a site not only from which I theorized other bodies, but from which I theorized my own experience as a researcher and also complicated the idea of producing "authoritative" knowledge from such an embodied subjectivity.

My daughter, Yoltzin, was born on my scheduled induction date, two hours shy of Leap Day in February. My labor was hard, unlike my previous induction. As she made her slow appearance, I looked down and found her looking right back at me, which meant she was positioned face up as opposed to the desirable position face down. Relieved that she was finally here, I began the next stage of her life by snipping the umbilical cord myself.

I returned to teaching ten days after the birth and passed my oral exam thirty days later. The entire time I was nursing. It was a messy time—shifting nursing pads under my shirt, leaking breasts, and baby spit-up on my blouses. Between my two consecutive classes, I would run out to the parking lot where my husband was waiting with the baby. I'd nurse for ten minutes, run back to teach the next class, and then run back out to drive him to work. For the next few hours, until it was time to pick up my other two daughters from day care, I'd work from home, writing at the computer while nursing my perpetually hungry daughter. I thought, "For a baby whose name, 'Yoltzin,' means 'little heart,' she certainly has a large appetite," but then I caught myself perpetuating the same gender norms that confine my own appetite.

When Yoltzin was five months old, the on-campus child-development center where my other two daughters were enrolled fortunately had an opening in their infant classroom, and I was able to return to working in my office. Colleagues regaled me with their horror stories of pumping in bathrooms or closets and graciously offered me their offices to pump. However, I wasn't quite sure how to admit that, aside from my own stories of pumping unsuccessfully, I was nursing for myself just as much as I was nursing for my daughter. Was it appropriate for me to admit, within the sterile spaces of the university, that breastfeeding made me "feel good"? I also considered how others would respond to my "need" to take time out of my workday to nurse. I eventually decided to continue breastfeeding Yoltzin. The breastfeeding–writing–teaching schedule was not "balanced," by any means, and I experienced heavy guilt as I dropped off my infant at day care before heading out to teach a room full of budding feminists-daughters in the course "Introduction to Women's Studies."

Then, halfway through this late morning class I would feel "it"—that tingly feeling in my chest that was like a cross between anxious anticipation and pixie dust. It was the feeling of little stars bursting, a crawly tugging feeling like new life sprouting. For the last fifteen minutes of class, I worked to retain my focus to conclude class as my body whispered its secrets of milk and hunger. Finally, class would finish, and I would ride the shuttle or walk-run the half-mile to the child development center. Most mothers who nurse their babies experience a sense of urgency in bodily ways. The weight of full breasts, the thought of a sudden, uncontrollable letdown of milk, the eagerness to satisfy a hungry baby, and the stimulation of lactation hormones lend themselves to a state of urgency that is completely embodied. Though I am no longer nursing, my body still remembers that feeling. I channel that urgency to propel me through my work and my teaching. It informs my research, fuels my passion, and binds my body to my research.

At last, I would reach the classroom where Yoltzin would be hungrily awaiting me. As I sat down with her close to me, the hearts in our chests still beating wildly, and begin to nurse her, a wave of calm would wash over both of us. Kerstin Moberg and Roberta Francis explain in *The Oxytocin Factor: Tapping the Hormone of Calm, Love, and Feeling* (2003) that these feelings of calm are most likely produced by oxytocin, a hormone that is released during milk secretion. In addition to contracting the uterus, oxytocin, also informally referred to as "the love hormone," has been shown to improve bonding between mother and child, lower blood pressure in mothers, increase feelings of trust, and reduce levels of stress. Breastfeeding, in short, made me feel good; it literally and figuratively lifted the weight off my chest. After nursing her to sleep, I was back at work, fulfilling my responsibilities as a teaching assistant and working on my dissertation, the oxytocin-induced feeling still lingering.

These bodily feelings are featured in a growing body of work on maternal eroticism that asserts, as Cristina L. H. Traina argues, "The experience of maternity as erotically pleasurable is not categorically perverse." Furthermore, the erotics of this intimate parenting "can be, in fact, a moral good," and Traina challenges scholars and the larger society to "revise our ideals and norms of mothering in order to account for it" (2000, 370). Amber Kinser also speaks of this maternal erotic, urging mothers and scholars to "locate mothering on a sexual continuum . . . to help us make sense of and work through its emotional intensity" (2008, 125). It is this "emotional intensity" that breastfeeding can enable mothers to transform into energy for pursuing a more socially just university and world.

GUILTY BY LACTATION: RECOGNIZING THE VIOLENCE OF RHETORIC AGAINST MOTHERS WHO NURSE

The enjoyment I found in nursing mobilized me to continue writing about and from my maternal body in both creative and academic writing. At the same time, I vigilantly reminded myself that the empowerment I felt from nursing was not an experience shared by all mothers. Nursing for pleasure, both emotional and physical, is highly stigmatized and in some cases criminalized. The vilification of mothers who choose to nurse past the recommended one year has turned the act into a practice equated with incest and child endangerment in the United States (Kendall-Tackett and Sugarman

1995). Because breastfeeding is often sexualized in the United States, mothers may feel the need to emotionally detach themselves from the experience or view themselves as objectified machines in order to avoid allegations of incestuous behavior. And although no one pays heed to the barely clad models on the covers of other magazines on the shelf, parenting magazines with close-up pictures of babies nursing continue to cause so much outrage that they are often removed or stylized in a way that disembodies the act of breastfeeding. I feel an especially close kinship with Jacqueline Mercado, a Peruvian immigrant in Texas who was indicted for a sex offense after photographing herself while offering her breast to her one-year-old son. At the time, Mercado's husband was trying to legally enter the United States and could not be present for his son's first year of life due to legal difficulties. As *Dallas Observer News* reported in 2003, after developing Mercado's pictures, Wal-Mart employees alerted the police because they deemed the images "child pornography" (Korosec 2003). Though the picture was meant to "re-create" an important moment that the child's father missed out on, law enforcement officials deemed the photos "sexually explicit" and pornographic, and thus child protective services removed Mercado's children from the home, separating them from their parents for months. The court failed to recognize the difference in cultural attitudes toward breastfeeding and the social constructions of motherhood and sexuality that shape our Western perceptions.

Another famous example of breastfeeding discrimination in academia is the case of Sophie Currier, the medical student who was denied extra time on her nine-hour medical licensing exam so that she could pump (Olson 2007). An exclusive breastfeeder, Currier was not physically able to abstain from expressing her milk for the duration of the testing time because of severe breast discomfort. Though the exam board eventually allowed her to have more time, the language that flowed during the debate signaled cultural perspectives about breastfeeding that lacked understanding of breastfeeding as a biological process and instead continued to vilify women's choice to nurse.

The mainstream rhetoric and discourse about breastfeeding attests to how mothers' bodies remain objectified. Nursing covers are referred to as "hooter hiders" and "titty tents." In addition, society continues to circulate the myth that pregnancy and breastfeeding "kills your brain cells," an experience sometimes referred to as "pregnancy brain" or "momnesia," despite studies showing how breastfeeding releases hormones that stimulate parts of the brain responsible for memory and cognition (Ellison 2005). Clearly, patriarchy, through the hypersexualization of women's breasts as well as the lack of accommodations in public and work spaces for nursing mothers, continues to perpetuate stereotypes of these mothers as objectified or deviant women in order to decenter women in the mothering experience and deny mothers the authority over their own bodies.

The precious year I spent traveling back and forth from my office to the child-development center was difficult. Ironically, however, it was within the realm of discomfort that I became more conscious of my privileged position in an institution that provided me with child care, a flexible schedule, and the freedom to raise my voice if I felt my rights were being threatened. The psychological stress I experienced did not compare to the psychological trauma experienced by many working-class mothers who lack adequate child care, legal protection (immigrant mothers), and access to education and who face domestic and workplace violence on a daily basis. Through my work and through sharing my *testimonios*, I labor to satisfy these mothers' hunger for social justice and the end to sexist practices as well. By beginning my work for social justice through my specific bodily experience, I hope that others may use their own bodies and experiences as points of entry into both political action and theory construction.

MAT(T)ERRING ACADEMIA

During pregnancy, a woman unlearns and relearns her body, discovering both its limitations and its possibilities. The process of unlearning and relearning has become a permanent part of my embodied ethos, which flows into my academic life. This embodied ethos demands that I use my body as an entry point into spaces of academic discomfort to challenge hegemonies and create paths of possibility. Though for some breastfeeding may be a "natural" act, for others who encounter resistance to breastfeeding in their careers or communities, it can serve as the beginning of radical counteraction, a point from which they can begin to challenge hegemonies that limit their choices and restrict their agency over their own bodies. For me as a scholar in Chicana and feminist maternal studies, the act of breastfeeding has enfleshed my experience as a researcher, adding the material weight to my theoretical and, at times, abstract work. Just as important, it has heightened the urgency I feel about my work, my status as a graduate student, and my employment as a low-wage teaching assistant, which encourages me to work harder so that I can graduate while meeting the needs of both the university and my family.

Breastfeeding fulfilled more than my daughter's hunger; it satisfied the hunger I felt in my own body and centered that body within the production of theory. As a student working within academic traditions and fields rooted in histories that marginalize women's bodies and lived experiences, I have found that nursing has given dimension to my learning, my research, and my mothering. I situate this work within the trajectory of Chicana body writing by Chicana feminists such as Gloria Anzaldúa (2007), Cherríe Moraga (2000), and Emma Pérez (1999), who write from their racialized, sexualized, and gendered bodily experiences. Breastfeeding has shown me that satisfying my own hungers is necessary in order to satisfy the hunger of others, for I cannot adequately meet the needs of others if I cannot meet my own. Breastfeeding has allowed me to recognize that my roles as researcher and mother are of the same skin and that in the work I do through both roles, lives are always at stake.

SUPPORT MOTHERS, CHANGE THE WORLD: TOWARD A MORE INCLUSIVE UNIVERSITY

Now, as I finish my dissertation on a Ford Fellowship, I reflect on my journey as a mother-scholar and the challenges and privileges that I have experienced along the way. I was a teaching assistant on a low-paying fellowship, but I was also married to a spouse who could work full-time. I had to pay for three kids to go to day care, but the day care was on campus and was affordable compared to other child-care providers in the city. I heard distasteful comments from students about my pregnancy and my role as a mother but was wholly supported by a department that encouraged my research and worked with my delivery date to ensure I could continue to teach and stay on the fellowship. My ability to breastfeed my daughter and receive the support of my department colleagues during this time significantly contributed to my feeling of satisfaction as a mother and a scholar, which further enhanced my scholarship and productivity.

In a discussion of Ann Crittenden's *The Price of Motherhood: Why the Most Important Job in the World Is Still the Least Valued* (2001) in my women's studies class, a student asked: "What can universities do to support mothers?" Looking at my pregnant student shifting her belly to the side while she sat in an old, one-armed desk, I responded, "Well, what does your desk suggest about the 'typical' university student? The 'typical' student, first of all, is not pregnant." The physical terrain of the university—the desks, the lack of diaper-changing stalls and pumping rooms, and the absence of high chairs in the dining areas—spatially and environmentally marginalizes mothers on campus, if not completely rendering them invisible. Professors or class policies that allow little flexibility for making up missed classes or assignments, especially when children are sick or when a woman has given birth to a child, further oppress undergraduate mothers. Universities that support their mothers (and fathers) by acknowledging their presence in positive ways will enable their student mothers to construct strong maternal identities that will empower them in their homes, in the classroom, and, it is to be hoped, in society at large.

Feeding my daughter allowed me to feed my body and soul. As a consequence, when I begin teaching again, I will create assignments that allow students to access and experience their bodies and thus their histories in ways that bring inspiration, pleasure, and even pain. If, as Gloria Anzaldúa (2007) writes in her work on the borderlands, it is first through the body that transformation of the mind and soul are achieved, then when a mother experiences her body fully, her potential to become an agent of change and justice for her family, community, and university is even greater and a benefit for all.

3

DIVERSE ACADEMIC SUPPORT FOR AN EMPLOYEE, MOTHER, AND NONTRADITIONAL STUDENT

Wendy K. Wilde

WHEN I BEGAN my employment in the English Writing Program at the University of Massachusetts–Amherst, a large, public university in New England in 1980, I was excited to be a secretary, following the footsteps of my mother, who was a secretary until she got married. I was nineteen years old. As I walked into 305 Bartlett Hall, the main office of a cluster of offices along the hallway, the atmosphere was casual and relaxed. Four women were gathered in the main office, sitting on the white, plastic bench or standing, drinking their coffee, talking about last night's episode of *Hill Street Blues*, oblivious to my entry. I was amazed by the female energy projected throughout the room; it was my first empowering experience on campus. Over the course of several years, I would be "mothered" by these women (referred to throughout this essay as my "aunties") while observing and learning from them.

My story here bears witness to the challenges I faced and the opportunities I embraced in the academy (first as an entry-level employee and then as a student) and demonstrates how the female relationships and connections I developed enhanced my life as a mother and woman. In many ways, my university aunties helped "raise" me because, many of them mothers themselves, they took on a maternal role in my life and served as role models. My aunties were in some sense like the "othermothers" whom Patricia Hill Collins (1994) portrays in her black feminist theory, those mothers who routinely take care of children in the black community even though their maternal ties are social rather than biological. My aunties also resemble the "fictive kin" Carol Stack (1975) portrays in *All Our Kin*—that is, black women who claimed one another as sisters as a way to assert the right to give and get care. My experience with aunties suggests that the figures "othermothers" and "fictive kin" can be utilized to understand other social and racial contexts. My aunties became the othermothers and fictive kin in my life and a key part of my survival strategy and success across work, personal, and academic environments. Yet my story is far from unique. I tell a highly gendered story, a story of the constraints routinely faced by working mothers (Garey 1999). I tell a story of social class, a story about the potent barriers—rooted in childhood, exacerbated in marriages, and amplified on the job—that make it more difficult for working-class mothers to reach what members of the middle class often simply assume or take for granted (Lareau 2003; Furstenberg 2010). I also tell a story of positive experiences shared by others who sometimes make the "hard choice," as Kathleen Gerson (1985) so aptly calls it, to deviate from their past and seize those opportunities and pathways that make it possible to overcome some gendered and class-based constraints.

After working more than thirty years in a university setting, I now realize that my initial decision to work rather than commit to a college education was the result of my working-class background, although at the time this reason was unbeknownst to me. My growing up on a dairy farm until the age of sixteen in a small, rural community formed many of my attitudes, beliefs, and early experience of life. Like most children of the working class (Gerstel 2011), I was related to practically every family on the street, with no connection to the outside world except for the bus ride to a school twenty-five miles away. Most of my cousins began to work right away upon their graduation from high school. My mother's exit from her early life as a secretary to a new role as a farmer's wife, where she labored around our home and farm, was expected and accepted. She was "doing motherhood" as needed in the culture of a rural agricultural community (Garey 1999).

I wanted to experience something different than my rural home life could offer. Although I was not sure what I wanted to do, I attended a local community college for a year and studied secretarial science with the help of a church scholarship. I continued to feel an urgency to make money, yet working part-time at the local supermarket while attending school was not getting me closer to my financial and personal goals. I was not entirely sold on the importance of a college education; it did not seem practical. Instead, I had dreams of finding a fulfilling job, getting married, and having kids. I wanted to move out of my parents' home, create my own home, and begin a new adventure outside my remote rural community.

One of my professors at the community college recognized my doubts about college and recommended that I apply for a job at the university. Luckily for me, there were many openings, so I applied in November 1980, and by December I was a university employee. At the time, I had no idea how my life's path would deviate from the culture of a working-class community and farm life where I spent my early years. As I began working in the Writing Program, I soon discovered an eye-opening life outside the farm.

My early aspiration of getting married and having a child came true six months later when I discovered I was pregnant at the age of twenty. This news was a shock to my parents because of their (conservative) Christian values so prevalent in rural communities, and so a "shotgun" wedding followed in November 1981. My university aunties, in contrast, reacted to my news with excitement but without judgment. I received so much love and support from the people I worked with in the Writing Program, including other staff, faculty members, graduate students, and especially my aunties. They were protective of me while also guiding me through this unfamiliar territory of becoming a new mom at such a young age. In May 1982, my son came into the world.

BECOMING A YOUNG MOTHER

Becoming a mom at the age of twenty-one was scary and overwhelming, especially because I had to go back to work a month after giving birth (by cesarean section). This was in the 1980s, when a growing proportion of working-class couples could no longer rely on only one income (Roos 2010). Working-class women could rarely afford to take more than a month off to care for their new infants, and I was one of them (Perry-Jenkins, Repetti, and Crouter 2000). Because I had not been employed at the university long enough to accrue even two months of sick or vacation time, I returned to work in early June, taking my son with me to the office. In addition, there was no alternative to going off the payroll system, especially if you did not have enough sick time accrued for maternity leave. Today, the university's Professional Staff Union manages a sick-leave bank where employee sick days are deposited each year, which allows new moms who do not have accrued personal sick and vacation days or have used them up to apply for additional sick days from the bank. Fortunately for me, my aunties in the Writing Program were sympathetic to my situation and welcomed my son into 305 Bartlett Hall. As a result, I brought my son and a playpen to work with me until he was old enough to be placed in child care. The director even gave my son "airplane rides" as he did his own son.

When my son cried and was hungry, I found the inside front of my shirt dampening as the overproduction of his nourishment couldn't wait until I found a private space to nurse him. One of my aunties, who had three sons, was especially helpful. She took me under her wing and easily shared her wisdom of motherhood as I juggled doing my job and caring for my son at the same time. She taught me simple parenting techniques such as setting feeding and sleep schedules and limiting my impulse to pick up my son immediately just because he was making a noise or fussing. All but one of my aunties were mothers themselves; they were fifteen to twenty years older than I, and their wisdom provided many layers of support. I see that perhaps I was subconsciously discovering my multiple intertwined identities as a woman, mother, and worker through the "fabric" created by my aunties (Garey 1999). My son soon became part of this close-knit community and reaped the benefits of having several surrogate aunties in Bartlett Hall who became a part of our lives. As I look back at this period in my when I became an employee of the university, I realize I was learning how to be a mom while working outside the home, all with my fictive kin's help.

One of the most difficult and emotionally draining tasks I faced was placing the care of my infant son in someone else's hands. The university did have a child-care center, but children weren't accepted until they were fifteen months old. The university's Skinner Lab accepted infants, but spaces were few, it was not full-time, and the cost was high. I always wondered why the university did not support more child-care for younger children considering that the maternity (unpaid) leave policy was only for two months. As I came to understand and a growing number of feminists are showing, the United States, when compared to almost every other developed country in the world, is exceptional for the absence of public support it provides to working parents (Heymann 2000).

As a consequence of limited child-care facilities at the university, for his early years my son stayed with various friends I knew who lived near my home and were stay-at-home moms. When my son was finally accepted to the university child care, I was so relieved; he would be close by, and the cost would be lower than other kinds of care. My relief was short-lived, however, when I received a call from someone at the child-care center saying that my son had injured himself. He had a cast placed on his leg and returned to the university child-care center two weeks later. After eight long weeks, the cast was removed. Two weeks after that I received another call in which they informed me that my son was now not walking on his other leg. My initial thought was, "Is he doing this for attention?" Yet after an X ray, we learned that his other leg was fractured; this second injury was again caused by unsupervised play on the same piece of equipment with the same boy. I admit that my son was a handful with a great deal of energy, but so are many other kids. I was beginning to understand that there was a systemic problem that made it impossible for him to obtain the attention he needed in this child-care center. State budgets have always been tight, but they seem particularly tight when it comes to the allocation of funds for services (in particular for child care and hiring of staff) that benefit employees (Clawson and Gerstel 2002). And the situation for our family unfortunately became worse.

Because the timing and circumstances around the second injury were so unusual, the hospital called in the Department of Social Services. Of course, both my husband and I were upset and angry. As I was in the hospital room with my son trying to calm and console him, the doctors and other hospital staff brought my husband to the X-ray room and proceeded to accuse him of causing these injuries to our son. How could Social Services accuse my husband when it was while my son was at day care that he injured himself and had to be carried out in my arms? The Department of Social Services came to do a home visit to investigate the cause of the injuries. I felt totally stripped naked, helpless and judged. We had to defend our home, which was under constant repair; not perfect, but it was home. We had a wood stove in the kitchen that heated our small cottage, with no fence or protective barrier to keep our son away. We had an opening in the floor in the living room that led down to an area we had just finished digging out, to accommodate our washer and dryer. Our fear was that the social worker would think that my son fell down the living room stairs.

This fear typically associated with the Department of Social Services and the accusatory fingers it points are not a consequence of our personal failings as parents. They are instead the result of a wider institutional disregard for those with few resources. Their response was just one more example of the all too common "blaming the victim," although it is a reality that child abuse exists (Ryan 1976). In the end, the Department of Social Services concluded that the injuries did occur at the child-care center and not in our home, but the child-care center was not charged with negligence. Furthermore, we had to hire a lawyer to remove my son from the list of kids who needed protective services even though we were not at fault. We had to withdraw him from the university child-care center, and for the next few years he went to several different licensed day-care providers' homes, where I thought he would get more individualized attention and care.

I learned, however, that using private, licensed providers was also difficult; they were unstable and different from child-care centers. I remember finding my son (he was about three) sitting in "the corner" at one such place. When I asked the provider, a grandmotherly woman, what he did wrong, she said a construction worker had found him at the nearby work site and had carried him back. He had wandered off because he wanted to see all the big trucks and backhoes. She was upset because he did not stay in the yard—even though she clearly wasn't watching him. I remember feeling lost and frustrated that once again my son could not get the supervision he needed. But I did not feel alone.

My aunties in the Writing Program were incredibly patient and supportive of my problems with child care. Their constant, straightforward advice to stand up for my son and myself helped ease the guilt I harbored for leaving my son in day care, especially the days after the aforementioned incidents and the guilt I felt for possibly having to miss work again because of no child care. My aunties tamed my overwrought emotions as they convinced me that my son's well-being should take precedence over any job and that the day-care provider was not competent. When my son began kindergarten, my stress lessened because he would be in school, and I had space to breathe. As he started school, I began to think about taking advantage of what the university had to offer while also setting an example for my son.

BECOMING A NEW STUDENT

I received more than emotional support while working at the university; working in an academic department was intellectually stimulating. There was an "aha" moment one day when as the usual summer lunch crew of graduate students and staff were sitting around talking about a particular book that I knew nothing about. I thought to myself, "I need to take classes so I can feel more a part of these conversations." So in the spring of 1987, when my son was five years old, I enrolled in an English literature class taught by one of the graduate students in the Writing Program. As one of my university benefits, I could take up to six credits a semester for free while working full-time. Taking a class was empowering because I was doing something for myself; it motivated me to step back and look at the broader picture of what opportunities could exist for my son and me. I was becoming part of the ever-growing group of "new traditional students" (once known as "nontraditional students")—those who were older than twenty-five, had a child, worked more than twenty hours a week, had a long delay between high school and college, and were now becoming a substantial part of the college student population (Belcastro and Purslow 2006). My taking classes improved both my and my son's well-being. He was happy because I was happy. He was a student, and I was a student. The Writing Program environment stimulated my interest in taking classes not only because it meant I could participate in and listen to fabulous conversations, but also because it challenged me in my work and gave me the freedom to grow.

Interestingly, when I started working at the university in 1980, I was the same age, if not younger, than most students. While they were embarking on college careers for the next four years, I was beginning a lifetime of work at the university. As I think back, I realize that my own lack of self-confidence was a constant battle, especially during my pregnancy, when I interacted with the undergraduate students who were my age. I felt they judged me—not only my physical state, but also my class status because I was not in college. However, when I was not pregnant and in my midtwenties and thirties while taking courses, I felt like a true undergraduate student largely because many did not know I was a mom or full-time employee.

By the fall of 1988, I was a stronger, more confident young woman and mother. With support and encouragement from my university aunties and coworkers, I found the strength to change the direction of life for my six-year-old son and me. The class I was enrolled in that semester was coincidentally "Introduction to Women's Studies," taught by a professor who would be part of my student life until I graduated in 2007. The campus's discrete Al-Anon meetings also empowered me to separate from my son's father and begin a new phase in my life. Becoming a single mother at the age of twenty-six was liberating, but it was also intimidating. My son and I struggled for a time, unsure of how to live as a family, just the two of us, but a huge burden had been lifted as I began the next stage of my life at the university. Just as I had walked down that hallway to Bartlett 305 on my first day of work eight years earlier, I walked down that same hallway the day after I left my husband. Some people said I was "glowing" that day as I walked with my head held high.

During the period after my separation and divorce, work and school became a haven for me, similar to what Arlie Hochschild describes in *The Time Bind* (1997), in which many employees experience the workplace as a haven because of stresses and hardships at home. The Writing Program continued to nurture me and to give me the autonomy and freedom to learn new skills and take chances with projects. My life continued to change personally and professionally. In 1992, I moved to a position in the English Department, leaving my aunties in the Writing Program. I felt as if I were leaving home. Yet as I moved forward in my career, I soaked up as much knowledge and took advantage of as many opportunities as possible, always remembering the lessons learned from my aunties. And as my network of women grew, my confidence also grew. Three years later, when my son was thirteen years old, I accepted a professional position at the university and met my current husband. I was indeed moving forward.

As my career at the university reaches thirty-one years, I am proud of the many things I have accomplished. I learned how to balance and navigate life between two worlds, work and home, and in the process I have raised an incredible son while also obtaining a bachelor's degree and moving successfully from classified positions to professional ones. Over the years, I have formed many professional and personal relationships, mostly with women, many of them mothers, and now I find myself also becoming an auntie and mentoring younger women.

BECOMING AN "AUNTIE"

Many working mothers share challenging experiences and missed opportunities that later become stories of triumph and accomplishment. This is especially true for those of us whose backgrounds limit our experience and understanding of such a diverse world. I believe my successes are rooted in the culture of higher education, which allowed me to grow intellectually, professionally, and emotionally through relationships with the women who worked and continue to work at the university. These women helped me raise my son and nurture myself.

My entry into the workforce at the University of Massachusetts–Amherst was molded through a working culture that enabled me to mature intellectually and emotionally while also empowering me to become a compassionate individual. At a young age, I knew I wanted a different kind of life than the one my mother experienced, and as I experience daily life on campus today, I am grateful for the larger network of women and mothers who are intellectuals, students, and employees and who influence my understanding of the world. My early network within my work environment in the Writing Program was limited in scope because the university had limited resources to support the women and mothers who were its workforce. The university still has limited resources, but today many of us take an active approach to creating support networks, and my own network now spans across the university. Working within campus groups such as the Community, Diversity, and Social Justice Committee (in which I was both member and chair), engaging in various studies, participating in courses, and sustaining personal activism in two labor unions have created spaces for me to share my experience and knowledge as a working mother. Although the university is a bureaucratic environment that is not always family friendly in terms of policies, it does offer a space for collegial collectivity among the people who share common personal and professional goals.

My personal experience of having low self-esteem and overcoming it became a useful tool as I advised students. I tend to attract students who are not typically supported in university settings—students from a working-class environment, students of color, first-generation students, and students who struggle academically. I can relate to them on a personal and experiential level. They, too, want to be successful in life and prove to themselves and their families that they can do it. And they can, just as I did.

4

BREAKING THE GLASS CEILING WHILE BEING A MOTHER

Parenting, Teaching, Research, and Administration

Kim Powell

FROM THE BEGINNING of my academic career, I was determined to stay single and childless, which would allow me to have complete focus as I worked on my M.A. and Ph.D. degrees and become a faculty member at Luther College in 1992. My first three years at Luther were fully concentrated on teaching and research; my career was my life. I heard female faculty with children talk about the struggles of balancing work and home. They would say they could not attend evening events, something expected as part of the culture of a small liberal arts school, and at the time I believed their use of family as an excuse not to fulfill their faculty obligations was absurd. Little did I know that within a few years I would have a more personal understanding of family obligations and the implications of the barriers mothers face in the academy (Gee and Norton 2009).

The term *glass ceiling* was used in a 1986 *Wall Street Journal* article to describe the invisible barriers that women face as they move up in corporate organizations. Twenty years ago women could see the top positions in a company but were unable to reach them due to unwritten rules based on gender and the assumptions about gender-specific roles such as childbirth and motherhood. In this chapter, I argue that the glass ceiling is still very present, especially in the academy, as witnessed by my own academic trajectory and decision to become a parent. For mothers interested in moving up the administrative ladder, there is always the concern of how the demands of motherhood will match up with the public expectations of high-profile positions. The tight flexibility of such positions has unfortunately limited my move into higher-education administration, even despite my being invited to apply for deanships. Being a mother ultimately imposes restrictions on women professionally because the demands of the work are not consistent with the time and effort it takes to be a good mother and maintain sanity.

FROM SINGLE AND CHILDLESS TO MARRIED WITH CHILDREN

In 1995, I met and married my husband. Though I did not want to have children when I married, the sudden death of my father-in-law focused my attention on family and having a child. When my husband and I discussed growing our family, I wondered how this decision would be viewed, given it was early in my career and the majority of faculty at my college was older with fully grown children. I sought the advice of one of the few female full professors with children in my department. She advised me to plan my pregnancy for a summer birth and emphasized that to be a successful academic, my career needed to come first. She said, without apology, that her children knew her career came first and her family second. That struck me as sad for the children (and for her). Although I said nothing, I did not believe in choosing between career and family but would aim to achieve a balance because both were increasingly important to me.

I did heed my colleague's advice about having a summer pregnancy because it is believed that having a child midsemester disrupts classes and needlessly burdens colleagues who have to step in to teach classes or find a replacement. Robin Wilson concurs: "It's become an unwritten rule in academe that female professors who can manage it give birth between May and August" (1999), when students are not around. Following this rule, my husband and I perfectly planned my pregnancy so I would give birth the week after classes ended for spring semester in 1997. I would not have to miss any part of the academic year, I would not inconvenience my colleagues, and I would be able to focus on being a mother for the summer because I did not teach during those months. However, as I would learn repeatedly in the coming years of child rearing, children have their own plans. On February 28, just four weeks into spring semester, at twenty-eight weeks pregnant, I became ill with HELLP syndrome (hemolysis, elevated liver enzymes, low blood platelets) and was placed on bed rest. HELLP syndrome is a reaction to pregnancy that causes the mother's body to experience liver failure, seizures, or even death if it is not caught early and monitored. Three days into bed rest, my condition became life threatening, and I was rushed to a hospital with a Neonatal Intensive Care Unit (NICU) for an emergency cesarean section. In early March, my daughter arrived at one pound, fifteen ounces, and spent seven weeks in the NICU, while I spent two days in intensive care and another three days in the hospital recuperating. Although my colleagues were very supportive, I was allowed only twenty-eight days of maternity leave, and only two of my classes were reassigned because the remaining third was a specialized course. At this small rural college, none of the local professors was qualified to teach my "Rhetorical Criticism" class. Therefore, despite being on maternity leave and recuperating from a cesarean, I taught the course via tape recorder soon after my daughter's birth, then in my living room for several weeks, and finally at the college until the end of the semester. I was traveling three hours roundtrip daily to the hospital to see my daughter in the NICU, so my full concentration was split, and I could not focus on my own recovery or my baby's; I was also grading papers and teaching a class required of our students to graduate. Thus, the struggle of being both mother and professor began.

By fall semester, I was back to teaching full time with my six-month-old daughter in day care. In retrospect, I wish I had been given more time to spend with her at home, yet getting a replacement for the fall semester proved to be difficult at my institution because no local adjuncts were available to teach my courses. In addition, part of my load was coaching and traveling with the college forensics team, which kept me away from home several weekends a year. Thus, if I wanted to keep my faculty position, I had to return to work full-time in the fall. It was necessary not only for my career, but also for my family economically. One solution that allowed me to adequately divide my attention between home and work was negotiating with the department head for a two-day-a-week teaching schedule. Challenging the traditional small college five-day schedule unfortunately resulted in some backlash from colleagues and students. Colleagues assumed I was not working as much as they were (though my teaching evaluations continued to be the highest in the department, as was my scholarly productivity), and some students said they could not find me in my office when they needed me (though I held as many office hours as my colleagues). These symptoms of the "maternal wall" (Porpora n.d.) are reactions stemming from assumptions that women with family are not or will not be as productive at work. Friends who were stay-at-home moms were also critical of my choice to continue my career because I didn't meet their expectations of a "good mother"—that is, one who prioritizes her children rather than her own needs, desires, and career aspirations (Mottarella et al. 2009).

Regardless of the criticisms and challenges I faced daily, my identities as both professor and mother were important to my own happiness. In order for my child and me to be happy, to occupy the "happy mother–happy child position" (Swanson and Johnston 2003, 68), I needed to have an identity outside motherhood. And although research by Debra Swanson and Deirdre Johnston suggests that full-time working mothers are not as happy as part-time employed mothers, I did not want to give up my career. Being a part-time academic or leaving academia entirely was not an option for me, either financially or emotionally; therefore, finding happiness as a full-time professor *and* full-time mom was necessary. During hiring discussions, I unfortunately often heard comments about women taking time off for family reasons and then hiring committees later assuming that these women had been fired or had priorities in the wrong places. Within this academic landscape (Hornig 2003), it became not only desirable but also imperative that I carve out a space to be an effective mother and professor if I were to succeed at both.

REDEFINING ROLES AS PROFESSOR-MOM RESEARCHER

In a faculty member's early years in academia, administrators and tenured faculty have the unwritten expectation that the member will be wed to his or her work and labor tirelessly to meet tenure demands. The tenure clock's overlap with childbearing years, as Cheryl Maranto and Andrew Griffin (2011) argue, is indicative of a preference in academia for workers without family responsibilities. This preference further solidifies a gendered glass ceiling because mothers may not advance as quickly as men or women without children. As Joan Williams argues, the ideal worker in academe is "someone who can move anywhere from Massachusetts to New Mexico, and can work like a fiend until tenure is granted—or denied—at around age 35" (2000). Furthermore, this ideal worker assumes an "open-ended time commitment of time, energy and personal resources" (Fothergill and Feltey 2003, 16). Giving birth while the tenure clock is ticking, however, is an interruption to academe's "ideal worker," of whom extensive research and publishing is expected. In my case, I had luckily met my publication requirements largely by the time my daughter was born one year before tenure review.

My research areas were political and social movement rhetoric, and although they were important topics, my areas of interest changed once my daughter was born. I redefined my academic practices in order to weave the personal with the scholarly. As my daughter watched *Teletubbies* and *Barney*, I studied gender depictions in children's media. Because she was premature, I researched the effects of prematurity on parents and eventually edited a book titled *Living Miracles: Stories of Hope from Parents of Premature Babies* (Powell and Wilson 2000). Being in the interdisciplinary field of communication allowed for my life as a mom and researcher to be interwoven and intersectional. Yet balancing teaching, motherhood, and research as well as coaching and traveling with the forensics team became too much to handle. Two years after my daughter was born, I approached my department head and college dean to ask them if I could step away from forensics to better balance my home and work life. Although my department head was initially supportive, I later learned that in my tenure letter he questioned my loyalty to the college and also falsely stated that I had been hired to be a forensics coach and that my desire to step away from this position was a breach of contract. The dean was fortunately supportive of my multiple roles and supported my tenure and promotion to associate professor. It was a real possibility that without a supportive dean I would have been denied tenure because of my decision to reduce my load to better balance mothering and scholarly production. This process was a life-changing lesson regarding the glass ceiling in academia: unless female faculty members who are mothers have strong advocates in positions of power who value working parents, they are particularly in danger of not reaching the rank of tenured professor because their very presence challenges the status quo.

FROM PROFESSOR-MOM TO DEPARTMENT HEAD

After I received tenure, the two-day-a-week teaching schedule I held in my first semester after my daughter was born was changed to a four-day schedule due to the visibility expected of a professor on my small college campus. Although my career carried on fairly well, in 1998 I became department head with no course release, which was not a consistent practice on my campus. Teaching seven courses a year, serving as department head, and attending to committee assignments accentuated even more the difficulty of the balancing act between career and motherhood. Although my husband was supportive, he also had a full-time job, and, as is often the case (Collay 2002), the majority of family and child responsibilities fell on me as the mother and primary caretaker. The successful continuation of my career required that I rely on day care. As Tondra Loder (2005) found in a study of school principals who were also mothers, educators at all levels rely on paid day care in order for their careers to continue. The fact that my daughter attended a quality day-care center that I had faith in made my new responsibilities possible.

As my career became increasingly rewarding, so did the desire to add to our family. Because my first pregnancy resulted in HELLP syndrome and another pregnancy would be life-threatening, we turned to adoption as an excellent alternative. In 2001, my husband and I became foster parents with the intention to adopt, and that summer, perfectly timed for the academic year, we adopted a pair of sibling boys, ages one and three. Our new sons came to us with many emotional challenges and developmental delays, including attention deficit hyperactivity disorder and oppositional defiant disorder. They had been neglected and abused in their birth home and had a great deal of anger they could not process or express verbally at their young ages. They would have screaming fits that could last an hour and would both lie and hoard. After three summer months of a challenging but rewarding adjustment, I returned to teaching full-time and used day care so that I could focus on work. As Swanson and Johnston have argued, "Full-time employed mothers try to justify their work decision by separating work and family spheres" (2003, 64). That is, in an ideal situation, while at work one thinks only of work, and while at home one thinks only of family. Although I was fairly successful at separating the spheres, the two once again melded in my scholarship as I researched the feelings of loss experienced by adult adoptees and the media representation of the U.S. foster-care system. An added advantage of straddling two spheres was that being a mother of children from challenging backgrounds made me a better, more empathetic teacher by enabling me to see each student as someone's child with unique gifts and challenges.

Despite my teaching and publication success, the stress of trying to balance work and motherhood was taking its toll. I felt immense pressure, leaving the office by four o'clock each day to be with the three children and prepare dinner and then later at night checking email, answering department head inquiries, and grading papers. One night my daughter said, "You are always grading papers and working. Can you pay attention to me?" I did focus on the children much of the time, but her words broke my heart and brought all the stresses I was experiencing to the surface, sending me to the dean's office the next day to ask for a reduced contract that would allow me more time with my children. At the time, I was not receiving a course release for serving as department head, so I negotiated a release and retained my position, which granted me more daytime hours to do my work at the office.

There was a five-day-a-week work expectation at my school, which I initially adopted as the department head. However, I began to challenge this unspoken expectation by carving out a day in the workweek to focus on my research and writing without having to hear the cries of my children, students, or colleagues. Wednesday was my quiet day to work from home, while my children were in school and day care. Although this practice was at first quite controversial in the culture of a small liberal arts college, many of my colleagues now work away from the office one day a week as well. In my case, the time lessened the professor-mom stress, fostered more productivity, and created opportunities to expand my administrative experiences.

PROFESSOR-MOM OF FOUR TO DEPARTMENT HEAD TO WOMEN'S STUDIES DIRECTOR

In 2003, we adopted our fourth child, a little girl from foster care with more severe developmental delays than our sons. As in the past, we planned this adoption to occur in the summer, which allowed me time to focus on the family without having to work. In the fall, however, I became director of the Women's Studies Program and continued to serve as department chair and teaching six courses. Adopting another child with special needs meant more than I initially realized. My daughter has gross developmental delays: speech delays, cognitive delays, motor skill delays, seizure disorder, and anxiety issues; at nine years old, she is two years old developmentally. The day care my other three children attended for after-school hours was not available, and the day-care centers in the area were not physically, emotionally, or medically equipped or prepared to handle my fourth child's special needs. The stress once again began to take a toll on me, resulting in headaches, sleepless nights, and heart palpitations. My work flexibility was beneficial for our family, but the trade off was that I worked well into the night at home, so the lack of sleep compromised my physical well-being. Faye Crosby (1991) found in a study of working mothers and the work–home spheres that when stress accumulates in one sphere, mothers buffer themselves by focusing on the other sphere. Although moving between spheres did give me a break from the stresses within each, I never had an alternative sphere/space of my own beyond work and home (Fothergill and Feltey 2003). At home I was thinking about work, and at work I was thinking about home. Like many academic parents, I did my research workload and class preparation at home, outside of the typical workday, so these tasks were often compounded by my parenting responsibilities at home (Maranto and Griffin 2011). I eventually managed by focusing on one task at a time, reducing my administrative load and ambitions, and interweaving my roles as much as possible.

Once promoted to full professor in 2003 and given a sabbatical, I was granted a Fulbright to study and live with my family in Dubai, United Arab Emirates, for the 2006–2007 academic year. Working in administration in Dubai energized me and fueled my desire to move into higher-education administration. Though offered dean positions at two other colleges once I returned from my fellowship, I made the difficult choice to turn them down because of the expectations placed on time: ten-hour or more workdays, presence at evening events, and weekend work. With four young children, all at this point younger than ten, I rethought my move into academic administration and decided to wait until my children were older. However, I must admit, at least once a day I have regrets about not moving into administration and feel in many ways stifled because I thrive on being a leader. I do not feel I am reaching my full potential in academia, yet I realize that teaching (rather than administering) full-time is the best work situation for my children and me at this time in our lives. I have reached a glass ceiling imposed by the demands of motherhood and therefore must postpone my career advancement for my children and for my sanity.

BALANCING AS FULL PROFESSOR-MOM AND EDITOR

Perhaps it is growing older and wiser, resetting priorities, or needing to reduce stress, but after my sabbatical in 2006–2007, I decided not to return as department head or women's studies director. Instead, I was back on the faculty ranks as a full professor. For me, this location is perfect for my motherhood: taking summers off and teaching during my children's school hours. This schedule still has me doing research, writing, class preparation, and grading in the evenings, but I am able to negotiate time around my family and thus am able to meet my obligations for both work and motherhood. Despite my professional and personal success, academia continues to be a challenging place for women because of all of the expectations outside of teaching. I realize my position as a full professor gives me the standing to choose my schedule and negotiate my time at the office in a way that is not entirely available for women in the other faculty ranks, especially due to expectations regarding time at the office and visibility on campus before tenure. The flexibility of being a full professor also allows for pursuing nonadministrative options for advancing professionally, specifically editorships. Editing journals—in my case the *Iowa Journal of Communication* and currently *Communication Studies*—is work that can be done around children's schedules in a way administration cannot. Editing journals and occupying organizational leadership roles also allow me to mentor other women and to support the type of scholarship that informs and is informed by parenting. Finding productive challenges and venues to expand my career's flexible hours offers an outlet and alternative to moving into administration in this new phase I am now entering.

MOTHERHOOD SHOULD NOT BE A GLASS CEILING

Airini and her colleagues (2011) found in their study of women in higher education five primary factors that hinder women from advancing in leadership roles, three of which relate directly to motherhood: university environment, invisible rules, and personal circumstances. The college or university environment calls for faculty visibility on campus and complete dedication to teaching and research, and there are also invisible rules or expectations regarding committee involvement and office-hours availability, all of which do not take into consideration personal circumstances or the demands of motherhood. In my experience, the current practices of higher-education administration leave out potentially powerful leaders because the hours expected are not compatible with a focus on family. A "good mother" is home with the children after school and in the evenings, whereas a "good father" can be at work for long hours to provide economically for the family. Women in higher-education administration have said that the work is not compatible with family life, which is perhaps why there are so many men in higher-education administration with wives who often do not work outside the home or women in administrative positions who are single or have adult children (Fisher 2007). A college dean, provost, or president is expected to spend more time in the office than at home. Therefore, being a "good mother" is not compatible with being a good academic administrator. I do dream of a dean's position with a nine-month contract and telecommuting option. Such a contract would give me time with the family, especially in the summer, while also breaking the glass ceiling so that more academic mothers will be able to enter into higher academic administration. This option is unfortunately not viable given the structure of academic administration as a twenty-four/seven job with on-campus presence and decision making needed on a day-to-day basis. Until the unrealistic expectations for an academic administrator are challenged and changed, the problematic notion of a "motherhood-imposed glass ceiling," especially in the area of administration, will remain in academia.

Although I do feel frustration at not moving into academic administration, I am thankful for how becoming a parent, especially the perspective of parenting children with special needs, has informed my scholarship and teaching; I see each person as a unique individual with his or her own talents and needs. Appointing people who are also working parents in higher level positions such as dean, provost, and president would bring more diversity, empathy, and broader perspectives to the problem of how to connect work and family lives, especially considering that the creation of family-friendly policies requires support from administrators (American Council on Education 2007). As a college administrator, I would support working parents by honoring a professor's choice to work at home on some occasions, by supporting alternative and flexible schedules so faculty members can be the best parents and teachers possible, and by sharing my own experience as a model of balance between home and work. In the meantime, I am using my position on faculty committees to develop and impact family-friendly policies. For example, I worked with the Faculty Interests Committee at Luther College in 2011 to create a new parental-leave policy that will now offer options to faculty parents. The flexibility of the college's new leave policy includes the option of a six-week paid leave or up to a three-course release over an academic year; the option to take the parenting leave anytime during the year following a birth or adoption; and committee-assignment relief.

As mothers in academia, we all can work to support each other, honor requests for creative scheduling that allow us to do our best work at home and the office, encourage diversity in our scholarship that weaves motherhood and research, and chip away at the glass ceiling so that motherhood becomes more compatible with higher-education administration. Although being a mother has postponed my move into higher-education administration, I am accepting that my role as a mother must be honored over my desire to advance my career at this point in my life. The glass ceiling imposed on motherhood is a real barrier, especially in academic administration because the job expectations prevent women such as myself from balancing the obligations of motherhood with those of the ever-present campus administrator. However, I know at some point I will break through. For now, I am thankful to have a career that allows me to support my family economically and emotionally while also intertwining my experiences as a mother, researcher, and teacher. This combination in itself is already challenging the status quo; every crack in the ceiling counts.

5

TO TELL OR NOT TO TELL

Single Motherhood and the Academic Job Market

Virginia L. Lewis

TWO THINGS have meant the most to me during my adult life: being a mother and being an academician. Without either of these roles, my self-realization would be incomplete. Although these specific roles are unique to me, they represent what philosopher Alan Gewirth (1998) designates "aspirations" that bring fulfillment to human beings and should be protected in any setting involving the safeguarding of human dignity. Although past models of academic performance have been developed based on male professors who do not bear primary responsibility for the care of children—men like my own father—there is increasing recognition that these models have resulted "in the loss of skills and talent to the scholarly enterprise" (Kennelly and Spalter-Roth 2006, 30) and that the right of primary caregivers, in particular women, to productive employment within academia must be protected.

Numerous organizations, such as the College and University Work/Family Association, work toward this end, emphasizing a goal very much in line with Gewirth's model of self-fulfillment: "lifelong holistic development and a healthy and productive environment for men and women across the lifespan" (College and University Work/Family Association n. d.). But there is much to be done, as my own experience in academia shows. There still remains the risk that primary caregivers such as myself, a single mother, will be regarded as "second-class workers" (Nussbaum 2006, 215) in the competition for employment opportunities in higher education. This state of affairs flies in the face of acceptable standards of human rights and social justice, and as Martha Nussbaum reports, the problem seems to be worsening (2006, 215).

The account I give here of the challenges I faced as a single mother of three young children (Asher, Deryn, and Culver) upon losing tenure and being thrust a second time onto the job market assumes that "a major aim of public policy ought to be the transformation of the workplace, through new flexibility and new ethical norms" (Nussbaum 2006, 215). Such a transformation should guarantee the access of all individuals to "core human entitlements," including productive employment (Nussbaum 2006, 70). When enacted in institutions of higher education, this transformation would then reap the benefits of the "skills and talent" that all professors—not just those who fit a certain profile—can bring to the scholarly community, regardless of their status as caregivers. This is the goal I seek to support with my contribution to this volume.

My journey as an academic professional began in 1989, when I was still "unencumbered," with only myself to look after. Earning tenure in my new position as a German professor became my primary personal goal as my career got under way. Following a proven model of career and family planning in higher education (Mason and Goulden 2002, 25), I reasoned that once I had tenure, I could then contemplate having the family I had always dreamed about because tenure would bring me the security I needed to pursue my companion goal of motherhood. My career went well in those early years—at the age of twenty-nine I had a tenure-track job and a bright professional future. I successfully earned promotion and tenure, and even though my efforts to find a mate dead-ended, I realized the good fortune of living in the 1990s, an age when pursuing motherhood as a single woman was a relatively straightforward option. And I succeeded: within four years of my promotion, along with being a tenured associate professor, I was also the mother of a wonderful three-year-old, with healthy twins on the way.

Five months into my pregnancy, the unthinkable happened. My dean called me and the other members of our department to a meeting and told us our language programs would be discontinued. The reasons cited included financial exigency in a move informed by corporate decision making: it would be cheaper to deliver our programs by outsourcing them with the help of computers and external teaching and evaluation resources than to continue providing them using professors in a face-to-face classroom. Of course, neither the fact of my pregnancy nor the welfare of my family was of any concern in this decision. My status as a caregiver did nothing to prevent the administration from eliminating the department, my position, and my livelihood. My myriad contributions to the institution and its students were no longer factors in a decision driven by the financial advantage to the university, as represented by the monetary value of my salary and benefits.

Thus, as a forty-year-old, soon-to-be single mother of three young children, I was thrust back onto the academic job market in the search for a livelihood. My credentials and experience were naturally assets in this situation, but what about my children? The question of how to handle my parental status while I was job hunting loomed large. A trusted colleague, who was concerned that potential employers would perceive me as a "second-class worker," advised me to hide the existence of my children from them. In fact, not one single colleague advised me to share openly the fact that I was raising three children on my own. This advice speaks volumes of the status of motherhood in the working world in general and in academia in particular at the turn of twenty-first century: being a primary caregiver constitutes a disability and a liability to be hidden at all costs. My heart desired to share the charming pictures of my newborn twins and their older brother with the parties who would interview me, but I violently suppressed this urge.

It is one thing to hide photographs stored away in one's wallet, but another to disguise the fact that one is nursing healthy twins and trying to pump milk on overnight journeys to keep up with their demand. This situation posed an enormous challenge to my attempt to conceal the existence of my children from interviewers, a challenge no male would ever face, reflecting the gender-based reality that places female caregivers at a disadvantage over male ones in the competition for academic employment. I still have vivid memories of the Modern Language Association (MLA) conference in December 2000, when my twins were three months old. The timing of my interviews had to fall in line with the regular appointments I had with my breast pump. After finagling this schedule, I then had to address the question of how to haul the pump around without it being recognized by interviewers for what it was. I counted on the unobtrusive black carrying case to accomplish this. To my knowledge, no one knew I was carrying a Medela® breast pump with me as I went from interview to interview. Of course, storing the milk was out of the question. I heaved a great sigh of sadness as I was forced to "pump and dump" ounce after ounce of mother's milk down the hotel drain. My goal was solely to keep my supply up so that I could continue to nurse the twins upon my return home.

None of my interviewers at the MLA conference asked the forbidden question concerning my family status. Questions about marriage and children are illegal according to federal Equal Employment Opportunity rules and thus among the "don't ask" questions listed by the MLA (2007). But the lie I was engaged in, denying the existence of my own children to these people, many of whom were parents themselves, ate away at my conscience. Even as I participated in the exchanges that would shape my future career, I questioned the advice of the colleague who had said I must not let on that I was a single mother. I found myself trying to read the attitudes toward parenting and children of those interviewing me. When it was clear that some of them were likewise fathers and mothers, I felt myself on safer ground and bravely shared that I, too, was a proud parent. It then dawned on me that my family and I would be happiest employed in a department where prejudices concerning the intrusion of family life upon one's accomplishments at work were negligible. Would I not be better off revealing my parental status and learning whether my potential employers stood on higher ground regarding primary caregivers as second-class workers?

Once I was invited to on-campus interviews, this question grew in significance. At first, I continued my cautious posture of pretending I had no children. Again I was confronted with the question of how to handle the needs of my nursing twins, whose demands had only increased, while I was away on interviews that extended over two or more days. It was one thing to hide my breast-pumping activities during interviews that lasted a mere thirty minutes; it was quite another to pull off this feat during a two-day interview. I was forced to grill my interviewers in advance concerning the schedule they were preparing for me. What breaks did they envision? Was there any room for a half-hour rest during the day to allow myself to "regroup"? Could I do this in a private location, preferably with an electrical outlet close at hand? Concealing the purpose of this time alone challenged my powers of invention to the extreme. And during these breaks, I lived in constant fear that someone would demand to know what in the heck I was up to and would find out the "horrible truth" of my babies' existence! This was, I realized, a sorry way to survive an interview for a job that must ultimately allow me the freedom and acceptance I needed to thrive not only as a professor, but also as a mother. And it angered me to realize that no man would ever have to endure such bizarre circumstances. Against this context, the conclusion that mothers of infants are less successful in their academic careers than fathers of infants is no surprise (Mason and Goulden 2002, 24–25). I felt awful, and I deplored the fact that my profession drove me to such depths of deceit.

Communications scholars have shown how the withholding of information in a market context bears certain "lying costs," including discomfort, guilt, shame, and other negative emotions (Demichelis and Weibull 2008, 1293; Kartik 2009, 1379). I can attest to the emotional pain I had to endure given my involvement in a job market historically tainted by injustices regarding primary caregivers. Even assuming my theatrics pay off and I am awarded the position I am interviewing for, I asked myself, when can I ever safely admit I am a mother? After my arrival on campus? After a year of successful employment? After I attain tenure again? It would be impossible in my new job for me to pretend I didn't love my children.

Interestingly, I was not offered any of the positions I interviewed for under the pretense of having no children. The reasons why candidates do not get certain jobs are always complex and often inscrutable. However, I came to the conclusion that lying was not working for me; the "lying costs" were too high, involving as they did long-term consequences that could hamper my success both as a professor and as a parent. I required a job that would allow me to be myself in both of these vital roles. In order to find such a position, I had to be honest about my family status. Indeed, I decided I would interview my potential future colleagues concerning their acceptance of parents with young children and the campus climate toward families. Would such openness about my family status doom me on the job market? I hoped not. During my last two on-campus interviews my first year back on the job market, I did just as my heart demanded. I explained that I was nursing twins and needed to access my breast pump during the day so as to avoid unpleasant consequences. The interviewers were gracious and understanding. My honesty made a positive impression on them. I ended up receiving job offers from both institutions and accepted a visiting associate professorship that seemed to hold promise for permanence down the road.

My journey to find the ideal position did not end there. But this account of my experiences during the trying year after losing my tenured position may suffice as an illustration of the awful dilemma faced by single parents seeking work in the academic job market. There are many institutions where the level of acceptance and understanding granted to parents of young children is limited to an extent that brings harm to the family and, I would argue, to the institution. I experienced an unhappy year at such a workplace when I was a visiting associate professor. I feel personally fortunate that the university where I am now employed has a strong family orientation and is therefore closer than many to realizing the just ideal of an academic community where all workers can thrive, regardless of their status as caregivers. The fact that the university has a program in early childhood education informs this acceptance. In addition, there is a large on-campus day-care facility, and young children are a frequent sight on university grounds. Many of our students are parents. For them, having a professor who is likewise a primary caregiver can be a godsend. I know exactly what they are going through when they must miss class in order to attend to a sick child or even bring a child to campus because a day-care arrangement fell through at the last moment. These students feel right at home with a professor who does not hesitate to circulate the latest pictures of her three beloved children for her students to admire as part of a get-to-know-you exercise. On our campus, many professors are also parents. They share my gratitude for a campus climate that not only accepts the importance of children in their lives but also makes room for these children at campus events, providing child care during faculty award ceremonies, hosting a campuswide holiday dinner where children are welcome, sponsoring children's events such as trick-or-treating in the dormitories, concerts for schoolchildren, swimming lessons, campuswide picnics, casual departmental get-togethers, and music camps.

Children are regular facets of campus life where I work, and my children are accepted as a part of that life. We all feel we belong at my place of employment. Although it would be a gross exaggeration to speak of a seamless integration of work and family on this or any other university campus—an impossible ideal given the separation of work and family that governs our economy—on my campus there is a ready acceptance of professors' roles as parents and an understanding of the need to put one's family first. I am grateful for the policies and practices that promote such acceptance on my campus. I teach at what in many ways constitutes a "family-friendly university," a privilege all primary caregivers deserve to have.

Acceptance is wonderful, yet it is really a bare minimum. Given the fact that raising a family constitutes a vehicle for self-fulfillment to which all humans ought to have a right, it is the duty of all public institutions to support this right. Concerned over low fertility rates, some nations go beyond passive support, effectively encouraging workers in their aspiration to become parents. A number of industrially advanced countries provide a range of benefits in the effort to promote fertility, including federally mandated paid maternity and paternity leave, cash subsidies, and publicly provided day care (Feyrer and Sacerdote 2008, 17). France and Sweden, for example, offer monetary incentives, flexible working hours, and up to eighteen months paid leave to encourage working mothers to have children (Bryant 2008). In such a society, would my status as a working mother be an asset rather than something to hide? Many scholars argue that beyond just meeting the exigencies of social justice, American universities can reap significant benefits by actively supporting the needs of employees who are also primary caregivers. By ensuring the broadest possible pool of talent from which to choose its employees, higher education ensures that it can fulfill its mission in the most effective manner possible. Steven Loomis and Jacob Rodriguez observe that homogenization constitutes a chief threat to higher education in an environment where franchising models of delivery are proliferating (2009, 480–481). This notion of diversity and complexity as an important value in education supports Nussbaum's call for a transformation of the workplace that will promote the inclusion of workers who are also charged with caring for dependents: "As young workers learn to think of care as part of their lives, they become less willing to accept rigid workplaces, and employers who offer flex-time and part-time options will attract the most skilled workers" (2006, 215–216).

In addition to my improved time-management skills since I became a mother, my rationales for producing scholarship in the first place has been drastically altered by my status as a caregiver. Writing with a view to making the world a better place has assumed great urgency for me because I now have offspring I will be sending out into this world to make their own way in it. Before becoming a mother, I wrote articles that would meet with acceptance among others in my discipline. Now writing as a parent, I seek higher goals to promote basic ethics of social justice and tolerance as well as to raise awareness concerning issues that interfere with the pursuit of flourishing and a meaningful life. Other scholars who are not parents undoubtedly feel the same higher calling with their scholarship, but I do feel there is a level of awareness in me now that was missing before I became a parent. As my children grow older, they serve as sounding boards for my ideas. Their constant inspiration motivates me to be an excellent role model. I want them to be proud of me, and I seek to earn their respect as they move toward adulthood. Every book I write is dedicated to them and stands on proud display in our living room.

Motherhood has had an enormous positive influence on my teaching as well. In my early years as a professor, I related to my students from the standpoint of my own experience as a student. During my years as a nonparenting instructor, I had an excellent rapport with my students, as any caring professor will and does. But now that my own student years lie far behind me, I find that my connection with my children allows me to connect with my students in a new and powerful way. As a parent with pronounced concern for the quality of the educators who teach my kids, I fully appreciate the trust granted me as an educator by other parents. In my effort to treat my students as I would wish my own children's instructors to treat them, I find I accord students high levels of respect, understanding, tolerance, and nurturing. Their crucial status as human beings worthy of dignity and respect is visible through the window of my love for my children. As a parent, I find that my urge to nurture students and promote their intellectual growth is keen because I seek the same advantages for my own kids. And students respond well to my interactions with them because they know that I see in them human beings first and German learners second. This awareness enhances their trust in my ability to nurture them intellectually in constructive and appropriate ways, as their evaluations of my courses show.

In addition, as my own kids' age nears that of most my students, my ability to understand students' mindsets, their experiences, and their educational needs and goals are enhanced. My children's experiences with the Internet, for example, help me engage the students in my classroom effectively. My son's desire to post his videos on YouTube opens my mind to the possibility that my college students may feel the same way. I encourage them to create projects for class that they can publish on YouTube, and they respond enthusiastically. Without my son's prompting, I would not have come up with such an assignment. Even a German-speaking Barbie doll, a Facebook quiz in German, an arts and crafts activity engage the learners in my classroom much as they engage my kids at home. Through my children, I have also developed close connections with our local schools, allowing me to organize practical experiences for my students to teach German to elementary school learners. This outreach is enriching our curriculum and strengthening our program's connection with the local community.

I have experienced for myself how parenthood has enriched my skills as a teacher and scholar. Motherhood has enhanced my professional success. It troubles me to imagine that should my own children choose to follow in my professional footsteps, they may find a job market even more hostile toward parenting than the one in which I have coped. After all, competition on the academic job market has in many cases become only stiffer, the stakes in our competitive economic system higher. The pressures placed on higher education by reduced funding and a market orientation make it even more difficult for primary caregivers to thrive, more likely that they will be regarded as "second-class workers." Full-time faculty positions are giving way to adjunct positions, which now compose 70 percent of the professoriate according to Loomis and Rodriguez (2009), and the centralization of work under an increasingly corporate model means that employers cannot always attend to caregivers' interests (Nussbaum 2006). The stresses endured by individuals compelled to put their offspring second in order to function adequately at work are dehumanizing and destructive (Jacobs 2004). I am fortunate to enjoy a position now that allows me to function well in both worlds, at work and at home. This state of affairs should be the norm, not the exception. As institutions invested in furthering human ends, academia and all work environments must support healthy families among their workers. When all job candidates can be forthright about their family status without fear of judgment, this goal will have been achieved.

6

CLASS, RACE, AND MOTHERHOOD

Raising Children of Color in a Space of Privilege

Irene Mata

WHEN I TELL people that I moved to Massachusetts from San Diego, California, I always get the same question: "Why?" Why would one choose to leave sunny California with its perfect weather for the cold of the Northeast? A valid question, but one that most young academics coming out of graduate school know too well is not really a question of choice. Always aware of the tight job market and the looming student loans that must be repaid, we go where the job takes us. The weather, however, is the more manageable of challenges I have faced in my relocation. The most troubling aspect of the move has been helping my children make the transition from the Southwest—a place of cultural familiarity—to the previously unknown world of affluent white suburbia in the Northeast. My formal education did not prepare me for the challenges of raising a family in a space where difference remains suspect and where real diversity is almost nonexistent. We feel as if we have stumbled into an alien world, where real Mexican food does not exist, where we rarely hear the sounds and rhythms of Latino music pouring out of the car windows, where the cadence of Spanish is nearly absent, even though Puerto Ricans have resided in the Northeast for many generations. In the neighborhood in which we reside, I find myself concerned with the project of raising children in a space of isolation and trying to find ways to help them survive the alienation. In this essay, I offer my *testimonio* of challenges and strategies of resistance in an effort to expand our dialogue of what it means to be a mother in academia and the role that intersectionality continues to play in the daily decisions we make in educating our children.

Making the transition from graduate student to faculty member is a challenging process rife with professional pitfalls. From learning to negotiate department politics to figuring out the balance of service and multiple student demands, the first few years out of graduate school are difficult, to say the least. When we add class and racial difference as well as the job of motherhood, one's professional life becomes that much more complicated. Women in academia continue to confront a system that persists in supporting a hierarchy of gender (Monroe et al. 2008; S. Warner 2010). A woman's advancement on the tenure ladder is further affected by the choice to have children. In their project "Do Babies Matter?" Mary Ann Mason and Marc Goulden endeavor to understand the role that family formation plays in the advancement of women in academia, specifically the University of California system. In their preliminary findings, they found that women with babies were 29 percent less likely than women without babies to enter into tenure-track positions (2002, 5). The same cannot be said for men: the project found that, "for men, being married with young children is the dominant mode of success" (4). Although men may now be more involved in child care, the gender gap remains; Mason and Goulden point out that "women with children clock about 94 hours per week between caregiving, housework, and professional responsibilities compared with a little over 80 for men with children" (2004a, 10).

The issues of race and class are also important factors in the rates of success of women in academia. In her essay "The Tender Track," Sara Warner points out that "women born into working-class and working-poor families are less likely to attend college, and those who do are less likely to pursue graduate school and to secure full-time employment in the academy than their middle-class and upper-middle-class peers" (2010, 176). In addition to the financial hardships faced by students from economically disadvantaged communities, what one learns in the classroom cannot easily compete with the inherited knowledge that comes with multiple generations of college graduates and academic families. When one considers the difficulties experienced by faculty of color in academia, it is easy to see why the dismal processes of hiring and retaining minority faculty continue to be such a problem (Delgado Bernal and Villalpando 2002; Segura 2003; Moody 2004). Given the intersection of these multiple factors, my professional life is difficult enough without the constant concern regarding my children's cultural survival. It is this worry, however, that most often occupies my mind.

In thinking of possible ways to help my family navigate the space we inhabit, I have come to realize that the most important tool at my disposal is my own family history—the background that helped me attain a tenure-track position at Wellesley in the first place. In *Telling to Live: Latina Feminist Testimonios* (2001), the Latina Feminist Group outlines the importance of using our own individual stories for resistance. This group of Latina feminist academics argues that in the process of using *testimonio*, or testimony, "the personal and private become profoundly political" (13). The group's work advocates for a reclamation of *testimonio* "as a tool for Latinas to theorize oppression, resistance, and subjectivity" because of its ability to "capture Latinas' complex, layered lives" (19). By using my own history to theorize and create knowledge around my experiences growing up as an immigrant in West Texas, I can offer my own *testimonio* as a way of teaching my children the tools to resist a homogenous culture that seeks to erase difference.

Moving from the southwestern United States to the Northeast may not seem like a big change. After all, it is not my mother's experience of migrating from one country to another. However, moving from an area with a diverse Chicana/Latino community to a homogeneous white Anglo community has been extremely difficult. The diversity we enjoyed in Southern California and West Texas is nonexistent where we now live. I have two children, one in high school (Alyssa) and one just beginning middle school (Jaime). In the town in which we live, most minority students in the public-school system are bussed in from areas in Boston through the Metropolitan Council for Education Opportunity program, a desegregation program that began in 1966 in the Boston area and is "intended to expand educational opportunities, increase diversity, and reduce racial isolation, by permitting students in certain cities to attend public schools in other communities that have agreed to participate" (Massachusetts Department of Elementary and Secondary Education 2011). These students might attend the schools, but they are not a part of the community because they are bussed out as soon as the school bell rings. It would be easy to dismiss my kids' marginalization in the schools based on their "new kid at school" status and claim that race doesn't play a role, but the longer they attend schools in Wellesley and the more contact we have with their teachers, the more convinced we are that their racial and class background plays a major role in their treatment.

The cultural model privileged in the town of Wellesley is one that positions whiteness and class at its center. Students of color are marginalized in this model, and they are taught to view the communities they come from as inferior because it is assumed that no persons of color live in Wellesley. One of Jaime's teachers actually asked a young African American boy what it was like to live in the "ghetto" just because he lives in an urban community in Boston. My son has been told by other students that "Mexicans are stupid," knowing that Jaime identifies as Chicano. My daughter's bus driver has made racist comments about "dirty Mexicans" and the swine flu. Even as these young students of color are being relegated to the margins, they are being encouraged to see themselves as "lucky" because they are attending an elite public school. When I mention to individuals that I don't like living in Wellesley, I usually get the same reaction: "At least the schools are good." I always want to yell in frustration. How can a school be good when it makes students of color feel ashamed? When it is a place where wealthy white students are taught to embrace their privilege without questioning structures of inequality? When economic disparities are blamed on individuals? The myth of meritocracy—the belief that the system rewards those who work hard—remains strongly entrenched in the larger surrounding community. According to many of my children's friends, poor people are poor because they are lazy. This is the message that Wellesley's "good schools" are teaching my children, and no one seems to be questioning their definition of success. As Angela Valenzuela's research on public schools in Texas illustrates, the labeling of teachers or schools as "good" is most often based on a "clinical definition of teaching" that "produces higher tests scores and other measurable outcomes in children" (2002, 236). Through her study of a "good" charter school in Texas, Valenzuela learned that "a 100% passing rate on the TAAS [the state's standardized test] does not necessarily a good school make. . . . Although technically speaking, the children appeared to be learning the three Rs, their harsh persuasion into a materialistic, status-seeking value system was profound" (2002, 237).

When we are thinking about which cultural models are valued, it is important to acknowledge the ways in which the ideas of cultural capital have positioned white, middle-class culture as the standard. In her critique of Pierre Bordieu's theories of cultural, social, and economic capital, Tara J. Yosso argues for an alternative understanding of cultural wealth. Drawing on critical race theory, Yosso introduces the concept of "community cultural wealth." She identifies six forms of cultural capital found in community cultural wealth: aspirational, linguistic, familial, social, navigational, and resistant (2005, 77–81). Aspirational capital is the value that the idea of hope holds for people of color. Instead of complacency, communities of color rely on aspirations for a better future for the next generation to keep motivated. Linguistic capital is the advantage that being multilingual holds for students of color. Unlike the racist rhetoric of English-only movements, Yosso relies on decades of research on the value of bilingual education to position linguistic cultural capital as an important part of community cultural wealth. Although teachers will often place the blame of a student's failure in school on the family, the concept of familial capital positions the family as the site of knowledge, community history, and memory. The family, defined as more than just the traditional nuclear family, is the place where students learn alternative histories and the importance of community. Social capital refers the networks of people and resources tapped into by communities of color in order to negotiate through systems of power. Navigational capital describes the skills used by communities of color to navigate through social institutions that have traditionally marginalized them. Resistant capital can be understood as a form of "oppositional consciousness," to use Chela Sandoval's words (2002, 2), a level of consciousness that allows for communities of color to challenge inequality and injustice. These different definitions of capital wealth serve to acknowledge the value that is found in the culture of communities of color. Such a framework rejects the practice of deficit thinking that blames these communities for poor academic performance. The amalgamation of scholarship that challenges hegemonic systems of thought with the alternative local knowledge passed down through our families creates a powerful tool for resistance and opposition. With Yosso's framework in hand, I now rely on my own familial and cultural background for support as I work toward tenure and create an environment so my children can be successful.

For inspiration in withstanding a discriminatory cultural model, I find myself thinking back to the ways in which my immigrant mother attempted to bridge the distance between my home and school life. As is the case with many women's stories, my *testimonio* is multigenerational and built upon the stories of the women who came before me. I struggle to ensure my children are successful in a school system that does not value who they are, while trying to keep them grounded in our own culture. I have had to learn to incorporate multiple forms of knowledge—academic and communal—and strategies in attempting to help my children survive the difficulties of living in a place where they will always be seen as outsiders. I am learning how to supplement their education with a type of knowledge that will help them reject damaging lessons imposed on them by an education system that promotes the myth of assimilation. I am working to ensure my children grow up to value their culture and embrace the idea of difference.

My mother was a strong woman, *una mujer con fuerza*. She raised me and my siblings in a working-class immigrant home in El Paso, Texas. My father worked the second shift at a cardboard-manufacturing plant, so we saw him only on the weekends. He was a good provider—a breadwinner—but daily parenting duties always fell to my mother. As an immigrant, she didn't speak English and felt uprooted from her home across the border in Mexico. She must have felt so isolated in the home, so far from everything familiar. Even though she never complained, she seemed so lonely. In Texas, her knowledge of *remedios* (cures) and food and tradition had little to no mainstream cultural value. She had only a third-grade education and would often be silent outside the home and with my teachers, but she was an intelligent woman, and inside our home her voice was strong. Although she regretted not being able to help us with our homework, she always encouraged us to be academically successful.

She loved us dearly, but I'm not sure she ever felt truly fulfilled by her roles as a mother and wife. It is one of the reasons I believe she emphasized graduating from high school and attending college. Like other mothers, she wanted her daughters to learn from her own experience. Sofia A. Villenas argues in her work on the teaching and learning that takes place between mothers and daughters that "somewhere in our living pedagogies, as we learn to 'see' and engage the often ambiguous lessons of our mothers' bodies, words, and silences, we find the decolonial imaginary" (2006, 157). Villenas employs Emma Pérez's (1999) concept of the decolonial imaginary to explain that out mothers' performative narratives offer "those shades of gray, those spaces of possibilities to make new meanings, to be creative and self-fulfilled" (2006, 157). For my mother, an education would make it possible for me to create a life for myself that would no longer be dictated by rigid gender roles, reliance on manual labor, and dependence on men.

In my mother's understanding, education meant more possibilities and choices, especially for her daughters. It was the inspirational capital she passed down to us. Unlike the stereotype of the Latino family that doesn't value education, for my family and so many others, the belief in education as a precursor to upward mobility in fact permeates our culture and has been embraced by many immigrant communities. The findings of a survey conducted by the Pew Hispanic Center indicated that "Latinos demonstrate an overarching faith in their local schools and in educational personnel and institutions overall. . . . Hispanic immigrants . . . profess particularly positive attitudes and a sense of optimism" (2004, 1). Although important differences exist between the foreign-born and native-born Latinos, "Latinos appear distinctly optimistic and eager to engage American institutions" (2). According to the survey, 95 percent of Latino parents believe "that it is 'very' important to them that their children go to college" (9). This is not to say, however, that Latino parents are not aware of difficulties encountered by their children in the education system. The survey also reveals Latino parents' "concerns that the educational system does not always treat Latino students fairly" (1). Education is supposed to help one achieve a better life than one's parents, but it is always a much more complicated process as one tries to negotiate different forms of knowledge and ways of knowing.

Like other immigrant parents, my mother must have felt challenged and sometimes even powerless to compete with the contemporary, white American influences we found at school. We came home speaking English and rejecting our native language, following our teachers' advice. If we wanted to speak without an accent, we were told to constantly practice our English, especially at home. Our mother's insistence that we speak Spanish at home could not compete with the message we received at school. After struggling for several years to keep us speaking Spanish at home, she eventually gave up, learning to understand our English while responding to us Spanish— her own small form of resistance. While picking up the basics in math, science, and English, we were also learning to see our parents' values as old-fashioned and antiquated. We were being exposed to values that were different from those taught at home. The strict rules regarding going out and hanging out with friends were based on my mother's own parents' ideas of protection and keeping children safe, but they only made us resent her and see her as out of touch. And school changed us. Our friends changed us. Our teachers—sometimes subtly, sometimes overtly—taught us different traditions, different worldviews. We came home different. We talked back, argued, and rejected her efforts to teach the skills we didn't learn at school. It must have been horrifying for her. How could she transfer her knowledge and values to us when our daily lives from 8:00 A.M. to 3:00 P.M. took us to such a different place? How could she teach us about the importance of family traditions when we were being taught to appreciate only the information garnered at school? The simple task of teaching her daughters how to make tortillas or gorditas, sharing recipes passed down for generations, became impossible. We were too busy with our schoolwork to make time for her lessons. Although she appreciated the fact that we were learning the skills necessary to succeed in the future, she felt rejected and came to resent the lessons cloaked in whiteness that we were learning at school.

I believe myself to be a strong woman in the model of my mother, and my experience with raising children in a wealthy white suburb has helped make me aware of how difficult it must have been for her to raise children outside of the space she considered home. When our daughter, Alyssa, began the eighth grade in the middle school in Wellesley, she transferred in with a straight A average. In California, she had tested into the state's gifted program and had been enrolled in advanced classes, including eighth-grade math as a seventh grader. Our son, Jaime, had also been in the gifted program and had done well in his elementary school. Entering the school system in the town of Wellesley proved a challenge to both of our children, however, and they struggled to acclimate to a very different school system. My conversations with some teachers made it clear that they believed Massachusetts' schools were much more rigorous than schools in other states and thus insinuated that Alyssa and Jaime's previous education was inferior. By the end of their first school year, our daughter began to lose confidence in her intelligence, and our son had started to develop test-taking anxiety. I now understood the frustration my mother must have felt being told her children were not prepared to enter English-speaking classrooms, the anger she must have experienced as she watched my siblings and I being placed in the more remedial Spanish-speaking classrooms. My mother believed in education, but it was the process of becoming educated that was the issue, as it is here in Wellesley.

Like my mother before me, I moved my family with the hope of providing my children with the opportunities I lacked. My multiple college degrees and tenure-track job—plus, my partner's career—have ensured our entrance into middle-class status, which would normally be considered a marker of success. Instead, our move has become a source of constant conflict. I watch as my children are being changed in negative ways to fit into a place that does not value difference. Just as my siblings and I were encouraged to give up our Mexican background, my daughter and son are being encouraged to lay aside their Chicana/o heritage in order to fit in more comfortably with an Anglo-owning class culture. If it is hard to see my children making choices about their cultural background and ethnicity in order to stand out less, I can now imagine how difficult it must have been for my mother to watch us reject our home culture in our efforts to assimilate. After all, our mainstream education system teaches that in order to be successful, one must fit into the mold already in place, a model of education that does not favor critical thinking skills or an investment in multiple knowledge traditions.

When I entered the education system in the United States, I came in with one year's schooling from Mexico. My mother was often told how lucky I was to be receiving a "good" education in an American school. What people don't know is that in the one year I had attended school in Mexico, I had learned the equivalent of three years of reading and math in the United States. Because my education had occurred across the border, however, it didn't count. Instead, I was immersed in a curriculum that demanded I forget the knowledge I had in order to become an "Americanized student." My mother stood by and watched me turn against my culture because she had been told this is what I needed to do in order to become successful. It hurt her to see me reject our traditions and thus, in essence, reject her. As Villenas argues, though, "Somewhere in the dark shadows of a woman's *sufrimientos* we might find . . . a mother's immense capacity to dream and prepare us for lives she could not imagine" (2006, 157). My mother's attempts to share family stories became less and less frequent, but the foundation she created—through the sharing of her knowledge—was strong, and although it cracked, it never fully crumbled.

In college, I began to question the assimilation process I had embraced and now came to begrudge. Being a Chicana studies scholar brought me back to my mother's cultural knowledge (her music, her stories, her language, her knowledge of *remedios* and different forms of healing), a wisdom I was once taught to devalue in favor of "American" (read "white, middle-class") models mass-produced and disseminated for a mainstream audience. I learned to embrace the language she loved and to read value in the stories she had once shared with me, recognizing them as a powerful *testimonio*. I rejected the ideological position that situates Spanish (and Spanglish) as inferior to English in a hierarchy of language and began to see my bilingualism as a form of linguistic capital. Although it was too late to learn to cook the many dishes I grew up with, I learned the importance of cooking with my own children and discussing the role food has in passing down family history and tradition—an important form of familial capital. In short, I became adept at recognizing value in our community knowledge and ways of knowing that are often marginalized and dismissed as inferior.

The knowledge that we can redefine the meaning of cultural capital has become an important instrument in resisting my children's "suburbanization." With this knowledge and the strategies it offers, I can more effectively challenge the traditional ideas of cultural capital taught in the school system. Knowing my mother's own struggles with trying to keep our family's culture intact, I sometimes find myself asking the same questions she must have pondered: How can I transfer my knowledge, traditions, and values to my children when they encounter and negotiate such different worldviews at school and with their friends? How can I encourage my children to be proud of their cultural roots and traditions when their schools do not or cannot overtly value them and promote them?

Rejecting the cultural model being promoted by the school system is somewhat easier when one has an alternative model to embrace. Whereas traditional cultural theory may not find value in the cultures of communities of color, Yosso's (2005) concept of community cultural wealth and the research it has produced provide us with ways to help children of color resist marginalization. Many of us already share with our children the six forms of capital that are present in the community cultural wealth model, but by explicitly positioning them in opposition to the traditional cultural model, we can more effectively challenge the race and class hierarchy perpetuated by our school systems. Understanding the ways in which our culture is dismissed helps Jaime and Alyssa fight for acknowledgment and recognition. They have begun to see this dismissal as another form of injustice, and so they employ resistance capital that allows them to rely on tactics used by previous social justice movements for opposition. They are learning to practice what education scholars Daniel Solorzano and Dolores Delgado Bernal have defined as "transformational resistance," a strategy of resistance that "refers to student behavior that illustrates both a critique of oppression and a desire for social justice" (2001, 319). The fight might not be easy for them, but it helps them develop the navigational strategies they will need to continue in an education system that often demands unquestioned assimilation. In her work on pedagogies of the home, Delgado Bernal discusses the ways in which Chicana students use biculturalism "to see things in ways that students of the dominant culture might not, and how their biculturalism can help others understand things from a different perspective" (2001, 630). My children are acquiring the skills necessary to shape an identity that helps them embrace the multiple cultures they inhabit—in both Texas and Massachusetts—without sacrificing their own cultural background. Our conversations about ways to talk back to racism in the classroom are preparing them to identify technologies of race and to recognize and navigate covert racism.

The survival of Alyssa and Jaime's psyches will be based on their ability to navigate the education system's strategies of cultural erasure. As Angela Valenzuela has observed, "Rather than building on students' cultural and linguistic knowledge and heritage to create biculturally and bilingually competent youth, schools subtract these identifications from them to their social and academic detriment" (1999, 25). I am always looking for ways of helping Alyssa and Jaime find pride in their Chicana/o background and reject the "subtracting model of schooling" (Valenzuela 2002, 236). Because we are so far from our community, the *cuentos* (stories) I share with them, versions of my *testimonio*, now take on an added importance. I keep our family history alive by constantly making connections to our past and ensuring they feel grounded in a space they do not daily inhabit. They do not need to be physically in the Southwest surrounded by our family and culture in order to feel connected to it. I have tried to find ways for them to remain connected to our community even while living in Wellesley. For the past several years, Alyssa has been dancing ballet *folklorico* with the Latina organization at Wellesley College. More than just dancing, she is learning a form of social capital from these young Chicanas/Latinas that is preparing her for the challenge of being a Chicana in college and teaching her the importance that community support will continue to play in her success. With each year that we are away, Jaime becomes more vocal about his Chicano background, finding his voice and learning to make alliances with other students of color. Although young, he is learning to implement navigational capital in creating support networks. Both of my kids are discovering ways to stay true to themselves and succeed in a system that does not necessarily value who they are and their background. They are developing and learning to rely on resistant capital, or "those knowledges and skills fostered through oppositional behavior that challenges inequality" (Yosso 2005, 80).

In addition to fighting marginalization in the school system, as a family we have also been struggling with the reality that we are middle class and have climbed up the social status ladder. Yet despite holding a class status different than my parents', Jaime and Alyssa nevertheless find it difficult to attend school with children possessing historical legacies of enormous financial privilege. When these kids return from school breaks, they share stories about their skiing vacations or Caribbean beach getaways. Their fathers are successful lawyers, doctors, and financial-sector employees who have the privilege of taking time off to vacation with their families. Most of their mothers revel in the economic freedom that allows them to be stay-at-home moms, with time and money to spare. I know it can't be easy for my children to encounter such privilege, knowing that they will never experience this type of childhood. Beyond getting them to accept this fact and not feel inferior, I am constantly struggling to help them develop a class consciousness that will prevent them from aspiring to be part of a system that rewards individual achievement over the value of community. It is too easy to equate the privilege of wealth with success. This is a challenge that many women academics of color face.

In a lecture given at Wellesley College in November 2008, Cherríe Moraga recounted to the audience her choice to send her teenage son, Rafael, to Chicano boot camp, a place where he would reconnect with nature while being surrounded by strong Chicano role models. She saw him as getting too invested in consumer culture and wanted to make an intervention. Although anxiety inducing, this intervention was about making her child uncomfortable about social and economic class. For many of us who were born into working-class families, the discomfort we feel in terms of class is something we intimately know, but as our children are raised in middle-class households, they no longer face the same struggles we encountered. On the surface, we can feel good about the fact that we are providing our sons and daughters with more opportunities and maybe more economic stability. However, the question now becomes: How do we instill in our children the same working-class values that built our character? Moraga argued in her lecture that "with our children of privilege, character building becomes more problematic because the only way to build character is by opposition . . . by discomfort" (2008). For Moraga, dislocating her son from the comfort of their home helped remind him of his privilege and denaturalized it. I am trying to build my children's character by helping negotiate the discomfort but not remove it. I cannot afford to give up my job in order to move them to a community in which they will feel more comfortable. Instead, by embracing a community wealth model, I am hoping to build in my children a strength they will carry with them through the many challenges they will face as people of color.

As I struggle to instill in my kids a strong sense of self and pride in our cultural background, I think of my mother and how hard it must have been for her to raise a family in an Anglo community so alien to her. Like her, I'm now away from my extended family and the support system they offer.

My faraway relatives are the individuals who keep our family history alive through their memories and *cuentos*. I find myself floundering and trying to re-create a sense of the familiar, attempting to fashion for my family a space where they will feel safe and at home. Without the cultural affirmation provided by my extended family and Chicana/o community, I sometimes fear my children will lose the sense of where they come from and the importance of their history. I now understand much better the anxiety my mother must have felt at having to raise us in a place that seemed so disconnected from her own background. I take heart, however, in knowing that I am not alone and that other dislocated Chicanas share this struggle. In "Building Up Our Resistance: Chicanas in Academia," Chicana literature and feminist scholar Anna Sandoval reminds us that, "as academics and third world women, we are constantly in a border space, straddling the elitism of the academy and the communities where we are raised. . . . For those who are isolated from any semblance of home . . . passion for one's community is rarely lost and comes from comfort with the familiar" (1999, 86–87).

I believe ultimately that I am making an intervention in my children's education process by making it difficult for those around us to dismiss our culture. For her tenth-grade thesis assignment, my daughter was handed a list of American authors to choose from for her literature project. Some African American writers were on the list, but no Chicana/o authors were included. I contacted her English teacher and argued that Alyssa be allowed to study and write on the works of Helena María Viramontes. Her teacher agreed after being reassured that I would help Alyssa with the assignment because no one else at the high school was familiar with Viramontes's work. As a result, Alyssa has been exposed to some wonderful literature, and the project has offered us the opportunity to discuss issues important to our community. She has also had to learn to explain to her classmates that a Chicana writer is an "American" author. My children are learning to stand up for themselves and defend their background. They inhabit a space of discomfort and are learning to be conscientious young people. In the process, I am learning to look back at memories of my own mother for lessons on how to raise strong children outside of the familiar. I am using my *testimonio* to help my children resist and create their own *testimonios* of opposition.

PART TWO

UNEXPECTED CHALLENGES AND MOMENTOUS REVELATIONS

THE ESSAYS IN PART II discuss some of the unexpected challenges and un anticipated revelations mothers in academia have encountered. These unexpected circumstances include cultural relocation and acculturation; terminal illness; overt and covert forms of racism, sexism, and classism; and the encounter with a deeper understanding of how motherhood creates moments of enlightenment and power. We begin this part with Vanessa Adel's essay "Four Kids and a Dissertation: Queering the Balance Between Family and Academia," which deals with family dynamics and an ethics of care as she deliberates the politics of transracial adoption. As part of a lesbian couple, Vanessa shares in her story the juxtaposition of being an unremitting graduate student with doing intensive reproductive labor in a racially segregated society. Susana L. Gallardo similarly discusses the corporeal experience of mothering in "'Tía María de la Maternity Leave': Reflections on Race, Class, and the Natural-Birth Experience." Her essay examines the politics of natural birth from a Chicana feminist perspective by offering reflections on her own pregnancy and birth narrative as a forty-two-year-old first-time mom. She interrogates how the birth process and motherhood are political acts, particularly for women of color and unmarried women, and seeks to deconstruct the popular narrative of natural birth as individual privilege and to reexamine it as a "raced" and "classed" reproductive right that is overmedicalized by the medical establishment. "Threads That Bind: A *Testimonio* to Puerto Rican Working Mothers" by Maura I. Toro-Morn explores the inclusion of Latinas/os intellectuals in American universities in a moment of increased corporatization and rising demands for more campus diversity. In that context, motherhood for Maura has meant trying to balance the growing workload in higher education with the challenges of raising a bicultural, bilingual son and the struggles of maintaining a transnational family. The intersections of race, class, and gender are also present in Olivia Perlow's essay "Parenting Within the Nexus of Race, Class, and Gender Oppression in Graduate School at a Historically Black College/University." She discusses how she developed strategies to help her overcome the structural, cultural, and institutional barriers that challenged her ability to balance academic life and family life successfully. Yet she concludes that although individual determination is important, more institutional support is needed for student mothers to thrive. On the topic of support, in "*Sobreviviendo* (and Thriving) in the Academy: My Tías' Counter*consejos* and Advice," J. Estrella Torrez weaves personal motherhood and activist narratives with critical interventions into academic perceptions of motherhood and "motherwork." She contends that Chicanas in the academia do not need to sacrifice raising families for a "successful" career in the academy. Our second section concludes with Allia A. Matta's chapter, "Revolving Doors: Mother-Woman Rhythms in Academic Spaces," where Matta shares her experience of returning to school at forty-two years old. She left job security, a rent-stabilized New York City apartment, and her sons to pursue her doctorate, a move many thought was not in her family's best interest. As an African American nontraditional graduate student, Allia contemplates how race, class, gender, and community are woven together and the ways in which the politics of mothering alter life-changing possibilities.

7

FOUR KIDS AND A DISSERTATION

Queering the Balance Between Family and Academia

Vanessa Adel

IN THE FALL of 2008, my partner and I were faced with a momentous decision: whether to welcome a fourth baby into our lives or not. We had three children, ages seven, six, and three at the time, whom we had adopted through social services. The youngest two shared the same birth mother, and she—a woman who had suffered a long history of drug abuse, violence, racism, and social and familial neglect—had just given birth to a baby girl, three months premature. Our social worker called us a little more than two weeks after the girl was born, asking if we would be interested in fostering and adopting our children's birth sister.

What to do? The first thing on our minds was the impact this new life would have on our routine: another mouth to feed, loads more dishes and laundry, additional doctor visits, less sleep, and the intensity of parenting a baby all over again. These concerns were compounded by the fact that she was a premature baby whose physical and developmental needs were unclear. How could we possibly manage this additional family member with our work, our careers, and our home? My partner has a taxing, more than full-time job as a sixth-grade social studies teacher in a nearby city. As a graduate student in sociology and a part-time lecturer with a full but flexible schedule, I shouldered the bulk of organizing and running the household. The mountainous bags of clothes that tumble down when I opened the closets in a frenzy to find sizable hand me downs every time one of my kids had a growth spurt became my visual symbol of being overwhelmed as I considered what welcoming a new baby would mean to me in our family system. The prospect of ever finishing my doctorate, let alone being able to successfully navigate through junior facultyhood, seemed absurd and laughable in the face of parenting one more child. This chapter bears witness to the process of deliberating whether to grow our family while I was in graduate school. As I tell the story of this decision-making process, I reflect on multiple layers and dynamics of ideology, structure, privilege, and penalty that drive its elements.

As a sociologist, I am acutely aware of how this deliberation represented an inherently social process in terms of the cultural narratives and meanings of family, identity, self, and career that my partner and I navigate and in terms of the social structures that shape our lives. Our relative positions of penalty and privilege as queer middle-class white women adopting transracially in a nuclear family system interlocked to shape both the decision-making possibilities available to us and the future ramifications of our decisions in different contexts (Crenshaw 1994; Collins 2002). The intersections of our social identity positions provide myriad data for reflection and analysis because they exist within and are constituted in and through dynamic contexts of ongoing and emerging institutional and social contexts and relations (Choo and Ferree 2010).

How we engage these positions in our interactions with others arises out of processes of power and garners outcomes that grease the wheels of power in the form of resistance or assimilation. My partner and I like to imagine ourselves as agents of resistance—a liberatory, radical couple pushing at the edges of ideologies of family, sexuality, gender, race, and blood ties. In reality, the processes of our lives involve both assimilatory as well as resistant dynamics of thought and action. That is, coming to be mothers of multiple children was born of intersecting power dynamics that we are embedded in and acting from (Hequembourg 2007). Although our gender, sexuality, and multilayered motherhood constitute perhaps the most vulnerable processes in my personal story, our race, education, and class are our most obviously privileged positions. In making the choices through which my partner and I came into motherhood with multiple children, "we create[d] the opportunity or space for movement within the process of subjectification" (Hequembourg 2007, 157), such that we opened up new understandings of ourselves as agents and parents and of myself as an academic and a mother.

Gender revealed its prominent role in the decision-making process as it made an evocative appearance in and through the contentious relations of my family of origin. When my mother learned of our deliberation, she emphatically asserted that I could not parent a fourth child; I needed to think about my own career and finish my Ph.D. Her response surprised me. In our relationship so far, my mother had never underscored, let alone emphatically expressed, the importance of career development for me or for any woman. As her daughter, I had always felt that she was intimidated by any professional endeavors I engaged in. I regarded this issue as deeply gendered because in my experience my mother seemed to regard the driven and successful women in her life with a mixture of insecurity and distrust. She came from a classically misogynistic family who, from my vantage point, successfully undermined her own desires for educational attainment and career development. Despite great talent, my mother did not professionalize her own passionate interests in interior design, education, and human rights. Instead, she structured her life as the wife of a UNICEF manager, staying at home to raise her children and to support her husband's and son's careers. Although my mother was a daily witness to professionals working for women and children's welfare, and although she spent many dinners discussing global women's rights, she herself gave feminism and women's movements for equity not much more than sideways glances, almost studiously avoiding their liberating potential for herself. In my own life trajectory as a queer woman, I learned to navigate the misogyny of my family of origin in contentious isolation from my mother. So when she expressed such emphatic concern for my career welfare, I was taken aback. At least for a moment, we shared a gendered concern that my motherhood responsibilities might prevent me from being able to fulfill my academic aspirations.

In the same conversation, my father interjected, "Well, maybe that's what [Vanessa] wants to do." For me, his words and tone, in the context of decades of tense communication between my parents, simultaneously cut down my mother's love-inspired wisdom and served to uphold the security of his own cultural and emotional attachment to an ideology of women staying at home. The swiftness of his response seemed like aggressive relief that his masculine-looking lesbian daughter might choose motherhood over a doctorate and a career as an academic. The effect of this comment and its delivery left little room for acknowledging and reflecting on the conflict for me, and by extension for many women, between parenting and work or, more specifically in this case, between parenting and graduate school. This tension is evident in the rise of attrition rates for graduate student mothers that recent research attributes to the conflict between the roles of mother and student, on the one hand, and the social structural environments of family and academia, on the other (Lynch 2008).

In a formulaic way, my parents' emotional responses correspond to the conceptual and experiential binaries of life choices for women, including those in privileged positions. It also highlights the remaining dichotomies between work and home at the level of both ideology and structure (Folbre 2001). For middle-class women, especially white middle-class women, with both professional goals and necessitated participation in the labor force, there is a tension between intensive motherhood and intensive professional life (Hays 1996; Gerson and Jacobs 2007). The gender ideologies that deem women as and push them to become primary caregivers create a binary that is often impossible to resolve in the current landscape of state and market policy. Many scholars show how women are bearing the brunt of this family–work conflict because of a marketplace that has not adjusted to working mothers' needs or family lives that remain largely gendered in their division of labor (Folbre 2001; A. Crittenden 2007; Gerson and Jacobs 2007; Stone 2007b). In the face of this conflict, many women turn to less-than-balanced resolutions. Recent research finds women doing the following in order to cope: leaving lucrative and top professional positions if they can afford it (Stone 2007a); spending more time and emotional energy at work than at home (Hochschild 2007); enduring long-term separation from their children as a result of transnational economic migration that sometimes lasts entire childhoods (Parreñas 2005). Even in workplaces with more generous family policies, the pressure to outperform at work leaves employees vulnerable to comparison with the performance of childfree counterparts and often resistant to taking full advantage of existing family-friendly policies (Glass and Estes 1997). In the context of higher education, graduate student mothers experience high rates of attrition because of the conflict between embracing intensive motherhood and navigating universities and colleges that implicitly regard family as a private, largely female endeavor. For graduate student mothers, there is the added stress of making significant time commitments to work that incurs child-care costs without also providing much in the way of income (Lynch 2008). Very little research explores the impact of parenting multiple children on motherhood and career balance, though it is not difficult to surmise that the tensions between home and work only intensify with larger families. Although my parents' conversation highlighted old dynamics of gender relations between us that my feminist analysis hoped to transcend, their reproduction and contestation of the dominant motherhood framework shape the processes and outcomes of my parenting experiences.

The decision my partner and I faced about whether to parent a fourth child was tougher than any we had made about our kids before then. It propelled us into a sphere in which we found ourselves confronting the limitations of our participation in the labor force in ways that were new to us, partially because we were used to the privilege of making deliberate choices that we felt we were in charge of. For our first child, we deliberated in the way of quasi-rational prospective parents of middle-class backgrounds in the contemporary United States. We wanted a kid, we had been together about ten years, we felt ready enough, and we had bought a house in preparation for growing a family. We deliberated the different options: birth children through insemination—known or unknown donor; adoption—domestic or international.

Much of our deliberation was in our minds; we analyzed what path would be best and which would be more suitable. We thought about timing from different angles, considering when having a child might be "too soon" or "too late." We were drawn to adoption because we felt that insemination was going to be complicated and expensive, whereas there were already children in the world who needed a home. We considered the politics of homophobia in our families and felt that adopting held the greatest possibility for creating more equity among all of us in our family unit than giving birth would, which might invite divisive attachments to genetic heritage as a marker of legitimate family bonds. For lesbian couples in which one partner is the birth mother, the nonbiological mother is often marginalized from full status as a mother, whereas the birth mother is seen as having a more legitimate claim to motherhood (Brown and Perlesz 2008). Research has also shown that lesbian couples are strongly committed to egalitarianism in their relationships, which certainly drives the way that we make choices about our lives together (Perlesz et al. 2010). Plus, we live in Massachusetts—a state where adoption by gay/lesbian couples assures that both parents are legal guardians of the adopted child, which is not the case in many states in the United States.

We deliberated about the politics of transracial adoption. As two white prospective moms, we thought deeply about whether it would be fair to adopt a child of color given the whiteness of our families and the country's racism and racial segregation. We weighed the meaning of being open or closed to transracial adoption and how we might wittingly or unwittingly participate in reproducing racism as a result of any of our actions. We had frank conversations with friends, who encouraged us to be open to adopting a child of color, to keep race on the table, to keep it in sight as a constant line of navigation. One friend, an African American transracial adoptee who is active in the transracial adoptee community, advised that if we were to adopt a child of color, we should adopt more than one so the children would not be alone in their identity and experience as people of color in our family. Another friend, a white mother of three adopted kids, also asserted the same wisdom: if you do adopt transracially, don't let any child be alone in her racial experience in your family. Numerous studies have revealed experiences of painful racial isolation and disconnect, especially when adoptees live in predominantly white communities (Benson, Sharma, and Roehlkepartain 1994; DeBerry, Scarr, and Weinberg 1996; Hollingsworth 1997, 2000; Brooks and Barth 1999; Huh and Reid 2000; S. Patton 2000).

In the end, we decided to go the way of foster-to-adoption via social services in our home state, which has legalized same-sex marriage, joint adoption, and foster care. We were open to any child age four and younger, of any gender or race, a single child or a sibling pair. In the fall of 2001, social services called us with the news that a healthy baby had been found in a church, parents and heritage unknown, and asked, Would we be willing to take her home tomorrow? This was the fortuitous beginning of our parenting adventure in the swift, surprise placement manner of social services. There are many stories to tell here, but nine months after welcoming our daughter as a several-days-old foster baby, we were able to adopt her, a precocious baby who was already walking just shy of ten months of age. We knew we wanted more children, siblings for our daughter. In agreement with the advice our friends had given us and what the literature reflected, we wanted to foster and adopt one more African American child with whom our daughter could share in the diasporic identity, solidarity, and strength of African American heritage and experience (S. Patton 2000; Lee 2003). After some unsuccessful attempts working with a private adoption agency and fostering two babies in quick succession who were successfully reunited with their birth mothers, my partner and I welcomed our son and second daughter into our home when they were ages three years and one month old, respectively.

The decision to have three children came relatively easily. We had previously been open to welcoming a sibling pair, and when our son and daughter's situation presented itself, it was not a leap from where we had already intended to go. We hadn't exactly planned on three, but it didn't seem too much of a stretch. With our fourth, however, the choice to parent catapulted us into a different sphere of decision making and orientation—out of the comfort zone of traditional nuclear family structure supported by our class and community culture that normalizes two-parent families with 2.4 kids. We deliberated for a long week, talking with close family and mentors, assessing every detail of how we might possibly be able to parent four kids the way that we like to parent and still do all the things we wanted to do, including for example, finishing my Ph.D.

Although we thought of ourselves as expanding notions of kinship in our lives as a queer, transracially adopted family, being confronted with the choice to parent our children's birth sibling revealed a certain attachment to blood ties. After all, social services had called us previously about children they had hoped to place with us. Our standard answer had been: "Please don't call us anymore; we're all set." Analyzed through the lens of intersectional power, this response can be read in different ways. On the one hand, our previous denials reflected reasonable boundary setting. On the other, they reflected the desire to maintain a privileged class status and a particular exclusivity over our family identity. Family is home, but it is also a bounded space from which some are inherently excluded (Espiritu 2003). In adoption, inclusion crosses traditional confines of "primary kinship" (Hicks 2006), but it is also a site where blood ties are implicitly excluded—in the case of birth parents, for example, and even in the case of birth siblings. My partner and I were compelled to consider inclusion of a birth sibling based in part on cultural notions of blood ties and in part on notions of the benefits of children's being able to share birth origins, especially in their navigation of potentially difficult identity work in coming to understand their birth histories (Benson, Sharma, and Roehlkepartain 1994; S. Patton 2000; Lee 2003). Blood ties are one way in which our own family choices are embedded in a field of power that has both liberating and oppressive directions. They were not the only factor compelling us, however.

We went to visit the baby in the hospital. She was doing incredibly well in the local Neonatal Intensive Care Unit (NICU) despite having been born at one pound, fourteen ounces. We held the baby and fed her onehalf ounce at a time of special premature baby formula from a tiny disposable sterile bottle. She was two pounds, seven ounces, when we met her, impossibly small to behold. One nurse in particular was quite overt in her opinion that we should foster and adopt this baby: "I could tell you some stories" (and she did). Her main point trailed a couple of horrific birth stories: "Sometimes I wonder how these babies are going to survive. I do hope you take her. How could you say no?" The intensity of sitting in the NICU with my children's birth sister made for a space in which the regular social rules of private self-presentation did not really operate. Add to that my transgender appearance, and my life became a performance to be commented upon. Holding the baby in my arms in an uncomfortable rocking chair, hot from the eighty-degree temperature maintained in the room, and the smock and mask they made me wear, I replied, "Well, it's complicated; we already have three kids at home." On cue, the baby erupted in a series of what the medical experts call gas-induced smiles, those presocialized upturns of the mouth, gummy and unformed by social expectations. The nurse noticed and added, "She's working on you. Did you see that?"

Cherríe Moraga writes about how her status as a birth mother changed her usual position as outsider butch dyke to insider mother in the NICU where her son spent his first four months. In contrast, her femme partner had to constantly prove her status as a mother, despite the way her gender expression conformed more closely to social expectations of motherhood (as cited in Tatonetti 2004). The nurse in the NICU where I held the baby knew nothing about me or my capacity to parent—financial, emotional, or otherwise. Indeed, I was sitting there internally wondering about my capacity to parent a fourth, but she read in my race and class markers sufficient cause for welcome and inclusion, to the point of insisting that I take on motherhood status. Queerness, whiteness, foster care, and adoption interacted together to position my decision making as partially public in nature, as a process to be commented on forcefully while echoing themes of compulsory and legitimized motherhood.

In fact, my partner and I initially declined the option to adopt baby number four after deliberating every rational angle. After meeting and feeding the baby in the hospital on more than one occasion, we called our social worker and said, "We can't do this, sorry." Then we felt sad. It didn't feel right. We deliberated all over again, this time much less linearly. We cried, we laughed; we wriggled with wrenching feelings of impossibility and possibilities. We called our social worker a week later and said, "We changed our minds, and we'll welcome the baby." And then we told our kids they had a new baby sister.

Taking a meandering intersectional look at our decision-making process, I find it hard to know exactly the nature of the reality I am viewing.

Indeed, saying this only reflects the multilayered, multivalenced nature of trying to be agentic within fields of power in and through which I am constituted. Gender, intersected with race, trumps our queerness to designate us as "good mothers," yet gender confines me to a largely private, altruistic role (Folbre 2001) that is barely supported in the academic workplaces where I study and teach. In the poker games of parenthood and academia, I have some ace cards and some low-numbered cards and even some cards that shift status depending on the context. I receive props for white motherhood, but that same motherhood limits my opportunities as an emerging scholar. My class position grants me an entitlement that enables a larger range of agency and choice, yet my choice to have four children pushes at the boundaries of middle-class norms and viability. As a queer adoptive family, we push at the edges of acceptability, helping to transform ideologies of family in living our daily lives, even while our middle-class nuclear structure supports oppressive hierarchies. The way that power and discourse prop us up or bring us down, sometimes simultaneously, and the way that we access privilege or suffer penalties form a shifting enterprise with some discernable and predictable patterns as well as occasional surprises.

Amy Hequembourg (2007) suggests that although lesbian motherhood (like any identity or position) is born out of relations of power, the choices that are made in the making of that identity create opportunities for movement and possibilities for change. The opening in my case is this: navigating through the unexpected parenting of multiple children has brought me to consider the way in which our decision queered our own positions by expanding our notions of love and our experience and reception of love. We smiled as we held Alia in the NICU because we felt love. We cried when we initially said no to adopting her, and we reversed our originally well-thought-out position because we loved her. As Moraga writes, "There is no accounting for . . . what finally makes a family, except love. [It is love that has] the power to queer cultural boundaries," freeing one to construct family identity in the queer spaces in between constraining cultural tropes and subject positions (quoted in Tatonetti 2004, 243).

When I first began parenting, one of my advisers reflected back to me that "children need a lot of love." It was one of those comments that have replayed in my mind as a kind of teaching, like a simple koan to reflect on in deeper and deeper ways.

Growing up in a family in which I experienced tremendous symbolic violence in my position as a queer woman, it wasn't so clear to me before I began parenting how much love there can be in everyday family life: how much love my kids give and how much love they love to receive; love in moments of play and engagement; love in its expression as attention, listening, snuggles, dancing, and the sharing of joy. My four-year-old snuggles with me, asserting, "I want you to stay with me forever." My eight-year-old writes me a card with a drawing and a caption that exclaims, "Everything you do means a lot to me." These days, our youngest is two years old, and when I'm flitting about trying to multitask, she turns to me and says, "Sit, Mommy, come sit," inviting me to be with her in quality presence and interaction. It's not always easy to stay here in this place of sweetness, but something is there that pushes and pulls at the rigidity of instrumental and dichotomous choices and decision making.

When we operate in congruence with mainstream ideologies of family and identity, our notions of parenting and relationships across age and nurturance suffer from constricting ideas about what is possible for us as people in terms of embracing relationships. In addition to encountering what we have not planned for ourselves, we might find ourselves participating in care work that we did not initially foresee given the narrowness of our conceptions of creating family structures, familial bonds, and caretaking arrangements. Making the "irrational" leap to parent a fourth child has nurtured and deepened decision-making approaches for me that consider putting the heart and meaning first, rather than instrumentality.

That said, parenting four children has made it more difficult to pursue my academic life, a life I identify with, am fulfilled by, and imagine myself good at. Despite my lofty talk about the significance of the heart and the importance of making decisions that defy mainstream capitalist rationality, I have incurred real costs for the commitment to intensive parenting. My dissertation has been in stasis for a number of years, and my income relies on insecure lecturer positions. It is hard to do much more than parent, run a household, and teach. Indeed, these tasks are already a hefty load. My life in academia is not progressing at a competitive rate in terms of publications, dissertation completion, let alone job security or adequate remuneration. My choice to parent multiple children is high-risk behavior, some might even call it professional suicide, in the context of an academic job market where graduates compete for dwindling jobs in a system in which one-third of full-time faculty are non–tenure track (Deresiewicz 2011). In addition, more and more institutions are relying on part-time adjunct labor, and public and private universities are facing monumental cuts that include axing entire academic departments (Deresiewicz 2011). Although the pay gap between men's income and women's income is narrowing within entry-level cohorts, the pay gap between mothers and nonmothers is growing, conferring an estimated wage penalty of 7 percent per child (Budig and England 2001). At times, I feel more as if I am dabbling in academia rather than really pursuing it, a victim of a gendered system with limited resources for mothers, many of whom are hanging onto professional status by a thread.

Without a doubt, I am caught in the binary between intensive motherhood and intensive academia (Lynch 2008). Although I suffer in terms of my level of competitiveness and structural position in the marketplace of academia, there are rewarding aspects to my life as an academic with multiple children. For example, there is a deepening of understanding and self-reflection that comes from long-term engagement as a graduate student, lecturer, and parent. My life as a parent feeds my sociological inquiry. Sociological literature helps me make sense of my life and challenges me to think through the social constraints of the choices available to me and the choices I am making. My students help me remain inspired to pursue the same questions from different angles semester by semester. My academic and parental experiences are woven in and through each other, even as the structures and processes of parenthood and academia do not mutually reinforce each other.

Deciding to parent our fourth was a multivalenced choice marked and made by gender scripts, racial scripts, family conceptualizations, work–family balance, motherhood practices, and social positionalities. The love that we sprang for is the queerest thing—irrational, unboxable—a gift that, if we can maintain the presence of mind to say, "OK, honey, I'll sit next to you," is the deepest and most capriciously enigmatic meaning worth engaging.

8

"TÍA MARÍA DE LA MATERNITY LEAVE"

Reflections on Race, Class, and the Natural-Birth Experience

Susana L. Gallardo

"YOU KNOW, have you checked with Faculty Affairs about maternity leave?" asked my colleague María. It was late September, and we were four weeks into the fall semester. I was somewhat successfully juggling three classes despite losing sleep, breastfeeding my two-month-old daughter, and breast-pumping my leaky boobs in the faculty office I shared with María and another colleague.

"Not Faculty Affairs," I responded, "but I've gone over the contract online, and there are only references to paid leaves for full-time professors." I had spent several hours doing that the previous spring at her suggestion and had promptly forgotten about it.

"Are you sure? It might be worth checking again. I had the impression there were some benefits for part-timers, too," she said.

"OK," I said doubtfully. "I'll have to do that."

It was another week or two later that I finally made the call to Faculty Affairs to ask tentatively if there were indeed any maternity benefits for part-time lecturers. I had grown up in a working-class suburban family where working any less than fifty hours a week was considered slacking. I have worked since I was twelve and my mom monogrammed my name onto a blue jumpsuit for me to wear Saturdays at the family auto repair shop, where I inventoried parts and filed customer invoices. I had absolutely no expectations of an unpaid leave, much less a paid one. My daughter was born August 3, and I had returned to work August 23 for the fall semester. If anything, I considered myself fortunate that I was working only part-time, officially 60 percent time, so that I could still spend plenty of time at home with my new daughter.

The call to the Faculty Affairs office was short. An administrator asked me when I was expecting ("last month") and asked me to come in the next day for an appointment. Thoroughly confused, I showed up the next day for a one-hour appointment that changed my life forever. It's still a blur how she presented paperwork that counted my years of service, accumulated sick days, and maternity leave and calculated that I could take the next three months off. Combined with the winter break, it meant I would be able to spend the next four months at home with my new daughter and receive full pay.

I was absolutely floored. I stumbled around in a cloud the rest of the day, and on the next day my department chair and I agreed that I would continue working another two weeks while he found substitutes for my classes. Maternity leave had to be taken within eighty days of birth—if I had waited any longer, I would have forfeited my benefits.

As I told my classes of the situation in the following days, I nearly broke down in tears, realizing the enormity of the situation. I was profoundly grateful for the union contract that guaranteed part-timers the same benefit package as full-time faculty. I was particularly grateful to my colleague María, who had insisted that I "check again." Ever since then, my partner and I have only somewhat jokingly referred to her as "Tía María de la Maternity Leave."

I open with this story against my better judgment because it reminds me of the complicated social location from which I speak. I am a Harvard- and Stanford-educated professional. I am a Chicana (Mexican American) and the daughter of a mechanic. I am also an adjunct instructor of social science and women's studies, an older than forty, first-time mother, and an unmarried mother by choice. I share my background not because I am necessarily representative of any of these group identities, but because I think they are relevant and crucial in my approach to researching birth experiences. Birth for me was a physically empowering experience that changed the way I thought of and related to my body. In particular, learning about "natural birth" and its inherent critique of modern ob/gyn medicine drew me into a convoluted web of associations about middle-class privilege, midwifery traditions, the practicality of pain and body issues, and global maternal mortality. Birth and motherhood have deepened my academic research and pedagogy in ways I could not have predicted yet are remarkably consistent with my long-term interests in Chicana studies, religion, and feminist studies. In this essay, I briefly outline my experience with natural birth and then address some of the interlinked issues of what I call the "feminist politics of birth."

FACING THE FEAR

Giving birth remains the most amazing thing that I have ever done. I was so terrified and skeptical of birth itself. I had always hated those women who smiled beatifically, saying, "Oh yes, it's hours of the most horrible pain, but it's all worth it." I don't like pain. Even though I was pregnant, I couldn't bear to think about what the actual birth would be like. I was horrified about where the baby would come out from my body.

I eventually faced facts, picked up an armload of books from the library, and started confronting my fear. A former student, Allana, worked as a doula—essentially a maternity labor coach—and had made presentations to my classes about birthing practices and feminist critiques of the medical establishment. She was the first to introduce me to the idea that there were multiple birth options for women to consider. She also made me realize how strange it felt to think about maternity and motherhood from a feminist perspective. I had been working in feminist and Chicana studies for more than twenty years, and I realized I had a huge blind spot, if not bias, against motherhood. I had been encouraging my women students toward college and economic independence for years, so I had little time to think about maternity and motherhood. That would also probably explain why it never occurred to me to become a mother until I was forty years old.

FAST FORWARD

Several months of research in birth guides, medical journals, feminist journals, and mommy memoirs found me at a very different place as I encountered two distinctly different approaches to birth. The first and most common is standard Western medical care, called "the active approach" and characterized by minimizing a woman's pain and accomplishing delivery "within a defined number of hours, usually twelve" (Feinbloom 2000, 182). Performed by an obstetric gynecologist in a hospital setting, the active approach routinely uses a series of medical interventions that work to facilitate or accelerate the birth process—such as labor induction, pitocin, epidural for pain, electronic fetal monitoring, episiotomy, and cesarean surgery. Indeed, these procedures were covered in the hospital childbirth class I attended in my sixth month of pregnancy.

Whereas the active approach foregrounds reduction of pain and timely delivery, a second model is "the unhurried approach" of natural childbirth, which is characterized by "the absence of an expectation for how long or in what way a woman should labor or give birth, and the presence of an expectation (call it confidence) that a woman has the capacity to handle the pain of labor without being traumatized in the process" (Feinbloom 2000, 182). This approach is best articulated by midwife Ina May Gaskin, one of the nation's most experienced midwives who has "caught" more than 2,200 babies in her lifetime: "The way I see it, the most trustworthy knowledge about women's bodies combines the best of what medical science has offered over the past century or two with what women have always been able to learn about themselves before birth moved into hospitals" (2003, xi).

This second approach implies a critique of the active approach at the same time that it assumes a reliance on the basic tools of modern medicine. Yet it gives priority to a woman's own body and unique experience in the birth process; a midwife assists as the woman herself delivers her baby. The difference is more than just language; midwives prioritize education and pain control through body position, environment, massage, acupuncture, and various other strategies.

Over the past twenty years, a significant body of national and global research on birth has called into question the U.S. overreliance on the Western model. With the best of intentions and despite cautionary guidelines by national medical bodies, the "option" of medical interventions has become the norm: one-half to two-thirds of all labors are artificially induced either by having the water broken or with synthetic oxytocin. Epidurals are given to more than 60 percent of birthing women (Osterman 2011) and episiotomies to almost 30 percent (Hartmann et al. 2005).

In addition, the rate of Cesarean surgery in the United States reached 31 percent in 2007, which signified a 50 percent increase from 1996 (Hamilton, Martin, and Ventura 2009). Cesareans are major surgeries that carry risks of infection, scar tissue, and complications, so that the World Health Organization (WHO) recommends that no more than 10 to 15 percent of normal births should require a surgical cesarean delivery (Gibbons et al. 2010).

Cesareans are linked to lower rates of breastfeeding due to maternal pain from the surgical scar, delayed access to the baby, and complications due to anemia or certain types of anesthesia (Dewey 2001; Zanardo et al. 2010).

American obstetric gynecologists are performing more procedures, earlier, and more often than ever before (Hartmann et al. 2005; Epstein 2007; Hamilton, Martin, and Ventura 2009; Osterman and Martin 2011). This practice might be acceptable if it meant that U.S. women and their babies were better off. Unfortunately, the United States is currently ranked second to last among thirty-three industrialized nations in maternal mortality, with a rate of eleven maternal deaths for every one hundred thousand live births (WHO 2007). We rank thirtieth in infant mortality, which has been steadily rising over the past twenty years. Journalist Jennifer Block notes that "[a]lthough we are superior in saving the lives of infants born severely premature, women are 70% more likely to die in childbirth in the United States than in Europe" (2007, xxi). Ireland's system of midwifery tops the list when it comes to reducing maternal mortality, with a rate of one maternal death for every one hundred thousand live births.

At the same time, some of the basic indicators of newborn well-being have been steadily dropping. Babies are arriving sooner, smaller, and less healthy. The rate of preterm birth (babies arriving at 32 to 36 weeks) was 12.7 percent in 2007 and has steadily risen since 1990 so that the average pregnancy length is now 38.7 weeks rather than the traditional 40 weeks (Center for Disease Control and Prevention 2005). The incidence of low birth weight has risen from 6.7 percent in 1984 to 8.2 percent in 2007 (Hamilton, Martin, and Ventura 2009). The National Center for Health Statistics notes: "It is becoming increasingly recognized that infants born late preterm are . . . more likely to suffer complications at birth such as respiratory distress, to require intensive and prolonged hospitalization; to incur higher medical costs; to die within the first year of life; and to suffer brain injury" (Kirmeyer et al. 2009, 1)

And even these overall numbers mask the inequalities of race and class. African American women are nearly four times more likely to die of pregnancy-related complications than white women (Amnesty International 2010). A New York study found that African American women are seven times more likely to die of complications. Women of color in general are less likely to be insured and to have regular access to good prenatal care.

The pattern of unequal access is replicated at the global level as well. Without dependable access to prenatal care and basic health care, women in developing counties are a hundred to a thousand times more likely to die from birth-related causes. Less than two-thirds of women in developing countries have assistance from any kind of skilled birth attendant (WHO 2008). Lack of access to health care means birthing women will die of hemorrhage, infections, eclampsia, obstructed labor, abortion, and other complications, at least half of which are preventable. Local community midwives in certain areas are making progress in some areas, but this progress only highlights the fact that good midwifery needs to happen in concert with good basic medical care; the relationship is crucial for women's birthing well-being. A midwife is not enough in an area that does not have minimal standards of hygiene, access to water, nutrition, and medical care.

Natural-birth advocates have documented the cascading effects of medical interventions—an induced labor is often stronger and more sudden than natural labor, so a woman is more likely to request an epidural, which in turn is more likely to lead to a cesarean (Block 2007; Epstein 2007), which increases risks to the mother and makes it more difficult for her to breast-feed her newborn. Women who can afford to hire a doula to help them understand this process will do better; they tend to remain at home longer and are less likely to need medical interventions and less likely to end up with a cesarean.

As for myself, privileged as an educated professional, I chose a doula and an ob/gyn to help me give birth in a hospital setting. I spent hours, days, trying to locate a midwife via my insurance provider before finally giving up in frustration and choosing an ob-gyn. She was wonderful but made it clear she did not appreciate my birth plan or my insistence on "questioning her judgment" when I refused to induce labor until I reached forty-one and a half weeks.

I became an avid natural-birth enthusiast and began incorporating the topic into my introductory women's studies courses. Yet as I continued to participate in discussions and sharing of natural-birth resources, I remained disappointed at the limited reach of the natural-birth community. Despite the best of intentions, an empowering natural birth seemed within reach mostly for educated, white, Internet-savvy, professional women. There is a too-small network of individualist "choice" discourse circulating within birthing communities that support women in this path. The excellent recent film *Business of Being Born* (2008), produced by Hollywood mom Ricki Lake and Abby Epstein, broaches many of these issues and follows a series of relatively affluent women as they deliver their babies at home with midwife Cara Muhlhahn. Less than one percent of babies are born at home in the United States. The follow-up book by Lake and Epstein, titled *Your Best Birth* (2009), also an excellent resource, still further signifies natural birth as an individual consumer product, to be chosen by those lucky enough to be able to "interview your ob/gyn." Professional doula Miriam Pérez comments, "Upwardly-mobile moms in New York City may finally be catching on to the benefits of midwifery and homebirth, but low-income women are still firmly planted in the hospital most often with medicalized births overseen by doctors" (2009).

Most every other industrialized country in the world bases its maternity care on the midwifery model, with ob/gyns reserved for only the 10 to 15 percent of cases with complications. Evidence from U.S. and international studies overwhelmingly shows that the midwifery model is the safest method of birth for mother and child —good for mom, good for baby, good for the nation (Büscher, Sivertsen, and White 2010). And yet we're not doing it.

The uneven access of women to adequate medical care in a world of inequality and the paradoxical results of access continue to be the greatest lesson I learned as a mother in academe. The obscene contrast between dangerously high levels of overmedicalized cesarean births among more privileged women and a basic lack of prenatal care among women of color in the United States continues to confound me. A WHO report starkly concludes that, at the global level, 3.18 million cesarean sections were needed in undeveloped countries in 2008, but "6.20 million unnecessary sections were performed elsewhere," a disparity with "negative implications for health equity both within and across countries" (Gibbons et al. 2010, 3).

Alison Bartlett, a feminist scholar who writes about the maternal body and breastfeeding, reminds me that the work of feminist academics is "still one of the few modes of employment which allows us to think subversively and to encourage others to contest dominant regimes of thought" (2006, 22). Groups such as the U.S. Sistersong Women of Color Reproductive Health Collective have begun to use the term *birth(ing) justice* to reflect work "for a better culture of birth and reproduction within an intersectional politics" (M. Pérez 2011). The First Environment Collaborative founded by Mohawk midwife Katsi Cook, for example, trains Native midwives in a project that reconfigures birth at the intersection of Native, environmental, and reproductive rights.

I initially wrote this article out of an incredible feeling of empowerment in motherhood and in my own physical body. I wanted to communicate that feeling to other mothers-to-be. Like a paid maternity leave, the natural-birth experience surprised me as an amazing luxury, something to which I had no idea I was entitled. I remain frustrated as I see birth being commoditized into an individual "choice," limited by access to privilege and at times discursively represented in language that plays on maternal guilt and control issues. We need new language such as *birth(ing) justice* that moves beyond "individual" consumer birth choices to productively engage dominant medical discourse and global patterns of medical access.

9

THREADS THAT BIND

A *Testimonio* to Puerto Rican Working Mothers

Maura I. Toro-Morn

Feminist scholars have written eloquent accounts describing and analyzing the dehumanizing and exploitative conditions found in the global assembly line (Fernandez-Kelly 1983; Bose and Acosta-Belen 1995; Safa 1995; Chang 2000; Parreñas 2001; Salzinger 2003; Nash 2005; Colón et al. 2008). In the past twenty years, a voluminous body of scholarship has helped map out the conditions of working mothers and daughters across Asia, Latin America, and Africa. We know that "women have become the new industrial proletariat in export-based industries" (Jaggar 2001, 305) and that gender stereotypes of Third World women workers as submissive, passive, and secondary earners continue to lure investors to the global South. Women workers across the global South have been subject to low wages, long working days, sexual harassment, horrid working conditions, and few prospects for advancement. Women across the world take these jobs out of sheer necessity, but also because it provides some meaning to their lives as women and mothers. The task of making visible the experiences of women workers in the global assembly line has sharpen the analysis engendered by earlier feminist work on the productive/reproductive continuum. Sociologist Joan Acker captures the issue best when she states that "women have been subordinated in both domains, held responsible for unpaid reproductive labor and consigned to positions with less power and lower pay than men within the sphere of production" (2004, 23).

At the other end of the global assembly line, feminist scholars have also called attention to the political economy of higher education and its connections to globalization practices. Chandra Talpade Mohanty writes, "We have witnessed a profound shift in the vision and mission of the nineteenth-century public university to the model of an entrepreneurial, corporate university in the business of naturalizing capitalist, privatized citizenship" (2003, 173). In the corporate university, race, nationality, and gender figure prominently as tropes of the new ideology of difference and multiculturalism and as systems of exploitation and subordination. As in the global assembly line, women—in particular women of color—play an important role in the corporate university. The contours of these processes cut through my own life in profound ways: I am part of the Latina/o "brain drain"—the movement of educated Puerto Ricans to continue our education in the United States, many of whom, like myself, have become incorporated as part of the immigrant professional social classes (e.g., college professors, engineers, and accountants, among others) (Toro-Morn 2010). In that context, motherhood for me has meant trying to balance the corporate university's growing demands with the challenges of raising a bicultural, bilingual son and the struggles of maintaining a transnational family. At the broadest level, my essay for this volume contributes in a very personal way to documenting how social class, race/ethnicity, and gender have shaped my experiences as an academic working mother in a transnational context. Here, I draw upon the feminist tool of *testimonio*. The Latina Feminist Group defines a *testimonio* as a "tool for Latinas to theorize oppression, resistance, and subjectivity," a way to capture "Latinas' complex, layered lives" (2001, 19). According to this group, "We all carry within us the memory of homelands, communities, families, and cultural traditions that situate us in our life trajectories as writers and teachers. Not merely celebratory or nostalgic, these 'stories' also capture the ironies and difficulties of becoming successful, accomplished women" (21). Made up of feminists and privileged academic women, the Latina Feminist Group introduced a new "praxis within *testimonio* traditions" as we Latinas make ourselves the subjects and objects of our own inquiry and voice, a practice I attempt in this account.

In keeping with this definition, my *testimonio* as a professional working mother in a midwestern university is connected to my mother, Rita Julia Segarra Ramos, a retired factory worker from the export-processing zone of Mayaguez, Puerto Rico, and to my "other mother," Chispa (her real name is Heremita Martinez, but everyone calls her "Chispa" as a nickname). Thus, it is an attempt to reveal and capture what connects us as workingwomen and mothers. It is a *testimonio* to their lives of struggle and sacrifice and to who I am today because of them. It is an attempt to capture this *herencia* (legacy), but, more important, it is also an attempt to recognize *el hilo que nos une* (the thread that binds us).

In the first part of this essay, I describe my mother's experiences as a working mother. My mother belonged to the generation of Puerto Rican women who became incorporated as a source of cheap labor in the modernization program Operation Bootstrap (Operación Manos a la Obra) that transformed the island from an agricultural to an industrial economy. Here, I claim my *herencia* as a "daughter of Operation Bootstrap," a name coined by Luz Acevedo (2001) to describe the experiences of many of us who came of age under the auspices of this modernization experiment that took place in Puerto Rico from the 1940s to the 1980s. In that sociohistorical context, gender and social class became salient characteristics of our lives. Next I describe and analyze my experiences as a working professional mother in the U.S. academy, arguably a different type of assembly line where race, gender, and social class intersect in significant ways. In the conclusion, I attempt to capture the threads that connect my mother's life and my own and the significance of this story at this historical moment.

THE MOTHERS AND DAUGHTERS OF OPERATION BOOTSTRAP

U.S. colonization of and imperialism in the Americas helps contextualize the role that Puerto Rican women across social classes have played in the global assembly. As Alice Colón-Warren and Idsa Alegría-Ortega (1998) point out, what we know presently as the maquiladoras in export-processing zones across the Americas were first adopted and tried in Puerto Rico under Operation Bootstrap. Puerto Rican women encountered different social and economic conditions that shaped their incorporation as workers throughout history. In the 1950s, they became an identifiable source of cheap labor for the industrialization model, Operation Bootstrap, the program that transformed Puerto Rico from an agricultural to an industrial economy (Ríos 1990). A gendered and racialized ideology underpinned much of the development model in that "the basis of these policies was the regulation of women's reproductive behavior, not the redefinition of gender relations" (Colón-Warren and Alegría-Ortega 1998, 105). Migration, a process connected to the development of export-processing zones, has also marked the experiences of Puerto Rican women and men across social classes.

My mother was part of the massive labor force of working-class and poor women and men who became the backbone of the industrialization model. My vivid memories of her life and struggles as a factory worker for Proper International, a manufacturing company making uniforms for the U.S. military, overlap with the ever-growing body of scholarship produced in the past twenty years that reveals the experiences of Puerto Rican working mothers (see, e.g., Ortiz 1996). But these memories—far too numerous to capture fully in this essay—are punctuated by pain, hers and my own. Daily and weekly struggles to meet production, frequent complaints and frustrations about management, and fears of being laid off impacted our lives in profound ways. Through her actions and dedication to being a mother and a worker, she modeled for me a way to reconcile these identities. Today I affirm my commitment to my work as a professor–intellectual worker with the same passion that I affirm my desire to be a good mother; for me it is not one or the other, it is both!

Yet in spite of a life of struggle and hardship, my mother's identity and affirmation as a working woman shaped my own awareness of Puerto Rican women's struggles and my evolving commitment to feminism. Work was oppressive, though she would not have used such a word. She "gave her life" to the factory (as she would put it, "Le di mi vida a la fábrica") As a single mother, she didn't have many options. She supplemented her wages by selling merchandise in the factory, an income-earning strategy that has come to characterize working women throughout the Caribbean (Freeman 2001). Among the happy moments at work was when los Americanos came to visit the plant, and she had an opportunity to interact with them. For a fleeting moment, their praise erased years of back-breaking labor, harassment, accidents on the shop floor, meager salaries, and the ever-present threat of closing—a prevalent tactic that continues to be used to keep the workers from organizing collectively.

A single working parent, my mother struggled to balance work and family demands, just as many women of her generation did in Puerto Rico and Puerto Rican communities in New York and Chicago. One strategy Puerto Rican working women have used to secure care for the children is to hire other family members or neighbors as help (Toro-Morn 2001). It is not clear to me how she became friends with Chispa, "my other mother," but I know that beginning when I was three years old, Chispa cared for me. Her family became my *non-blood-related extended family*, a term I coined to explain to friends my complex family arrangements. She began to care for my brother, Jose, when he was only days old because my mother had to return to work shortly after his birth. To this day, my brother calls both Chispa and our mom "Mami."

Chispa and her husband, Pablo, a police officer, lived down the street from our house and represented the model of the "traditional family" that is frequently praised and celebrated as the backbone of Puerto Rican society. Chispa and Pablo had three kids, Marlyn, Miriam, and Pablo, whom today I consider my siblings and their children my nieces and nephews. My mom waited for her ride to work every morning in front of Chispa's home, which added some security to the dangers of waiting by the side of a country road where cars frequently exceeded posted speed limits. Chispa was a devoted wife and stay-at-home mom. She did not learn to read and write until she was an adult, in contrast to my mom, who had an eighth-grade education. As far I can remember, Chispa never left the house or went to town alone during my formative years. After her husband died, she started walking to town and enjoying more freedom. She represents what has been depicted in much of the social science and popular literature by and about Puerto Ricans as "the traditional Puerto Rican mother" (Safa 1995). I know that my mother gave Chispa a little bit of money from her paycheck every week, offering evidence that challenges cherished notions that mothering equals being a non–income earner. Puerto Rican feminists and scholars have worked very hard to demystify gendered tropes of "traditionality" that defy the lived realities of Puerto Rican women (Toro-Morn 2008). Chispa and Pablo provided for us the safety of a nurturing home and siblings who became college educated and served as role models. All of them went to college and became part of the growing professional class of Puerto Ricans on the island, a celebrated outcome of the Bootstrap model.

As I write these notes, more details about this part of my life continue to surface, too many and too complex given the space limitations of this essay, but a few words about my father are necessary here. The story is far too painful to "birth in writing," but suffice it to say that my mother could not marry my father because he was already married when they became involved, revealing yet another untold dimension of many Puerto Rican families—the "other woman" phenomenon. My father was not completely absent. We visited him and my loving paternal grandparents frequently, but he was not willingly involved in our care and well-being. Although my mom initially resisted the idea of taking him to court to force him to own up to his financial responsibility as a father, she eventually relented. His financial support, even when enforced by the court, was inconsistent and uneven, though.

I struggled through the formative years of my life with the gendered tropes of motherhood (re)constructed against the backdrop of a modernizing Puerto Rican landscape. I know that part of my own awakening as a woman and as a feminist was a complete rejection of the gender socialization I received in Puerto Rico from my mom, my other mother, my extended family, school, and larger community. I don't know if my mother understood what getting an education meant and how that came into conflict with the tropes of being a good wife and mother that seemed to be so cherished historically.

I also know that my mother wanted something better for me. She did not want me working in the factory. In many ways, she had internalized a new paradigm for Puerto Rican women: "Estudia por si acaso tu esposo te sale malo" (Educate yourself in case your husband turns out to be a bum) (Acevedo 2001, 144, translation added). Women of my generation coming of age in the late 1970s were told to perceive education as a fallback in the event that their marriage falls apart (Acevedo 2001). It is ironic that I didn't feel ready to be a mom until I was supposedly "medically" passed my "reproductive childbearing age"— that is, forty years old. Although getting pregnant was not easy, once I became pregnant, I turned to the task of motherhood with the same discipline and dedication that I turned to my doctoral dissertation and academic career.

EDUCATION, MIGRATION, AND WORKING IN ACADEMIA

Education became a modernization trope that was hard to escape. "Tienes que estudiar y hacerte una mujer profesional" (You must study and become a professional woman) was the constant cry from everyone in the barrio, my family, and public-school teachers. I began my educational journey as a political science major in a small liberal arts college, Interamerican University, on the western coast of Puerto Rico. I wanted to go to college in Ponce, forty-five minutes away from my home, but in keeping with my mother's deeply gendered notions, it would have been unthinkable for me to live away from home. I could go to college, but I had live at home under her watchful eye. Education fueled my budding feminist consciousness in ways that my mother had not anticipated, however, creating many conflicts and tensions between us. By the time I had finished my undergraduate degree, the pressure to fulfill traditional gender expectations had become unbearable for me. My ticket out was doing exactly what they wanted me to do: "hacerme una mujer profesional" (become a professional working woman).

I added a chapter to the family's (and the country's) history of migration when the opportunity to pursue graduate studies in the U.S. Midwest presented itself. My migration, however, was part of what I have come to identify as part of the " Puerto Rican brain drain," the movement of educated Puerto Ricans to continue our education in U.S. universities (Toro-Morn 1995, 2005). In fact, the migration of educated and professional Puerto Ricans became even more pronounced in the 1980s and 1990s (Aranda 2007). According to anthropologist Jorge Duany (2010), this migration has intensified in the past five years and has shifted to a new site of settlement, Orlando, Florida. The movement of working-class and educated Puerto Ricans and their incorporation in the U.S. labor market have been connected to the failures of the modernization program in Puerto Rico, the ongoing colonial situation, and current globalization processes.

From 1983 to 1993, I pursued graduate studies at Illinois State University, the University of Connecticut, and Loyola University. As a graduate student, I entered an ethnoracial landscape shaped by social class and racial dimensions that were foreign to me at the time. I have devoted my academic career to studying migrations, people in movement, crossing borders real and imagined. I, too, have crossed many borders in an attempt to find an intellectual home in sociology, ethnic studies, feminist studies, and more recently Latino studies. Each space has been complicated for me as a Puerto Rican/Latina woman for different reasons. Sociology was a complicated space for me because I selected to study topics that at the time did not seem mainstream (gender, migration, intersectionality), and I sought to deploy principles and assumptions drawn from my engagement with feminist theory and methods. I became adept at crossing intellectual borders, at speaking different languages, and at recognizing potential dangers.

As a Latina/Puerto Rican woman, an immigrant, a Spanish-speaking daughter of a factory worker in an export-processing zone, I became part of a corporate assembly line at a time when "diversity talk" became a significant ideological trope in universities across the nation (Dominguez 1994a, 1994b). Diversity talk has become an institutional way to organize strategic planning, hiring documents, curricular offerings, and vision statements.

With diversity talk comes the celebratory perspective that erases the socio-historical experiences of the many groups that have been part of the U.S. experience, and in the process a new form of marginalization has developed. This ideological trope of the corporate university contributes to what Alyssa García has labeled the "commoditization of race and gender" and "cultural taxation" processes encountered by faculty of color across academia (2005, 261). More broadly, faculty of color are recruited to address problems of absence and underrepresentation in academic institutions and—though frequently not overtly—to serve as tokens. A vast number of studies shows that once recruited, faculty of color frequently find themselves isolated, ghettoized, and overburdened with committee and service assignments (Segura 2003; García 2005), problems I myself have faced in the twenty years I have been part of academia.

In the United States, universities are highly stratified institutions subject to change under the auspices of local, national, and global privatization strategies. In the global assembly line of the professoriate class, the pressures of quality control and productivity come in the form of yearly academic evaluations, publish-or-perish imperatives, student evaluations, and demands made on one's time on the basis of diversity initiatives. These issues for women, in particular working mothers, become a source of a great deal of tension, anxiety, frustration, and institutional discrimination. Throughout my career, I have faced my share of problems and difficulties that stem from my position as a woman of color in the university assembly line. One difference between my own situation and my single working mother's is that I have a husband's economic and emotional support, which allows us a comfortable and modest middle-class existence.

EL HILO QUE NOS UNE . . . THE THREAD THAT BINDS US

The thread that binds working women is that, whether we are aware of it or not, we are (have been) actors in the global assembly line. By working in an export-processing zone, my mother played an important role in the industrialization model that "modernized" the island. She occupied a space in the global assembly line shaped by social class and gender exploitation. Her working experiences shaped her own social class awareness of struggle and sacrifice, values that also came to characterize her mothering practices. She knew she was exploited and mistreated, and she sought refuge from that in her identity as a working mother. To her death, she was proud of her work *en la fábrica*, in the factory. She was also keenly aware of the struggles and problems she faced as a single mom and tried to balance work and family roles. My other mother, Chispa, supported her family and ours with her reproductive labor, which included not only cooking and caring for us, but, more important, emotionally dedicating herself to us, even though my brother and I were not her biological children. I, too, have ironically come to occupy a peculiar space in the corporate assembly line that characterizes U.S. universities today. As a Latina/Puerto Rican academic, my experiences are shaped by race, social class, and gender differentiation as well as by the microaggressions that characterize life in academia for so many women of color (Toro-Morn 2010). But I love what I do! Although there have been much pain and confusion and many emotional scars, I return to the classroom every year renewed by the conviction that our society requires an educated population, critical thinkers and citizens capable of speaking truth to power.

I have recently come to discover that my life is connected to the women of my mother's generation in even more profound ways. On Father's Day 2008, my mother suffered a debilitating stroke that left her bed ridden and paralyzed. A fiercely independent and physically active woman now faced the fourth stage of her life with a fortitude that is admirable and at times defies explanation. A few days after her stroke, I flew to Puerto Rico to care for her, unaware of what this meant for us and my families, the one I left in the United States and the one I was returning to on the island. In the most recent chapter of our lives, a transformation in our roles as mothers and daughters unfolded. I have become part of a large group of Latina women, transnational mothers, caring for families on both sides of the ocean, in my case my aging mother (Alicea 1997; Aranda 2007). For a Puerto Rican woman living and working in Illinois, this physical and emotional work is done in a transnational space, an added dimension to my evolving responsibilities as a working mother.

At my mother's hospital bedside, I rediscovered her friends from *la fábrica*, women whom I knew by name from my childhood, but whose faces I did not recognize. They collectively belong to a generation of Puerto Rican women who found themselves as historical agents in the development of export industrialization in Puerto Rico. As women workers, they were subject to hard working conditions, humiliation, and exploitation—problems that have been well documented by feminist scholars both in Puerto Rico and the United States. A quality that has always impressed me about these women workers is their strong sense of identity as working mothers, their solidarity as workers, and their long-lasting friendships and sense of obligation to each other. Their resiliency, commitment to and pride in their work, and sense of justice are values that connect them to women workers across the hemispheres.

In the past two years, there were many close calls, many moments in which it is clear that my mother was saying good-bye and coming to terms with the inevitability of death. It is in those moments that she and I were able to speak openly and honestly to each other and recognize how much we mean for each other and how in spite of a life of struggle, conflict, and pain, it was our deep sense of love via our mother–daughter bond that continued to sustain us.

My mother died shortly after midnight on September 23, 2011. I wish I could tell you that her passing was peaceful and quiet. It was not! As a working-class woman, my mother labored through her death like she did through most of her life. But I do know that she faced it with valor and strength, qualities that characterized her. My mother was a very strong, resolute, fiercely independent, generous woman who loved deeply and passionately. More than two hundred people came to the funeral and paid their respects. The mayors of Cabo Rojo (our hometown) and San German (my brother's place of residence) came, as did our islandwide senator and many of her coworkers at Proper International, the factory where she worked for more than thirty years.

I spent night and day at the hospital with her during the last week of her life. I bathed her everyday and fussed to make her comfortable. During most of that week, she was in and out of consciousness. The parallels between birthing and dying are striking. I became a different woman the day my son was born. The day my mother died, I also became a different person. The world is not the same without her. Meghan O'Rourke's account of her mother's passing in the book *The Long Goodbye* captures the experience best for me: "Nothing prepared me for the loss of my mother. Even knowing that she would die did not prepare me. A mother after all, is your entry into the world. She is the shell in which you divide and become a life. Waking up in a world without her is like waking up in a world without sky: unimaginable" (2011, 10).

I cared for my mother in a transnational space; now I must learn to grieve her *entre mundos* (between worlds). There is so much missing here that I feel lost. Where do I put my grief? What do I do with myself? Where can I go to see her, to remember her? The cultural differences in how people grieve are also striking. Here in the United States, grief is private, personal, contained. There in Puerto Rico, grief is open, public, ritualized, and communal. As an intellectual who has devoted a significant part of my academic life to exposing the intersections of social class, race, and gender in the Puerto Rican experience, I wrestle with scholarly notions that continue to portray women as stripped of agency because of culture. I know that my mother did not have many options—such are the hidden injuries of social class—but she made the best of her situation. Today my brother and I are evidence of her life of struggle and her agency as a woman and a worker. It is an agency that I affirm today as a professorial worker and claim as *mi herencia como mujer y madre* (the heritage passed on to me as a woman and a mother).

10

PARENTING WITHIN THE NEXUS OF RACE, CLASS, AND GENDER OPPRESSION IN GRADUATE SCHOOL AT A HISTORICALLY BLACK COLLEGE/UNIVERSITY

Olivia Perlow

THIS CHAPTER provides a personal account of my experiences as a mother and graduate student attending a historically black college/university (HBCU). I trace my narrative through the critical theorizing of black feminist scholars who have examined the ways in which whiteness, patriarchy, and capitalism are interrelated systems of oppression that mutually reinforce one another on multiple levels (Collins 2000; Landry 2007). Societal institutions such as universities act as conduits through which the oppressive values of these systems are often transmitted to its members on macro-, meso-, and microscales (Landry 2007). It is my contention that although HBCUs were designed to provide black people with the opportunity to achieve upward mobility, my experience at the HBCU where I attended graduate school was that it perpetuated race, class, and gender oppression and thus became a hostile environment for me as a mother. Through face-to-face interactions with peers and professors and encounters with administrators who exercised an authoritative commitment to the university's policies, I experienced how other academics internalized society's racist, patriarchal, and capitalistic value system and thus oppressed students like myself. This chapter therefore demonstrates how my social location as a low-income, black female hindered my ability to navigate motherhood in this context and exposed me to multiple oppressions within and outside of the HBCU. I conclude by exploring the ways in which I and other women like me combated these challenges.

Intersectionality, as a feminist framework of analysis, is a powerful lens through which to understand how one's social location is determined by various intersecting identities (i.e., race, ethnicity, class, gender, sexual orientation, age, disability) that over time have cumulative effects (Davis 1981; Combahee River Collective 1982; Lorde 1984; Spelman 1988; Christian 1989; Collins 2000; Landry 2007). My race, gender, and class, for instance, interacted to create a unique set of challenges for me as a parent. Due to the history of slavery and the commoditization of black women in the United States and across the Americas, racist assumptions about black motherhood have been created (Lewis 2001). Pauline Terrelenge Stone states that black women's experiences are different from white women's in "the peculiar way in which the racial and sexual caste systems have interfaced" historically (quoted in Berry and Mizelle 2006, xv). Patricia Hill Collins agrees: "African-American women occupy this center and can 'feel the iron' that enters Black women's souls, because while U.S. Black women's experiences resemble others, such experiences remain unique" (2000, 39). My story is unique, but like all student mothers, I ultimately share in the struggle to achieve a successful balance between academic and family life. The difference is that I believed the individuals at my university, as an HBCU, would work in solidarity with me because they know all too well how interlocking systems of oppression have created barriers for black people. My intersecting gendered and class experience sadly demonstrates, however, that I was incorrect.

AFRICAN AMERICANS AND COLLEGES/UNIVERSITIES

HBCUs have historically appealed to African Americans because of their "supportive campus environments and open opportunity structures" for students of color (Boyd 2007, 547). It is well documented that many alumni, students, faculty, and administrators at HBCUs have been leaders in the fight against racial inequality and injustice (Reviere and Nahal 2005). I attended an HBCU with the expectation that the institution would shield me from racial oppression and live up to its historical legacy of embodying a commitment to social justice. To the contrary, I found that although my HBCU may be ahead of predominately white institutions in challenging racism, it has lagged behind in confronting sexism and women's issues (Bonner 2001; Reviere and Nahal 2005; Gasman 2007). As at many other educational institutions, the black men (and women) at this HBCU also reproduced the larger society's patriarchal power structure (Guy-Sheftall

1995; Collins 2000). Florence Bonner concurs: "In terms of barriers to promotion, exclusion from the curricula, a chilly climate in the workplace and
classroom, and sexual harassment, African American women face the same
obstacles at HBCUs as they do at [predominantly white institutions]" (2001,
188). Gender issues within black institutions are "swept under the rug" in
order to highlight issues of racial inequality within the larger society (Gasman 2007, 760). Thus, the goal of racial solidarity requires black women to
remain silent around issues of sexism, even within black institutions (Fordham 1993). One of the manifestations of this silence is that very little scholarly inquiry regarding black women at the HBCU exists despite the fact that
they have historically been the majority at these institutions (Gasman 2007).

As a case in point, the absence of a women's studies program until recently is an indication of my university's neglect of gender issues (Reviere and
Nahal 2005). Further evidence of patriarchy is the existence of a glass ceiling;
positions of administrative power are heavily dominated by men, and women
are most heavily concentrated in the lowest-ranking and typically pink-collar
and service positions (Bonner 2001). Despite these and other inequities at
my university, women, even those in high positions, have not significantly
challenged the administration to redress gendered issues. Signithia Fordham
explains that, according to Jo Anne Pagano, "women pawn their collective
voice in exchange for success in the existing patriarchic structure. By engaging in such practices, she argues, women ensure the continued existence of
authority in the male image and their (women's) complicity in the lie that
asserts that they are naturally silent. She concludes by asserting that women
who either remain or become silent are instrumental in maintaining female
dependency and invisibility in the academy" (1993, 10).

In my experience, many of the black women in upper administrative
positions within the university refused to challenge their own gendered
subordination and failed to support female students, including student
mothers. The needs and interests of this particular population (i.e., child
care, family housing, flexible schedules, mentorship, etc.) were not met
as a result of a male-centered ethos that did not regard student–mothers
as a priority for the university. In fact, the fiercest opposition to motherhood that I received within the university came directly from black female
administrators. I was surprised and shocked by what I perceived as a high
level of internalized sexism.

In addition, instead of adhering to traditionally African-centered principles of cooperation, interdependence, and collective responsibility, my

HBCU promoted the dominant ideology where hegemonic ideals of success are based on Western capitalistic notions of liberal individualism, conformity, and a staunch commitment to an impersonal bureaucratic structure (Johnson 2003). In an effort to challenge this ideology, bell hooks argues, "Collectively, Black folks could progress in our efforts to achieve Black self-determination if we repudiated bourgeoisie values. The bourgeoisie knows this, which is why it wants all Black people to believe that material success is all that matters" (1995, 258). According to James Teele's analysis of the writings of E. Franklin Frazier, the first black president of the American Sociological Association, the HBCU's real goal, instead of empowering black communities through a commitment to social justice, is in fact the shaping of a "Black bourgeoisie," and the educational tradition is "to mold [students of color] in the image of the [owning-class] white man" (2002, 146). For example, HBCUs have been a significant pathway for blacks into the U.S. business elite (Boyd 2007). Thus, despite a stated mission of empowering students to recognize and fight against their oppressions, the main goal of the HBCU at which I attended graduate school was to create, consistent with capitalistic principles, an avenue of upward mobility into the middle and upper classes for black students, but with little or no regard for how to use their education or new positionality to effect social justice.

According to Collins, "In some fundamental ways, moving into the middle class means adopting the values and lifestyles of White middle-class families" (2000, 196). In terms of being a good mother within white, middle-class, traditional American culture, this means adopting what Sharon Hays refers to as "intensive mothering," an idealized gender role that expects women to be selfless, investing an extraordinary amount of time, emotional and physical energy, and financial resources into their children (as cited in Lynch 2008, 586). The dominant cultural portrayal of motherhood is one of sacrificial commitment, and even white middle-class mothers struggle with such level of engagement. In the same vein, the dominant script for what it means to be a good student, especially a graduate student, is also one of selfless commitment. In this regard, the dominant cultural expectations of graduate school and motherhood place these two roles in direct conflict with each other because each one requires so much attention and effort.

Race, class, and lack of mentoring also exacerbate the challenges of mothering in graduate school (Koro-Ljungberg and Hayes 2006; L. Patton

2009). Because academe is a microcosm of the macrosystems of oppression, black students are forced to deal with various factors such as others' perceptions about their scholarly ability, which then impacts their academic achievement (M. Williams et al. 2005). For black female students, these issues are further complicated by their social location. As Himani Bannerji states, "One can only think of racism, sexism and class as interconstitutive social relations of organized and administered domination. It is their constantly mediating totality which shapes people's perception of each other. . . . They see her as a *Black woman*, in the entirety of that construction, about whom there are existing social practices and cultural stereotypes . . . [and] racist sexism . . . [that] have had an overwhelmingly negative impact on her economic and personal life (1995, 127–128).

Angela Davis ([1971] 1995) further argues that African American women bring to academe a unique history of womanhood that strikingly contrasts to that of white women. For one thing, black women have historically been forced to work outside the home in large numbers and have thus had less time, energy, and financial resources to devote to motherhood (hooks 1981; Collins 2000). More important, black motherhood has historically been inextricably linked to the sexual politics of black womanhood in which black females' sexuality and fertility has been controlled to enable the systems of whiteness, patriarchy, and capitalist exploitation to operate more effectively (hooks 1981; Collins 2000). As a consequence, the white male elite created and reserved the definitions of womanhood, in particular the "cult of true womanhood," for white women, who were perceived as inherently good, including in their role as mothers. In contrast, black women have been regarded as the antithesis of womanhood, historically devalued as persons since slavery, and considered bad mothers (Christian 1989; Collins 2000, 79; Jordan-Zachery 2008). It is not surprising, then, that negative hegemonic images of black mothers as the Mammy, Jezebel, Sapphire, Matriarch, Welfare Mother/Queen, and Teen Mom describe them as promiscuous, sexually uncontrolled, abundantly fertile, irresponsible, immoral, and lazy. According to Collins,

> These negative images provide ideological justification for the dominant group's interest in limiting the fertility of Black mothers who are seen as producing too many economically unproductive children. . . . The image of the welfare mother fulfills this function by labeling as unnecessary and even dangerous to the values of the country the fertility of women who are not White

and middle class. . . . [S]tigmatizing her as the cause of her own poverty and that of African-American communities shifts the angle of vision away from structural sources of poverty and blames the victims themselves. (2000, 87–88)

Therefore, such images of black mothers benefit the white elite's political, economic, and cultural interests (Morton 1991).

The internalization of this macrosystem of oppression is apparent within black middle-class institutions that have struggled to establish cultural boundaries between themselves and the lower class. By serving as juxtaposition to middle-class values, the aforementioned negative images of classed sexuality and fertility are examples of what black women should not to be. The moral policing of black sexuality can paradoxically be seen even within black institutions in that they often attempt to counter these negative images by imposing conservative restrictions on black women's sexuality—that is, by promoting a "politics of respectability" (Collins 2005, 139).

In keeping with the internalization of hegemonic images of black women and of the middle-class value system, black student motherhood is highly frowned upon because it plays into notions of irresponsible and unrestrained black sexuality and is an aberration in the normative middle-class sequence of education, financial stability, and individual achievement promoted at the HBCU I attended. Black student mothers are often demonized as irresponsibly producing children that we cannot afford (Collins 2000). Many professors communicated their disapproval of me and other black student mothers through both verbal and nonverbal insults. For example, I can recall the negative glares I received from some professors as I strolled my infant daughter through the hallway. Some were notorious for having strict "no children allowed in class" policies. I can also recall one professor forcing a student to leave class when she brought her infant son because she didn't have any child-care options. Professors would often make snide remarks to student mothers, such as, "You shouldn't have had a kid if you can't take care of it." Because we were seen as responsible for our own plight and thus unworthy of assistance, very few professors showed compassion and leeway in terms of attendance or due dates for assignments if our children were ill. Instead, we were often accused of making excuses or being incompetent.

Although peer support has been shown to be essential for student mothers, research shows that the "chilly climate" they experience can contribute to unfair treatment by peers (Van Stone, Nelson, and Niemann 1994;

Colbeck, Cabrera, and Terenzini 2001). Many of my peers consistently expressed their disappointment in my decision to have a child while attending graduate school. Within my program, I can recall my closest peers' reactions when I first told them that I was pregnant. Instead of viewing my pregnancy in a positive manner, they made comments such as, "Are you sure you want to go through with this?" and "Wow, this is a really bad time to be having a kid" and "How are you possibly going to manage?" Instead of offering me assistance as well as much-needed emotional support, my closest peers within my program all but disappeared after my daughter was born. Thus, I often felt stigmatized and isolated within my program (Kurtz-Costes, Helmke, and Ülkü-Steiner 2006). Consistent with the internalization of the middle-class value system, my HBCU peers were concerned that motherhood would interfere with the completion of my degree, and in their eyes I embodied the irresponsible, bad black mother.

The abject criticism and opposition I received from administrators, professors, and even my peers for my decision to have a child while attending graduate school demonstrate how negative hegemonic images of black women converge with the white, middle-class value system to oppress black women, even within black institutions (Archer 2010). One multifaceted experience particularly stands out as a beacon of my oppression in graduate school. I was the recipient of a fellowship from the graduate school that required me to work, which became challenging to me as a new mother with an infant. I therefore sought the assistance of a black female administrator with significant power in hopes that she would empathize with my situation and assign me a flexible work schedule to accommodate my circumstances. She responded to my request by stating condescendingly, "You have a prestigious award. What do you want to do, just be a floater? It was your decision to have a baby in graduate school!" She was apparently imposing her middle-class values of individualism and self-reliance on me by further perpetuating the notion that I was irresponsible for having a child and thus undeserving of assistance. I once again found myself being labeled as a black welfare mother looking for handouts. She treated me as if I were looking for an easy way out or trying to get over on the system. As the protector of this system, this female administrator was not going to help me out. This sort of treatment, bell hooks argues, occurs because "American women have been socialized, even brainwashed, to . . . uphold and maintain racial imperialism in the form of white supremacy and sexual imperialism in the form of patriarchy. One measure of the success of such indoctrination is that we perpetuate both consciously and unconsciously the very evils that oppress us" (1981, 120).

The administrator who chastised me (along with many of the black female administrators in top positions within the university) ironically seemed to embody the prototype of a "black lady" or a "modern mammy," a middle-class black woman who is "tough, independent, smart," displays "undying loyalty to the job," uses "standard American English," and has a "dignified demeanor" (Collins 2005, 140–141). She had "arrived" and had done everything the "right" way, meaning that she had completed her education and obtained a well-paying job *before* having children. However, she failed to recognize how her careerist orientation perpetuated racism and sexism and how she was participating in the oppression of black women.

Carol Davies has coined the term *condification* to refer to black political figures such as former U.S. secretary of state Condoleezza Rice and administrators like the one I encountered: "'Condification' defines the process of the conservative Black and/or female subject in power working publicly against the larger interests of the groups to which s/he belongs. . . . Thus, 'con-di-fi-cation' carries within it the 'con' of conservatism; the 'con' of being conned, along with the resonance of commodification, in the sense of being bought and/or sold for a particular interest. It also suggests the Fanonian self-alienating psychology of 'conditioning' and 'confusion' that is ultimately the product of racism" (2007, 395).

When I complained to a black male dean within the university about the incident, he casually dismissed my grievance. I felt beaten and betrayed by an institution where I believed the mission was to empower black students in ways that challenge the status quo as opposed to maintaining it. The eradication of patriarchy and class inequity was quite obviously not on the agenda.

The disregard for students with children extends beyond the personal judgments of individual administrators, professors, and peers. Rather, it is part of a larger institutional culture that follows the status quo of most university settings (Lynch 2008). Thus, although concessions are made for students with disabilities, student athletes, and other student populations, in my experience the special needs of student parents are often given inadequate attention within the administration. Student mothers at my university constantly expressed their frustrations to the administration about issues such as the lack of family-friendly restrooms on campus and the lack of flexibility in class scheduling. Karen Danna Lynch (2008) found that lack of financial aid and child care were the two most common issues faced by graduate student mothers. My university's failure to assist students in meeting challenges surrounding access to affordable quality child care is another prime example of how it in general failed to provide support to students who are parents. Without financial assistance, there was no way that I could afford the great expense of child care. I can recall having to nurse my infant daughter in one hand while typing my master's thesis with the other because I lacked access to affordable day care. Many of my peers who were mothers faced the same dilemma, so we often brought our children to school with us out of desperation, despite the negative consequences. My university was not child-friendly; infants and children were not allowed in many of the workspaces there, such as the computer labs, which created additional dilemmas for student parents without child care.

Even at the graduate level, education at the university is clearly geared toward traditional students: young, middle-class, single students who may receive assistance from their parents and are able to survive with few monetary resources or both. These students are able to cut costs by eating "college food" (i.e., cereal, noodles, etc.) and renting a room in a shared apartment or house. However, students who are parents are often not able to make these types of sacrifices without endangering their children's health and well-being. The lack of resources available to students with children, especially those who are already economically disadvantaged, at the university (i.e., affordable family housing) places a great deal of strain on their ability to navigate academic life and parenthood successfully. Lynch found that most graduate student mothers felt that the structural avenues of support in graduate school were insufficient: "In the absence of these more traditional systems of support, female students with children face a tough and lonely road to degree completion" (2008, 603).

Black women are disproportionately low-income and single mothers forced to bear alone the burdens of mothering and therefore are also disproportionately impacted by the lack of resources available to students with children (Haleman 2004; Duquaine-Watson 2007). Recent welfare reforms have placed even more barriers in front of women in poverty who wish to participate in higher education (Duquaine-Watson 2007). Before the reforms, because there were few systems in place within the university, many black student mothers, especially those who were single, sought out government assistance in the form of food stamps, subsidized housing, cash assistance, Medicaid, and child-care subsidies (Adair and Dahlberg

2003; Duquaine-Watson 2007). I participated in several governmental and nonprofit subsidy programs in order to sustain my family and myself while earning my degree. However, some black student mothers refused to take advantage of this option due to the stigma associated with black women's accepting public assistance. Some of these black student mothers internalized the patriarchal tradition of black mothers making it on their own (i.e., the hegemonic image of the black superwoman), which had a detrimental impact on their physical and emotional well-being (Collins 2000, 188). However, some student mothers who were not able to make ends meet were forced to send their children away to extended family members while they attended school, sometimes for the entire duration of their student career.

My university administration's neglect of the circumstances of students with children and failure to address our complaints led me to become extremely vocal in my attempts to challenge them, which ostracized and placed me within the category of "troublemaker." Whereas rabble-rousing has traditionally been rewarded as championing black issues outside of the HBCU, I was expected to remain silently in my place within the university when it came to gender and motherhood issues. Yet this silencing of black women is counterproductive to social change. Within the chilly university climate, black female students and student mothers have typically turned to women-centered networks (M. Williams et al. 2005). I, too, found much-needed support in such networks within the university that did not include black women administrators. For example, I joined an informal student-run support group for student mothers (which was not funded by the university). Through the group, I received information regarding resources ranging from child care to activities for children. I also found support from several peers who were mothers in graduate school and had experienced or were experiencing the same types of issues as I. These groups of women became "safe spaces" (Collins 2000, 111) that served the important function of providing the opportunity for black mothers to have their voices heard in an environment that otherwise ignored and belittled them. Expressing concerns, frustrations, and even positive experiences validated our worth amidst hostility.

The National Center for Education Statistics found that mothers in graduate school are at one of the highest risks for attrition and that faculty support or lack thereof can impact these rates positively or negatively (cited in Lynch 2008, 585). Research also continues to demonstrate the positive impact that mentoring has on black graduate students (M. Williams et al.

2005). Beth Kurtz-Costes, Laura Helmke, and Beril Ülkü-Steiner state: "In addition to influencing the quality of training the student receives and access to professional opportunities, the mentoring relationship often shapes motivational and affective aspects of the student's progress, such as his/her level of self-confidence, commitment to the field of study and whether the student persists" (2006, 139).

Arwen Raddon (2002) further demonstrates that female mentors may be particularly significant for women who have children or plan to have children. Evelynn Ellis (2001), however, found that black women often did not have mentors or faculty who took an interest in their well-being. Although I feel that the majority of the faculty at my university did not support student mothers, I did find some to be extremely helpful in both my academic and my family endeavors. Rather than viewing student mothers as failures or as statistics, they admired our ability to succeed despite the many obstacles that we faced. Over time, a few of my professors (both men and women), most of whom had children themselves and empathized with my circumstances, made allowances to help me combat challenges by allowing me to bring my daughter to class, being more lenient with me in terms of deadlines, and allowing me to complete some of my work from home.

Because my relatives lived far from me, some female professors who served as mentors and some of my peers assumed fictive kinship relationships with me and my daughter, placing her picture in their offices, inviting us to functions outside of school, and even becoming "othermothers" and sharing in her care. Collins states, "The resiliency of women-centered family networks and their willingness to take responsibility for Black children illustrates how African-influenced understandings of family have been continually reworked to help African-Americans as a collectivity cope with and resist oppression" (2000, 197). Without the support of these networks, combating the opposition that I received and the challenges that I faced as a student-mother would have seemed unbearable. However, the abundance of time and energy it takes to seek out external resources detracts from academic endeavors and causes unnecessary burdens to student-mothers that the university might alleviate by providing supportive services to students with children.

In conclusion, I have no doubt that HBCUs have been highly successful in producing an outstanding number of black (male) leaders and remain an important source of cultural capital and economic development for black communities (Freeman and Cohen 2001, 586; Boyd 2007). However, the

HBCU still has a great deal of work to do in its fight to end all forms oppression, especially with regard to gender and parenting, in order to achieve
equality for all students and people overall. As Shirley Chisolm put it, "In
the end, anti-Black, anti-female, and all forms of discrimination are equivalent to the same thing—anti-humanism" (quoted in Collins 2000, 47). By
neglecting the needs of black student mothers, my HBCU squandered the
opportunity not only to support and strengthen black student families, their
communities, and the larger society, but also to fight against oppression and
injustice within their own walls. Black liberation cannot be realized without
addressing whiteness, patriarchy, and capitalist exploitation within black
institutions. Cole and Guy-Sheftall posit that black "communities are not
served by any of us keeping racial secrets. We will fare much better when
we commit ourselves to dealing openly and honestly with what harms us—
whether it is racism in the majority culture or sexism in our own backyards"
(2001, 101). Thus, the HBCU cannot achieve justice if it continues to over-
shadow issues faced by black student parents, especially mothers. Likewise,
all men and women in the academy, including HBCUs, must mobilize to
provide supportive environments for women, especially those with children,
and advocate for much-needed social change. Only then will our intersectional positionalities be viewed as strengths rather than as burdens to society
or to the university.

11

SOBREVIVIENDO (AND THRIVING) IN THE ACADEMY

My Tías' Counter*consejos* and Advice

J. Estrella Torrez

I WATCHED HER rise, weary of the potential comments that were intended to intimidate me or challenge my beginning years as an academic. Although I didn't know her well, and we hadn't been formally introduced, I did know of her politics (which diverged from my own). She was an elder, a Chicana from the 1960s who had cracked the glass ceiling of academia, and for that reason I respected her, but the academy had killed her radicalism and left her cynical. As cliché as it may sound, the newly retired dean had become what she at one time fought against: a gatekeeper. It was clear a *comadre* (mentor) had fallen. If I had been around in her younger years, I think we might have been friends, bound by spirit, working arm and arm to tear down the ivory tower brick by brick. Instead, in her older age, she was helping barricade the doors of the ivory tower with patriarchy while many emerging scholars of color struggled to scale the walls.

Standing in front of the room of thirty *mujeres* (women, young and old), I waited for her comments on my presentation "Remaining a Xicana Activist While in the Academy." The tone in her voice indicated she was scolding me: "No, I think you're wrong. This may have worked for you, but you are the exception, not the rule. I tell my students to have fun with someone but don't get involved. Wait for kids; you don't need them when you're trying to get through school. Have fun but don't get attached." In that moment, she, a retired academician and highly respected Chicana dean in the sciences, aimed to shoot down my perspective as an activist-mother-scholar and thus to discredit my entire academic ontology. In many ways, she attempted to disprove my scholarly proposition that Chicanas (and women overall) do not have to hide our children and discontinue community ties for the sake of our academic careers or be placed on the "mommy track." I looked at her, unsettled but not deterred, and said: "I respectfully disagree. Although I was fortunate to be in an amazingly encouraging graduate program with brown, black, and Native *mujeres* who saw my children as an asset and not a detriment, I refuse to think that I am the exception. In fact, I think that my experience can and should become the rule. It is up to us as black, Latina, and Native women within the academy to keep the doors open and allow women with similar experiences become the rule. Once we sever our ties to our families, friends, and communities, we not only deny our communities by uprooting ourselves but also allow for few exceptions. No, thank you for your wisdom, but I respectfully disagree."

My encounter with the Chicana dean firmly established my position as one in opposition to mainstream university ethos. It is also an opposition imparted to me by the women in my family through their astute and multi-generational guidance, and this narrative is an attempt to bridge their wisdom with that provided by institutionally educated Chicanas and Latinas over the years.

THEORETICAL FRAMEWORK: (RE)CREATING MY LENS

The work of black feminist Patricia Hill Collins (1994) and Chicana feminist Dolores Delgado Bernal (1998) were particularly useful for me in reflecting on my position as a Chicana scholar-mother-activist. Motherwork is those practices that move "beyond ensuring the survival of one's own biological children. . . . This type of motherwork recognizes that individual survival, empowerment and identity require group survival empowerment, and identity" (Collins 1994, 47). It is by way of Collins's work that, as both a mother and a scholar, I can negotiate the academy, whose hierarchy is often rigid and sustained by rewarding individual scholarly production rather than greater communal implications. Collins further notes, "Themes of survival, power, and identity form the bedrock and reveal how racial ethnic women in the United States encounter and fashion motherwork" (1994, 49). Invoking her ideas has allowed me to challenge an institution that assumes a homogenous faculty devoid of racialized and gendered bodies.

Dolores Delgado Bernal provides the foundation for Chicana feminism in the academy. She describes a Chicana feminist epistemology as being "concern[ed] with the knowledge about Chicanas—about who generates understanding of their experiences, and how this knowledge is legitimized or not legitimized. . . . [Chicana feminism] also acknowledges that most Chicanas lead lives with significantly different opportunity structures than men" (1998, 560).

For Bernal, Chicana feminist epistemology is founded on ideas presented by black feminist and grounded in Chicanas' unique life experiences. It is these lived realities that Chicana scholars are able to call upon as their historical legacy of resistance in the pursuit of social justice in both research and scholarship (Delgado Bernal 1998). The layering of these theoretical frameworks has allowed me to create a unique model to examine my experiences in the academy, including the ways that I approach scholarship and community engagement, as the following sections show.

LOS COUNTERCONSEJOS

Despite the senior scholar's misinformed observations aimed to undermine the advice I was presenting through my talk, I refused to let her discourage the other participants in the workshop from maintaining meaningful relationships or from allowing their children into their lives in the academic world. In fact, my undergraduate and graduate school mentors, all strong women of color with tenure, taught me differently. It is with their guidance that I continue to survive within the academy while keeping my children nearby, maintaining a loving relationship with my partner (also an assistant professor), and working closely with local Chicana and Native communities. By combining my mentors' counter*consejos* (counterstorytelling and advice) with my family's words of wisdom, I hope to promote a healthy balance of family love, community involvement, and self-assurance. Although traditional academics' advice assist in my logistical navigation of the academy, it is my family's counsel that has anchored my sense of self in the ivory tower.

My *abuela*, *tías*, and *amá* (grandmother, aunts, and mother) taught me that the severance of familial or community ties was a negation of one's very being as a *mexicana* and therefore a disrespectful act against their invaluable wisdom. Listening to my family's counter*consejos* that challenged dominant views, I knew that the Chicana administrator was wrong in her support of the status quo. Being a successful scholar and mother does not have to be the exception if we mothers-scholars-activists work together. Experiences such as mine can be the rule. In turn, we may model a union of community knowledge with academic knowledge, eventually creating a space where students of color will not feel divided between home and school ecologies and they are respected in university spaces.

It is through this well-respected counsel (sometimes solicited, other times not) that my survival skills were developed and refined. These survival skills have guided me through the tumultuous world of the academy while solidifying my relationship with surrounding communities and reaffirming my labor as "motherwork." In my own motherwork practices, identifying and actively working to resolve systematic educational issues within Latina/o and Native communities are tantamount to my own personal survival. My scholarly practices strive to nurture classroom spaces where students are encouraged to listen, agree, disagree, confront, and reflect while abiding to communally constructed rules of engagement couched in community-based knowledge. The women in my family encouraged confrontation of difficult topics as a means to build strong trusting relationships, an ideal carried into my teacher–student interactions. By binding home pedagogies that lovingly connect our households to my own classroom teaching, I learn to transcend the archetypal professor who believes serious rigorous scholarship and community development are mutually exclusive.

The "uneducated" women in my family recognized that we were, as Delgado Bernal states, creators and holders of "unique ways of knowing and understanding the world based on the various raced and gendered experiences of people of color" (2002, 107). As a child growing up in rural Michigan, I found it easy to recognize my difference. Being one of three *mexicano* families in the area and the only seasonal farmworkers, we knew that ours was a knowledge unknown to our white neighbors. Our language, food, family, music, *bodas* (weddings), and affinity for loud volleyball games were our secret from the larger Anglo-American community.

In my family now and then, as with many families in the region, to be *mexicano* indicated a specific relationship to Mexican heritage as opposed to a citizenship status. The term moves beyond national identity, instead connecting families to socially constructed Mexican traditions, cultural practices, and, at times, language usage. These practices are regionally situated within the experiences of farmworker families living in the rural Midwest and are therefore heavily influenced by life in America's Heartland. Our language and food are peppered with Anglicism from words such as *wacha* (watch) to venison tacos; *la cultura mexicana* is a unique blend of rural America and the Rio Grande Valley of South Texas.

However, our family did not completely succumb to normalized household conventions, especially white middle-class representations of gendered practices. We severely deviated from the machismo that situates men as domineering within the household, thereby challenging those natural practices. Sociologist Pierrette Hondagneu-Sotelo comments on the misplaced assumption of gender roles in her study of migratory Mexican families: "This image consists of a caricature-like portrait of excessively tyrannical men and submissive women. It is based not only on the notion that immigrants preserve intact cultural traditions but also on the belief that machismo is 'traditional' among Mexican families" (1992, 397). Like the Mexican women in Hondagneu-Sotelo's investigation, the women in my family held the reins.

The Torrez women were not isolated in the home, sheltered from the harsh field labor, nor were they relieved of household chores. My grandmother (a mother of sixteen children) worked alongside her husband in the fields, sewed her children's clothes, fed her family traditional foods (*frijoles*, tortillas, *carne asada*, etc.), and never let anyone step out of line, including the men in the family. She unknowingly served as a model for younger *mexicanas* on how to raise a family: work hard, expect your husband to contribute, and maintain high expectations. In reflecting on my family's experiences, I have realized that the *mujeres* in my family were operating within a Chicana feminist epistemological paradigm, although they would not self identify as either Chicana or feminist. The Torrez women associate the ethnic term *Chicana* with an overtly political connotation and therefore refrain from identifying as such. Instead, they continue to identify as *mexicanas*, regardless of their citizenship status. In fact, my family has been on the U.S. side of the border since before the Treaty of Guadalupe Hidalgo split Mexico in two in 1848.

The women in my family, like Rosi Andrade and Hilda González Le Denmant's mothers, "practiced what was necessary to push us in [a Chicana feminist] direction" (1999, 155). In their own ways, the elders were intimating empowerment and cultivating a strong sense of self in the younger women; they were unknowingly guiding us along a Chicana feminist pathway. Our mothers created a background by which we, as future mothers, could challenge patriarchal traditions. In those moments, we learned of the strength of motherhood, community, and ourselves.

It is within this framework that Chicanas have become agents of knowledge and through intellectual discourse forge connections between experience, research, community, and social change. As modeled by my family, storytelling became one such outlet allowing for the practice of Chicana feminism in which women's lives were (re)told, (re)examined, and (re)modeled. Older women were able to share their stories through words used only among other *mujeres*, and younger women were able to interpret those experiences through their own ideological lens.

Counter*consejos* were used within my family as words of wisdom passed down from mother to daughter, challenging dominant ideologies meant to discreetly (albeit crudely) categorize *mexicano* communities as inferior, uneducated, criminal, and provincial. The lessons learned through these particular counter*consejos* nurtured young *mexicanas* to confront patriarchy and the constraints of socializing scripts, which discredit our value within larger society. Counter*consejos* are rooted in life experiences; they are tools imparting survival skills as well as knowledge systems of how to be a *mujer* in multiple spaces. These spaces may occur while women are *chismeando* (gossiping) around the kitchen table or sharing stories among mixed company in the summer heat. I find that my family's wisdom follows "an understanding of *educación* that was *mujer*-centered and based on women's culturally specific knowledge and practices" (Elenes et al. 2001, 597). In this way, counter*consejos* advocate survival and more powerfully urge *sobrevivencia* (beyond survival to thriving). Ruth Trinidad-Galván identifies *sobrevivencia* in her work with a group of transnational mothers from Guanajuato, Mexico, as "what lies ahead and beneath plain victimry, our ability to *saciar* (satiate) our hopes and dreams in creative and joyful ways" (2001, 163). The women in my family depended on counter*consejos* to move future generations out of anger and self-destruction caused by the Anglo community's alienation and violence. The knowledge imbedded in the Torrez women's actions and words reminded us that we could create intimate spaces to flourish, laugh, and love. Indeed, the women in my family shared their counter*consejos*, their form of counterstories, with narratives detailing their experiences and histories as Chicanas in America's midwestern heartland. Richard Delgado, founding Latino/a critical race theorist, describes counterstories as those that "can open new windows into reality, showing us that there are possibilities for life other than the ones we live. . . . Their graphic quality can stir imagination in ways in which more conventional discourse cannot. . . . They can show us the way out of a trap of unjustified exclusion" (1989, 2415). My family's counterstories narrated the lived realities that could not be seen through *la mente del bolillo*, the term we used for "white" perspectives. The counter*consejos* that emerged from these stories underscored our survival, love, and celebration of life. Highlighting both the injustices perpetuated against *mexicanas/os* and our perseverance in becoming part of the rural community, counter*consejos* have led our family to healing, liberation, and strength. Through the process of counterstorytelling, spaces were opened that challenged social norms while simultaneously creating a richer new world.

Through individual counter*consejos*, the women in my family ripped open our realities as *mexicanas* while blurring the lines between their harsh experiences and the possibilities for change. Sharing stories of physical and emotional abuse inflicted by school personnel, the women reminded their daughters of the ever-present racism permeating their lives. Rather than getting thrown against lockers, being called "Spic," or being denied the opportunity to participate in sports, the new generations experienced racism through tracking, blatant disregard, and labels such as "educably impaired." Our elders' counter*consejos* reminded us of this institutional racism but likewise informed us that we could subvert those powers through pride of who we were as *mexicanos*. My mother let me know, "No te peleas con las maestras, pero no les permites robar tu mexicanidad" (Do not fight with the teachers, but do not let them take away your *mexicanidad*). Although the schools attempted to shame my family regarding their *mexicanidad*, my family reminded us that it was a source of strength to be embraced. As a professor raising two daughters (Reina and Mexica) in a midwestern town, I have passed on the same counter*consejos* to my children because the reality for *mexicanas/os* in the United States has changed very little. In fact, for the next generation, counter*consejos* are not simply direct instruction for entering a hostile educational system blind to the value that students of color bring to campus. Rather, my daughters are currently learning how to confront the false notions of living within a tolerant and multicultural world. My counter*consejos* illuminate the dangers of "teaching tolerance" and "embracing diversity," particularly when little has changed in much of a white-dominated, patriarchal ivory tower. Although these counter*consejos* may not appear to differ greatly from those that my grandmother and mother shared with me, they shift the discussion to a contemporary vernacular used within popular discourse.

Yet despite the racially charged oppression of the present and the past, I, too, want to share the counterstories of survival and celebration, just as my *abuela*, *amá*, and *tías* did with me. Linda Tuhiwai Smith, the brilliant Maori pedagogue, explains that "celebrating survival" is a means for Indigenous people to focus on the events and histories that highlight the positive in their lives (2001, 145). For Smith, as for my own family, celebrating survival that has transcended injustices meant to systematically oppress colonized people honors both "our resistances" and "the mystery of life and the journey that each of us takes" (145). Through our cultural practices, we were not only actively resisting the hegemonic discourse that negated our familial existence, but also celebrating our strength as *raza y familia*.

My family's counterstories had a dual function. First, the stories celebrated our survival in an environment vacillating between hostility and alienation. Second, they formed a security blanket protecting my siblings and me from an academic system that constantly marginalized us. The rural educational institution, much like the greater community it represented, wanted to ignore our existence in the community. The teachers, principals, and students disregarded our work and agricultural labor as meaningless. In response, the counterstories gave us strength as they positioned our families within an oral history that was otherwise absent in mainstream historical accounts. Moreover, these counterstories reaffirmed the country's economic need for our community (as farmworkers). Through all of this, new generations of Chicanas/os were co-creating an education that sought to challenge and negotiate interactions with Anglo community. Meshing knowledge learned from previous generations with new experiences, each subsequent generation molded linguistic and cultural practices to maneuver through their own relationships with the Anglo-American community.

Working in the fields alongside my grandmother, *tías*, mother, and cousins made an indelible impression on me for a number of reasons. My parents never allowed me to forget: "Mexicanos nunca olvidan sus familias y nojotros somos mexicanos. Sin familia no tenemos nada!" (Mexicans never forget their family, and we are Mexicans. Without family, we don't have anything!) As I bent over the crops with a hoe in my hand, the sun at my back and flanked by the matriarchs in my family, this epistemology was cemented into my very ontology. Each time I walked the endless rows of sugar beets, I armed myself with powerful weapons in the creation of an arsenal that I would later use in the war against academic violence inflicted upon our communities and myself and that one day might perhaps be inflicted upon my own children as well. While *jalando* (working) side by side, these women provided me with "pedagogical moments," as Sofia Villenas calls these "unintentional" moments of teaching and learning (2006, 153).

Such powerful and pedagogical moments sadly ended the summer after my nineteenth birthday, when my grandmother, then in her eighties, could no longer work. That same summer I began work as a teacher's aide in a summer migrant education program, the same program I had attended as a child until I started working at age eleven. Although I no longer worked alongside my grandmother, opportunities for learning and revolutionary love emerged in another form while we sat around the kitchen table. Revolutionary love, as conceptualized by Paulo Freire, serves as a testimony to the suffering and struggles endured by those who refuse to lose spirit or become extinguished from historical memory (McLaren 2000, 172). The fluid code-switching between English and Spanish emphasized the unremitting struggles the elders in my family had endured in keeping our *mexicanidad* alive despite the outside pressures to abandon it.

LOS CONSEJOS DE LA ACADEMIA (THE ACADEMY'S ADVICE)

Carrying these powerful and loving counter*consejos* deep within the fissures of my soul, I entered the world of academia as a junior faculty member at a research-intensive institution. Upon my arrival, my intellectual definition of community quickly expanded and soon became interchangeable with the definition of family. My farmworker epistemologies based in extended family relations unfortunately clashed directly with the epistemologies maintained by the university's ultracompetitive and territorial culture. This confrontation was concretized during my inaugural year as an assistant professor. Although I never doubted my oppositional positionality within the academy, I was astonished when the few Chicana faculty members were the first to raise their eyebrows in dismay at my own motherwork and especially at being a mother myself. Instead of providing models that could guide and refine my work overlapping family, community, and scholarship, these academic women had sacrificed community betterment for an isolated research agenda. My colleagues offered advice about working as a paid consultant for community projects as opposed to sharing experiences of best practices in working with community members.

The patriarchy that permeates all sectors of society, including academic institutions, sadly invaded the space that I had previously thought to be safe: a circle of *comadres*, Chicana mentor academics like myself. In contrast to my experiences as a professor, my graduate studies in the Southwest never questioned the obvious intersections between academic and family life or suggested (let alone encouraged) that either family or community activism be disassociated from my scholarship. It seems that the women I encountered in the southwestern university I had attended already knew, as Patricia Hill Collins does, that there is no rigid distinction between the arenas of work and family, but rather that these spheres always intimately overlap (1994, 59). Once a professor and reflecting back on my graduate training, I realized that my thesis and dissertation committees never questioned how familial and intellectual labors were inextricably intertwined, therefore reciprocally informing one another. In fact, while I was at graduate school, the counter*consejos* of my *abuela*, *amá*, and *tías* served as the foundational methodologies of my research agenda and my decision to become a mother while still in school. In accordance with their advice, working with and from communities is expected — "No olvides de dónde vienes" (Do not forget where you are from).

After all, without familial and community relations, I would be engulfed by the oppressive weight of academia. Cutting community connections would sever my motivation to remain within a university system that has historically marginalized Latino students, and thus yet again another faculty of color would be forced out the academy. Similar to the experiences of many junior faculty and doctoral women of color, my initial intent in entering the academy was altruistic and meant as a conduit to allow me to better serve my community. My connections with community concurrently served as a source of intellectual and emotional strength, a guiding, illuminating light in the dark times in an alienating system.

Returning to the *consejos* offered by the retired Chicana administrator who reacted so negatively to my presentation and reflecting on other negative interactions with Chicana faculty, I realize that these women did not reaffirm the subaltern knowledge created in my working-class *mexicano* home. Not many years ago, these women protested against an establishment, but they now complacently served it. My own experiences with home pedagogies inversely privilege *mexicana/o* collective memories by placing the survival skills and memories of our communal accomplishments over the academy's marker of legitimate knowledge. Unfortunately, the university structure rewards individual achievement as the marker of professional success rather than recognizing communally based accomplishments (considering the two to be mutually exclusive). Perhaps these women have forgotten the struggles of working-class women of color in their ascension of the economic ladder.

Acting as "mentors," some of the Chicana academics I have encountered as a tenure-track assistant professor have offered advice on how to evade the "mommy track" and the label "not seriously academic." These women's *consejos* attempted to guide me through a "professional world" biased against women generally and against mothers specifically (Correll, Benard, and Paik 2007; Panofsky 2007; Varallo 2008). Their words of wisdom, although well intentioned, suggested two main points. First, I must never bring my children to university functions, nor should I share with colleagues that I have children. Second, I must work in the community as an *expert* in the field, clearly establishing a hierarchy, with me at the apex. Although I understand that these women were speaking from their own experience, their *consejos* seemed antithetical to my own community-based epistemology, which does not dichotomize or prioritize various forms of education or expertise. With a community-based research framework, how can I divorce my academic life from my children and community?

In the *consejos* offered by the retired Chicana administrator, I am reminded of how Latina students frequently find themselves marginalized within mainstream institutions even by Latina/o faculty. Instead of a situation in which the hegemonic society guides us to the periphery, with these ill-advised *consejos* we complacently place ourselves on the fringes—happy just to be invited to the table. These women seem to have forgotten the powerful words offered by Audre Lorde: "The Master's tools will never dismantle the Master's house" (1981, 99). As women of color in the academy, we are obliged to transcend the marginal spaces silencing us from the larger discourses. We must insert our unique voices and experiences in the fabric of the academy (Souto-Manning and Ray 2007), while dismantling its facade as meritocratic.

Instead of resorting to the models of success presented by my "career-oriented" colleagues, I turn to my mother, who established that there is more at stake than a "successful career." Despite becoming a mother at age sixteen and being subsequently forced from her home, my mother garnered strength from this powerful role. Through her own motherwork, she became a fearless protector, engaged in the intellectual activities of teaching her children survival skills while simultaneously earning an income to help sustain her family (see Udel 2001, 50). Although the survival skills I learned are different than those I teach to my own daughters, the cultural survival and gendered resistance seamlessly binds together these two sets of skills and experiences.

My intellectual labor, as a component of my motherwork, is founded on the vernacular epistemologies passed through informally educated women's counter*consejos*. Through this integration, I remain centered and able to confront the unending pressures of the "tenure clock." In bell hooks's *Teaching Community: A Pedagogy of Hope* (2003), she advocates that we must stop teaching toward death and begin learning to live (2003). She uses "teaching to die" to describe how many professors vow to start living after successfully completing each institutional hurdle set before them (finishing the dissertation, securing a tenure-stream position, being reappointed, attaining tenure, and being formally awarded promotion to associate professor and then full professor status). However, as we wait to "live" our lives, authentic living will simply pass us by, and if we are mothers, our children's lives will likewise pass as well.

I refuse to teach to die while waiting to live! Life is too important; my daughters', my mother's, and my own lives are too important. Disregarding those ill-advised, albeit well-intentioned *consejos*, I choose to incorporate my daughters into every academic activity possible. They have nursed at my breast while I attended graduate seminars, sat through academic and activist conferences, listened to speakers, attended protests, and even sat on my lap during a meeting with a university president. My family, teaching, scholarship, and activism intersect in robust ways and therefore cannot be discreetly divided into (un)equal parts if my motherwork is to function properly.

Throughout graduate school, I was surrounded by women of color who refused to bifurcate their academic and family lives. In fact, these women were strong (and successful) voices within the academy and therefore served as the quintessential models of activist–scholars. Their work did not privilege scholarship over activism; rather, it allowed for the intersection of family, scholarship, and radical social change—all positively impacting one another. Similar to my own family's knowledgeable advice, the counter*consejos* told by their families also worked for communal survival. In her discussion of contemporary Native women activists' departure from white feminist movements, Lisa Udel articulates the value of collectivism versus individuality in the work of Native mothers. She writes, "While individual achievement is sought and recognized, it is always within the context of the collective that such endeavors are valued" (2001, 50). My pedagogies of the home, like the practices of Native mothers in Udel's discussion, associate communal survival with success, serving in direct conflict with the university's focus on individual profit as the marker of achievement.

MIS **COUNTER**CONSEJOS

Using a Chicana feminist epistemology learned from my *tías*, I am determined to create a constellation where my scholarship, community work, and motherwork intersect, all while moving through university tenure-stream requirements. Working alongside community members has presented sufficient possibilities for scholarship, especially when these projects are grounded in grassroots and systematic change. Engaging in this work not only grounds me in the reality of life off campus but continues to serve as motivational knowledge. In the end, these humble experiences have revealed that it is essential for women of color to create a balance within in their lives while continuing to create spaces where work and family are central.

We women of color who are scholars, activists, mothers, daughters, nieces, *comadres*, and granddaughters cannot continue the cycle of patriarchy. It is our responsibility to acknowledge that *nuestras comunidades* (our communities) are holders and creators of knowledge (Delgado Bernal 2002). We must recognize our constant negotiation of a space meant to exclude our knowledge base and struggle to open those spaces for future scholars of color. I find Juan Carlos González's concluding remarks quite poignant:

> Academic leaders and institutional change agents need to understand that the face of today's colleges and universities is changing rapidly, and in order to serve the students of tomorrow they need to build environments, enact policies, and create the type of culture that will sustain our higher education systems and allow all students to participate. . . . In particular, the fast growing Latina intellectual community is beginning to acquire the type of social, cultural, and intellectual capital to penetrate higher education forcefully and change those institutions from within, and many other students of color are engaging similarly. (2007, 298)

As mothers-scholars-activists, we are responsible for disrupting a system that is blind to its ever-changing student and faculty body. Each year we gain institutional experience that allows us to negotiate through the academy, which, coupled with our mothers' counter*consejos*, we can use to interrupt the legacy of marginalization.

Remembering my *abuela's* words, "Nunca olvides que tú eres mexicana, tú eres de esta familia" (Never forget you are Mexican, you are from this family), I must reiterate: I am a *mexicana* farmworker from rural Michigan, a daughter of a young mother, a granddaughter of a woman who nursed sixteen children, and a mother of two loving daughters. My most revolutionary act as an activist-scholar is one that bridges my family (as community) with my labor in the academy. As in Lorde's (1981) assertion, the "Master's house," the mainstream university, must be dismantled, and it will be my *comadres* (any women ready to disrupt the process as it stands) and I who will rebuild a new structure by including our families in this process.

12

REVOLVING DOORS

Mother-Woman Rhythms in Academic Spaces

Allia A. Matta

"THE SEMESTER BEGINS. The planning, the teaching, the grading of papers, the dinners to cook, the homework to check, and the reading to do,
and then even more reading. I now use a rolling briefcase bag because of all
of the books and papers I have to carry across campus. This is my new life
in New England in the academy. I have journeyed far to get here. I open
the door to the university's seminar room. I am the only woman in this small
cohort of graduate students. I am also the oldest student. I arrive early, and
I am excited. I have new notebooks and pens, and I am thrilled to begin
this Ph.D. in Afro-American studies. I am also nervous, single, and in a
new town. I now have a roommate and live in a nearby apartment that does
not remotely resemble the apartment or the neighborhood I left behind. It
is peaceful. I am grateful. I am lost. My children are not with me. I have
stripped myself of my mother identity because of the choice to enter this
academic door."

This chapter bears witness to my educational and professional movement through doors that appeared to be shut for a woman like me. The
retrospective narrative discusses key shifts in my life history and contributes to the broader conversation of the "black womanist narrative"—that
is, the acknowledgment of black women's testimonies as "grounded in
personal histories of racism, classism, and sexism, as well as experiences of
marginality and alienation" (Henry 1995, 280). My personal history illustrates the emotional and spatial rhythms, difficulties, and opportunities of
shifting work, domestic, and familial spaces as I pursued higher education

after marriage, child rearing, and divorce and tried to stay grounded as a woman, mother, and academic. In this chapter, I examine the complexities of focusing on my academic and professional life and the choices that led me to decenter and reprioritize my role as a mother, which has always been crucial to my identity and self-worth as an African American woman. By bearing witness to my own life, I ultimately make a small contribution to challenging how womanhood, motherhood, and mothering are constructed by history and culture. As Andrea O'Reilly notes, scholarship in "motherhood studies" questions the ways in which "motherhood is used to signify the patriarchal institution of motherhood, while mothering refers to women's lived experiences of childrearing as they both conform to and/or resist the patriarchal institution of motherhood and its oppressive ideology" (2010a, 2). In my examination of my own mothering, I would like to do the same.

Nancy Chodorow's seminal book *The Reproduction of Mothering Psychoanalysis and the Sociology of Gender* interrogates and contests the core ideals of "traditional" Western and perhaps Anglo constructions of motherhood as initially defined by the nineteenth- and early-twentieth-century ideals of true womanhood. This ideal—that women were innately maternal and would care for the children and exclusively manage the private domestic sphere—is also fostered in the construction of "'the true black woman' ideal of the twentieth century[,] [which] recasts the nineteenth-century concept of true (white) womanhood" and reinforces the notion that "black women would advance the race simply by being a good mother and creating a good home life" (Dallow 2004, 90). Those social messages certainly affected me, and as an African American woman, I am further plagued by the historical function and expectations of black mothering. For instance, although education was always the cornerstone of economic upward mobility and communal prosperity for black people, "black women's educational decisions and career choices [were] not for individualistic gain, but for black community empowerment" (Henry 1995, 288). Thus, the decisions I made for my personhood directly corresponded to my role as a black woman and mother. However, when I chose to pursue higher education later in life and subsequent employment in the academy, my movement away from the traditional mother normative challenged the community space I inhabited; my reinterpretation of black mothering was in fact viewed as contentious. I consciously chose part-time mothering, which was also regarded as a taboo in my community and as conflicting with the socialized ideals of being a mother. Yet my choice was about personhood; my own survival and my children's survival were at stake.

REDEFINING WOMANHOOD AND MOTHERHOOD IN NEW YORK CITY

"This street will never look the same. I stroll down Fulton Street, cross to Willoughby, and walk down to Flatbush Avenue headed to the job I am leaving in a few days. I am leaving my job as the associate director of the campus Writing Center and my rent stabilized apartment in Queens. I am also leaving my children. I will be entering a Ph.D. program on a fellowship at age forty-two. I am moving to another state, leaving the children with their father because they are not remotely interested in moving to New England from New York City, and leaving a life of certainty for a place and space that seems so foreign to a woman like me—a divorced African American mother of three sons. Yet this is perhaps my last chance. Many in my family thought I was crazy and selfish for supposedly abandoning my children. How dare I, a mother at this age and stage of my life, pursue a Ph.D.? They speak a silence through facial expressions that emote, 'Why can't you wait until your boys are older?' 'You're leaving them and moving to go to school?' 'What are they going to do without you?' These family members act as if my boys do not have a very capable, competent, educated father who wants the opportunity to have them full-time and in fact suggested that they live with him."

Black communal spaces, though historically engaged in antiracist struggles, can also foster conflict when community members challenge the status quo within those spaces. As Patricia Hill Collins indicates, "Rather than seeing family, church, and Black civic organizations through a race-only lens of resisting racism, such institutions may be better understood as complex sites where dominant ideologies [such as gender, sexuality, and class] are [also] simultaneously revisited and reproduced" (2000, 86). Though my decisions and choices as a black woman seem personal, they are part of a larger historical trajectory that has aimed to empower families and communities. My academic studies have helped me realize that I am one of those "Black women [who] learn[ed] skills of independence and self-reliance that [have] enable[d] African American families, churches, and civic organizations to endure" (Collins 2000, 86). I am similarly also affected by those very same communal spaces that perpetuate self-sacrifice and the curtail-ment of personal aspirations or interests, while foregrounding those of the larger black community (Collins 2000, 86). These social structures impact black women in particular because African American communities have never completely relied on the traditionally nuclear family model to raise children. For many of us, othermothers and the extended community of grandparents, aunties, uncles, and cousins have been active participants in child rearing.

In my case, my children's daddy (i.e., my former husband) also offered my children emotional support and financial security even though we were no longer a couple. I had been the primary caretaker for many years, and perhaps it was now his turn. Although this positive arrangement comple-mented my journey into higher education, the communal and extended fa-milial backlash reinforced Nancy Chodorow's (1978) assertion that women, as opposed to men, are stereotyped as the only possible caretakers. Thus, there is a problematic assumption that mothers are primary, and fathers are not. In my community, the role of the black mother similarly became the primary defining aspect of my identity, yet this definition was directly op-posed to the historical realities of the function of black women in the com-munity that extended beyond motherhood. Without a doubt, my desire for graduate studies extended my identity beyond motherhood, and it became increasingly clear I needed to follow my dreams.

In 2000, at the age of thirty-eight, I entered a New York City–based grad-uate program in English to focus on creative writing. Three years into single parenthood, I was now a graduate student and a working mom. My for-mer husband, a highly educated and professional man who was Latino, was a valuable support during this time because he understood the historical importance of education in our respective black and Latino communities. Twelve years earlier, while we were married, he had watched me attempt a graduate degree in political science, but at the time my second son was only two months old. I worked full-time and attended classes at night. Although my beloved grandmother and othermothers helped care for my baby during the day, and his dad cared for him until I came home, my son cried the entire evening until I arrived. Needless to say, I had to leave the political science program and rethink my dream of attending law school when I be-came pregnant with son number three.

Yet like many black women, I refused to give up and insisted on my right to define my own reality. The journey to graduate school in creative writing (through the stolen moments of writing poetry) was the important event that circumvented my emotional breakdown and created a pathway to pursue higher education. My former husband knew I was committed to the graduate program as well; he cared for the children every weekend when I had to work as a writing tutor to secure funding while taking graduate courses. When I was offered an opportunity to teach composition as part of my funding, I quit my well-paying job, which was a difficult financial sacrifice. I realized that completing my graduate degree was more urgent. In addition, I was working in a somewhat racially hostile environment, and though economic stability mattered, my health and well-being mattered as well. Collins's assertion that "African American mothers are complex individuals who often show tremendous strength under adverse conditions" (2000, 75–76) resonated with me and served as a reminder that in a different historical moment I may not have been able to choose.

After quitting my full-time job, I worked part-time and lived on child support, fellowship awards, and student loans. I was able to maintain a solid graduate school record and devote more time to my children's growth and development. The situation wasn't always smooth, but it was calm and relaxed. I was adapting to this new rhythm and could breathe a little easier. As a single parent and full-time graduate student, I was ironically able to manage successfully the duties that are ascribed to the traditional mother-normative role. I graduated with my master's degree and took a position at the same university as the associate director of the Writing Center. The shift I made to my dreams paid off. For two years I thrived as an administrator and writing teacher, but my journey needed to continue, and so I decided to aim for a doctorate degree.

NEW BEGINNINGS IN NEW ENGLAND

"I open the seminar room door, but after the first session, I am in shock. The seminar was good, and I think I will love the program, yet I am lost. I have classes two days per week, and that's it. No cooking for anyone, no homework to check, no one to clean up after except for myself. I decide to go food shopping on the way home from class. After unpacking the groceries, I open the refrigerator door and stare inside. There is so much going on in there, so much, juice, milk, fruit, and fresh vegetables. I close the door of the fridge and open the cabinet door. It occurs to me that I am in the apartment alone. My children are not due to visit for weeks, yet I have stocked the place as if they are still living with me. I close the cabinet door and retire to my room. I am a mess. A moment later I have a flashback. I'm at home in New York. I blow cigarette smoke out of the bathroom window, and I write poems. My youngest son is two years old and a very active and vibrant boy. He knocks on the door screaming for me to come out; I promise to do so but stay in the bathroom longer. When my second cigarette is extinguished and the whole poem is on the page, I exit the bathroom, fix dinner, bathe the boy, set the other two up for their respective showers, and put everyone to bed. Flash forward . . . "

My admittance into a doctoral program causes me to redefine myself as a mother and as a woman. This is the first time in my adult life that I have the luxury of thinking about myself first. My core identity has been defined by fulltime motherhood, and now that I am the part-time parent, I am lost. I feel the sentiments expressed in Joanna Clark's "Motherhood" when she decides that she needs a break from her children to save herself from physical exhaustion and an emotional breakdown. At every institutional turn, she is reminded that she is a mother and that she is abandoning her children, even when she tries to leave them with their father (1970, 80). Clark points to the circumstantial difficulties of mothering when one is not emotionally or financially intact and the negative societal response when a mother decides to give up her children, nervous breakdown notwithstanding. I circumvented my emotional breakdown by writing poems in the bathroom, on the train, and any other time that I could steal to write, which led to my access to higher education. Perhaps if I had exhibited an obvious emotional breakdown—wearing no clothes and shouting incoherent words in the street—my leaving the children with their father would make more sense to other people.

The black community unfortunately exists within the larger societal narrative that has created negative images of black women and perpetuated problematic stereotypes such as the mammy (the "good" black mother in white homes) and the black matriarch (the "bad" mother figure in black homes) (Collins 2000, 75). These figures still plague the societal positioning of black women and impact the social messages and symbolism around black motherhood. Furthermore, the backdrop of these images directly influences how some of us subscribe to traditional mother-normative behavior as a means of debunking the mammy and black matriarch images even when in reality we should opt for an alternative model that better suits our particular families. Such alternatives are indeed possible despite "the fundamental injustice of a system that routinely and from one generation to the next relegates U.S. Black women to the bottom of the social hierarchy" (Collins 2000, 72). In that case, what do we have to lose?

MAKING IT WORK, TRYING TO THRIVE

"My oldest son is in crisis. If he doesn't come to live with me in New England, I am not sure what his life will look like. Therefore, he moves in with my roommate and me, and I enroll him in the local community college. We are sharing my room. This is my last year of coursework, and I can barely afford to pay his tuition. My adjunct salary pays his tuition, and he looks for work. I am struck by the difficulty of my current predicament. He is with me because I am his mother and must rescue him or lose him to an unproductive life or perhaps even the street. It is a difficult road. My roommate understands that I am a mother and does her best to support me, though this move is somewhat of an infringement on her life and space. We all make it through this very tense period, and my son moves in with a roommate and continues to go to school. He works part-time, but I am still financially responsible for his tuition and his rent. At the end of his second year at the community college, he decides that he is done with school and wants to return to New York City and work full-time. He returns to his father's house. He is now twenty-two years old. He is grateful for my support and understands the sacrifice that I have made. I realize that because I am his mother, I did not have a choice."

My lack of choice when it came to saving my son reflects the truth about the difficult of mothering children, especially African American children, in the twenty-first century. According to Audre Lorde, "Raising Black children—female and male—in the mouth of a racist, sexist, suicidal dragon is perilous and chancy. If they cannot love and resist at the same time, they will probably not survive. . . . [M]others teach—love, survival—that is self-definition and letting go" (1984, 74). Though my son was twenty years old, I knew that I still needed to teach him self-love and how to survive the plight of being an African American man in a society that has placed a bull's eye on his back. My son had been raised well; he was not a negative black male statistic (incarcerated, on drugs, or dead), but he was fading fast. However, college was not part of his agenda, and he was unable to keep a service job, which was the only job he could secure. He was becoming disillusioned by the realities of racism and capitalism and muted by alcohol. He didn't love himself, and I was increasingly concerned that he would not make it. This is why I had no choice but to love my adult son unconditionally and have him live with me.

The dilemma of making sure a male child does not become a negative statistic is nothing new for mothers of color, including black mothers. Despite differences in class backgrounds, many black mothers fear that their sons will not make it. When faced with the possibility of this dilemma, they choose to privilege the needs of the family and community and forgo their own personal choices. I was no different. The community needs thriving black men who can flourish in society and contribute to the community's empowerment and prosperity. I understood the urgency of my choice. I knew black women who had used their life savings or homes to post bail and to pay for a good lawyer, visited their incarcerated sons in upstate New York, and were putting money in jail commissary accounts for luxuries such as toothpaste, candy, cigarettes, notebooks, and pencils. These women were dealing on a daily basis with the racial and class injustices of the legal system and attempting to remain whole in the midst of trying saving their sons from getting hemmed up on charges that would destroy their lives even if they were not living a criminal life.

My son was getting used to being stopped and searched on the street in front of his father's middle-class suburban home, and I was afraid that he would make the wrong choices if further humiliated and pushed to the edge. He needed to be loved by me, up close. He needed to understand that he was entitled to the time to grow into a mature and positive man. He needed to understand that he could not only survive, but also thrive. Like Lorde, "I wish[ed] to raise a Black man who will not be destroyed by or settle for, those corruptions called power by the white fathers who mean his destruction as surely as they mean mine" (1984, 74). My son needed his mother, and I reached out to him. In the time that he was with me, I thought about Lorde's comment that, "for survival, Black children in America must be raised to recognize the enemy's many faces" (1984, 75). My son survived, and he now recognizes the "enemy" as well as those of us who have his back.

Again, I have shifted to another stage of motherhood and mothering while pursuing higher education and, more specifically, my doctorate. I assisted in the recovery of my oldest son's humility, productivity, and self-love; I am working full-time to put my middle son through college; and my youngest son is moving to New England to live with me in order to tackle his high school academic underachievement. The journey has once again changed, and it is tiresome. In three years, I have gone from being a single-parent mother of three to a full-time graduate student and then again to being a single parent navigating work responsibilities, school obligations, my youngest son's life, and my life. I have struggled as a woman to maintain my personhood and be a good mother. At times, the struggle for personhood trumped motherhood or at least mothering in a conventional way. Yet I am a better mother when I am in touch with myself and my emotions. I was not a good mother when I compromised my happiness, creativity, and personal development. I equated motherhood with the sacrifice of one's desires. Many of the women in my circles were unable to consider their personal selves because motherhood overwhelmed personhood. I have watched folks fall into the challenges of parenthood because they were missing some crucial pieces of themselves.

The way in which my life has shifted and transformed is evidence of what I see as an important truth: when one's sense of personhood and the self are intact, parenting is pleasurable even when difficult. We must consider ourselves first, and it is important that as mothers we don't self-judge, self-critique or self-condemn. It is the striving for whole personhood that has in fact made me the best mother that I can be regardless of what it looks like to the community or larger society. I know that I am a good, solid mother. My now grown-up children have character, believe in humanity, and are creative and critical thinkers. They supported my personal and academic journeys. They understood the importance of my life choices and realized that they benefitted from these shifts as well. They witnessed the evolution of their mother. My sons' love and support are why I was a solid graduate student in both programs in New York and in New England. Although the evolution wasn't easy, they eventually understood what was at stake! These traumatic and life-affirming moments taught me (and my sons) the value of self-definition and resilience—in particular, educational resilience. My mothering bears witness to the importance of stepping out of prescribed boxes in order to make things work and of not compromising one's sense of self.

FINAL MEDITATION

"I open my office door. I now fully understand that my life as a woman, mother, graduate student, and teacher has been fully enriched by the emotional trauma of my experiences. Had I been completely comfortable in one space, I would not have been able to move, enter, or exit through the many doors that have brought me to where I now stand. The journey has been difficult, funny, painful, and ridiculous. I have achieved many things— earned a master's degree, sent two sons to college, published a few poems, established a pretty solid teaching record, and started writing a dissertation. Though I consider myself a budding scholar, I am a solid woman-mother. I have been fortunate to come out on this side of my personal womanhood and mothering."

My positionality as an African American, working-class yet educated female poet fostered my journey into higher education. I come from a long line of African American women (my grandmothers, aunties, cousins, and even my mother) who were not able to reshape their lives because they could not fully satisfy their inner desires. I know many of them could actively contribute to this reflection on mothering, although they never complained about the sacrifices of motherhood that impeded their dreams and desires. They did not have the educational luxury to contemplate on their multiple spaces, but I luckily do, and in so doing I bear witness to their lives as mothers, too. Many of us honor the privilege of mothering but have a harder time acknowledging the ways in which motherhood can take over personhood and identity (Brown and Amankwaa 2007). As women, we often dwell in the emotional flux and in-between spaces of motherhood and mothering and the social politics surrounding these spaces, but we do better for our children and the communities we live in when we emphasize loving ourselves. I am a first-generation doctoral student and the first in my family to have the drive, opportunity, resilience, and resources to fully realize both mothering and personhood without forever compromising my identity. My presence in the academy as a mother is important because it represents a journey that challenges the status quo and is an embodiment of knowledge instilled by my familial foremothers and othermothers that I should not sacrifice my inner desires.

Nevertheless, I am still challenged by the pressure to (re)prioritize mothering, especially because I am fully engaged in the academy. After a long day of teaching and trying to work on my dissertation, I am often very exhausted. Yet when I come home, I must give the time and energy to my teenage son, who is navigating life and high school. In addition, when my two adult sons call and want to talk, I listen, encourage, and advise with an open heart. In many ways, my children are still competing with my academic responsibilities as a teacher and graduate student as well as with my creative and personal worlds. Some days I do it well, others days I do not, but I am largely happy trying to manage adequately all of my multiple rhythmic spaces as a woman, mother, teacher, and graduate student. In essence, I am becoming a whole person.

Many of the women in my family and community unfortunately could not do the same because of a lack of resources and space. They may have worked, but they often did not choose the types of work they were doing. They had dreams that were extinguished by motherhood just as I extinguished cigarettes in the bathroom. I offer my story as a way to think about the ways in which motherhood can challenge personhood for some women and as a prescription for the possibility of creating or re-creating spaces and new rhythms. I am a stronger woman and teacher because I am an experienced mother. I do not mother my students, but mothering influences my interactions with them, my listening skills and ability to read facial expressions and body language. Watching my own children grow up has also helped me develop a keen interest in students' intellectual growth and development. The lesson I learned by way of my experiences is that as a woman, mother, teacher, graduate student, and person, I decide which doors I will enter and which spaces I will shift. None of them has to be extinguished for the other to exist. The mother-woman rhythm I want in my life is finally contingent on me.

PART THREE

CREATING MORE PARENT-FRIENDLY
INSTITUTIONS OF HIGHER LEARNING

AS IN THE FEW existing anthologies that focus on the work–life balance for mothers, we conclude our volume with solutions for creating more parent-friendly institutions of higher learning in order to change the ivory tower. This final part begins with a very concrete example of how contemporary libraries are developing policies that are more compatible with women's service needs and research interests and by extension their families' needs. One policy and ideological change that Gilda Baeza Ortego addresses in "Academic Library Policies: Advocating for Mothers' Research and Service Needs" is the need to examine critically how academic libraries have historically supported intellectual pursuits of primarily male library users. Ortego's suggestions are followed by a conversation between a graduate student, a tenured academic administrator, and a pretenure professor. Throughout their essay "Reimagining the Fairytale of Motherhood in the Academy," Barbara A. W. Eversole, Darlene M. Hantzis, and Mandy A. Reid weave personal experience with a discussion of how university policies impact mothers in the academy and how mothers in the academy can affect policy.

Next, Sandra L. French and Lisa Baker-Webster's essay "Tales from the Tenure Track: The Necessity of Social Support in Balancing the Challenges of Tenure and Motherhood" explores the social networks that tenure-track women create in order to succeed both at work and at home. Although female professors' social support networks are useful to all tenure-track women, they are crucial to women balancing the challenges of tenure achievement and motherhood. In "How Higher Education Became Accessible to

Single Mothers: An Unfinished Story," Summer R. Cunningham highlights issues for graduate students with regard to a work–life balance, social support, financial obligation, and administrative policy in an academic culture that oftentimes does not seem conducive to single motherhood. She tells a story about overcoming obstacles, but also a story that exposes the root of those obstacles in the hope that we might work to remove them in order to create a smoother path for other mothers. Another example of working collaboratively to support each other's work is Erynn Masi de Casanova and Tamara Mose Brown's essay "Making It Work: Success Strategies for Graduate Student Mothers." They outline six "do's" and "don'ts" that graduate students can follow to negotiate mothering while in school and that aim to motivate graduate students to finish their coursework and dissertation as they take on one of life's most challenging jobs: parenting. In "Academic Mothers on Leave (but on the Clock), on the Line (and off the Record): Toward Improving Parental-Leave Policies and Practices," Colleen S. Conley and Devin C. Carey explore the issues academic mothers face in negotiating maternity leave. It reviews various policies and practices, relates personal accounts of successes and challenges, examines the outcomes of various leave policies and practices, and offers recommendations for supportive policies. This last part ends with "Supporting Academic Mothers: Creating a Work Environment with Choices" by Brenda K. Bushouse, in which she mixes her personal history with a review of family-leave policies. The mother of twins, Bushouse concludes with a discussion about the need for advocates to support successful implementation of family-leave policies and continued support throughout the tenure process.

13

ACADEMIC LIBRARY POLICIES

Advocating for Mothers' Research and Service Needs

Gilda Baeza Ortego

ACADEMIC LIBRARIES have often been referred to as the heart of the university. This designation has been attributed to Charles William Eliot, a nineteenth-century president of Harvard University (Brophy 2005, 1). During that era, academic libraries served principally as the central depository for collections that supported the intellectual pursuits primarily of male faculty and students. The predominance of men in higher education was a phenomenon of social norms that prevailed early in the history of higher education. As Dale Gyure has noted, colleges in colonial America were established for "training ministers and gentlemen" (2008, 110). Although colleges' mission gradually diversified to include a broader audience, men continued to be the prevalent beneficiaries of higher education for nearly two hundred years. As a consequence, academic libraries have traditionally been focused on men's scholarly information needs. This chapter examines how feminization of higher education has impacted academic libraries by making traditional library practices and policies obsolete. In particular, I focus on the importance of advocating for student and faculty mothers' library research and service needs in the context of male domination in higher education. Serving as my inspiration is the groundbreaking work of Nancy E. Dowd (2010), who explores masculinities analysis and feminist theory in critical legal scholarship.

Dowd asserts that one must consider "the man question"— that is cultural and social constructs that define "manliness"—as well as the impact of the "man question" on male power and the subordination process and how masculinities analysis can further feminist theory. She also argues that "when one sex is dominant, sometimes gender issues are rendered invisible" (2010, 416). If one accepts this notion, one can see why gendered practices and policies characterized male-oriented academic libraries of yesteryear and how these practices and policies continue to be sustained despite their dubious relevance in a more feminized academic culture.

The heart of scholarly endeavors, academic libraries, did change dramatically in the last three decades of the twentieth century, however. The most obvious change was the introduction of technology into library services. Driven by the need to serve students and faculty in distance-education programs, innovative technologies are now being used to design library services in a virtual environment. Richard Bazillion and Connie Braun note, "Electronic publication, full-text databases, worldwide interactive interlibrary loan, hypertext, and broadband networking now define the world of academic libraries" (2001, 1). The contemporary academic library is no longer identified as a facility stocked with printed materials. Furthermore, the execution of library services has ceased to rely on the physical proximity of patron and library staff member, an accidental boon to women engaging in scholarly research from afar. In my years in library administration, I have witnessed how this accidental boon has changed how women, especially mothers, have been able to avail themselves of library collections and services.

As I know full well, women, many of whom must juggle research time with family time, have greater access to information than at any other time in the history of higher education. Mothers, like all library patrons, are now able to take advantage of many library services from their homes and at more convenient hours. They can locate full-text journal articles, complete supplemental reading assignments through e-reserves, use online features to renew books and request interlibrary loan materials, ask reference questions via e-chat and social media, and access thousands of digitized books and government documents via computer or mobile devices such as smart phones and iPads.

However, the availability of library services and resources does not relieve women of "second-shift work" (i.e., household duties and child care), described by Arlie Russell Hochschild in 1989 (see Hochschild and Machung [1989] 2003). Technological innovations have certainly eased the burden of physical access to library collections and services, but at the same time they have done little to modify gender-specific social responsibilities. O'Reilly poignantly illustrates this point with an anecdotal account of when participants of a national conference on motherhood empowerment were asked to submit postconference images of their households in disarray. She posed the questions: "Why should the mothers come home and find their house in such a state after a two-day conference? Should fathers not be expected to competently run a household in their absence? And why was their 'incompetence' to do this considered funny?" (2010b, 26).

Indeed, I ask: Is this situation an extended manifestation of Dowd's core propositions that the definition of masculinity is "not to be like a woman" and "devaluing of things associated with women," such as housekeeping (2010, 418)? Are women partially responsible for their subordination by not demanding that men contribute to household chores when the women cannot, as O'Reilly asks?

Like many in my middle-aged generation, I confess that I am a "digital immigrant," a person who has adapted to technological innovations as they developed and were introduced (sometimes forcibly) into my work responsibilities. With much pain and consternation, academic libraries' acceptance of innovations in information technology was slow to evolve. In fact, technology posed a serious threat to libraries. Lyndon Pugh (2005) eloquently discusses how centuries-old library management theory was forced by necessity to formulate a new identity. For example, collection-development policies of a by-gone era reflected a "just in case" perspective in which libraries collected relevant resources "just in case" they would be needed by a library user. The escalating costs of printed materials forced library decision makers to abandon this policy in favor of the "just in time" policy in collection development. Pugh postulates that academic libraries are now entering the "just for you" era that is made possible by distributed information resources. Not only have I accepted my digital immigrant status and its limitations, but I have come to see that the "just for you" approach has exciting possibilities for women library users and researchers, especially mothers within academia. I doubt that my male counterparts in library administration even realize that mothers as library users are a historically underserved population group, but they cannot embrace what they cannot see. To adapt Dowd's (2010) comments to my librarian perspective, mothers as library users have been "rendered invisible"—that is, until now.

More subtle than the technological transformation is the fact that academic libraries are experiencing a gender shift in its dominant user group. According to the U.S. Department of Education, women currently constitute the majority of university students and will grow another 16 percent in the next decade (Bailey and Hussar 2009, 9). Women are also more present among the professoriate (Wolf-Wendel and Ward 2006, 487) and at the higher-education administrative level (Skandera-Trombley 2003). Progressive campuses are finally awakening to this reality and are beginning to develop policies that are more compatible with women's service needs and research interests and by extension their families' needs (Patterson 2008).

Research suggests that women have paradoxically been both enriched and penalized by the growing opportunities for education attainment and career achievement. As Elizabeth Hayes describes the situation, "The tensions experienced by women between their family roles and learning in higher education provides a particularly prominent example of the gendered nature of these conflicts" (2000, 47). The expectation is not only that they can "have it all," but that they can do it all in an academic cultural context that favors men's lifestyles, reproductive abilities, and behavioral patterns. For years, academic libraries continued to fit themselves to their parent institutions' gendered mold.

Therefore, it is by default, not by design, that library technical innovations benefit mothers' research and library service needs. Men who did not acknowledge gender differences developed these innovations. Studies in information-seeking behavior suggest that women often seek information more frequently than men and usually use more resources than men in their information quests. Lori Ricigliano and Renee Houston (2003) were among the first researchers to explore how library technologies impacted social relations and dynamics in library settings. They conclude that, contrary to improved expectations, technology in academic libraries has contributed to wage disparities among male and female employees and has given rise to gender segregation in the academic library workplace. The integration of library technologies sprouted another male-dominant enclave, the information technology staff. Aloha Record and Ravonne Green (2008) report that men still dominate as library administrators and managers. These two studies provide evidence that even though academic librarianship consists of more women than men, men still have the power in decision making and in designing and managing technical innovation. This phenomenon can be explained in terms of Dowd's masculinities analysis. She includes work segregation and income inequality as among the consequences of male privilege and female subordination (2010, 420).

Although the mode of information delivery has been transformed, academic libraries have not taken into account that women seek and use information differently from men. The professional literature addressed this issue with the publication of "Gender Issues in Information Needs and Services," a special issue of *Library Trends* (Ingold and Searing 2007). This special issue explores gender-related considerations in frequency of library visits, politics of information, and topics of interests to women. However, it is directed primarily to the social milieu of public libraries rather than of research or college libraries, where academic mothers most abound. Nevertheless, my experience as library administrator and researcher make me believe that the gender-related considerations it discusses apply to the academic environment as well.

Perhaps the male-dominated decision making in academic libraries has been tolerated because higher education as a whole is slow to change. Anne Stockdell-Giesler and Rebecca Ingalls note that despite the support of female scholars by the American Association of University Professors and other professional groups in academia, "the ethos of the scholar in the modern university remains that of a solitary male thinker who, upon producing enough intellectual work on a strict schedule, is rewarded with a lifetime position" (2007, 38). Indeed, the "Rodin Perplex model" (my name for the solitary male thinker) has guided library policies, services, and use of space. Interestingly, Dowd (2010) has identified the gendered use of space as one of her core propositions in masculinities analysis, which includes the presence of children in those spaces.

Academic libraries have historically gained notoriety for issuing policies that prohibit or discourage children in their facilities. Library administrators justify antichildren policies by referring to liability concerns, the traditional paradigm about the need to maintain a quiet environment, and the need not to have to deal with issues such as Internet filtering. Because not all library services and information resources are accessible through technology, student mothers with library needs are thus stymied with the challenge of finding child care simply in order to use the library. Women professors face the same dilemma. They, too, have research obligations that cannot be met in light of library policies toward children and noise.

Yet as I have found as university librarian of the Miller Library at Western New Mexico University (WNMU), accommodating mothers' needs in academia is often simple and inexpensive. The Miller Library serves as a testimonial to making facilities and services more mother-friendly. In 2009, I appointed a staff committee charged with creating a lactation space called the "Mothers Comfort Zone" in which nursing mothers can either feed their babies or pump their breasts in a safe, private setting. Drawing on their personal past experiences as nursing mothers, the committee researched, designed, and furnished the lactation station for less than one thousand dollars. Until then, WNMU did not have a designated space for nursing mothers anywhere on campus. The Miller Library was the ideal location because the facility is centrally located on the campus and maintains the longest hours of operation. The staff committee regularly represents the university at meetings of the Southwest New Mexico Breastfeeding Council. Their attendance assures that the university is kept updated on legal and community developments pertaining to the rights of nursing women. To compliment the Miller Library's mother-friendly services, WNMU's Office of Multicultural Affairs and Student Activities organized a breastfeeding support group for students, faculty, and staff. The Southwest New Mexico Breastfeeding Council recognized the university and the Miller Library with a well-publicized Community Breastfeeding Promotion Award for their efforts in promoting and supporting breastfeeding to WNMU mothers (Southwest Breastfeeding Task Force New Mexico 2009).

By creating a special space for university nursing mothers, the Miller Library is respecting that the library user, whether student, staff, or faculty, is not a "bodiless scholar" whose sexual identity must be negated in academia, as Catherine Waldby has described the perceived norm (cited in Bartlett 2006, 23). Furthermore, in a reflective work published in the *Chronicle of Higher Education*, Laura Skandera-Trombley discusses the agonizing dilemma she experienced in her dual roles as academic administrator and nursing mother. She points out that "fundamental biological distinctions between men and women" cannot be denied, nor should they cause embarrassment (2003). With the creation of the lactation space and a campus breastfeeding support group, WNMU is acknowledging with dignity that nursing mothers cannot ignore milk-engorged breasts while pursuing intellectual pursuits.

Just as the Mothers Comfort Zone and the support group address the biological functions of motherhood, the Miller Library also considers mothers' lifestyles in offering traditional library services. Like other academic libraries, it offers a library instruction program in which students are taught as a class to conduct library research. Initiated by individual faculty members, the instruction is typically scheduled at the beginning of the semester and usually takes up one class period. Prior to class time, the library instructor and the faculty member agree on content and length of instruction, which ranges from fifty minutes to one and one-half hours. Librarians and students have called attention to the inadequacies of time limits on library instruction, but most faculty members do not want to dedicate more time to it. To that end, the Miller Library has expanded its instruction program to allow students to make an appointment for instruction outside the classroom context. Modeled after Pugh's "just for you" concept, the individualized library instruction program is serving students well. Another initiative is using software such as Lecture Capture to create online modules that students can view at their convenience. Returning students on our campus, many of whom are mothers who postponed their education to raise families, especially welcome these expansions of our library instruction program.

Miller Library personnel found that returning student moms were experiencing disproportional information overload and frustration because of their unfamiliarity with navigating new information technologies. Unlike their children, not all student moms are digital natives. Coupled with the anxieties of adjusting to the campus environment, they are often overwhelmed when faced with a research assignment. While teaching them important library skills on a personalized basis, Miller Library personnel often discover other issues that impede student moms' academic success They most often find that returning mothers are not confident in their writing skills and are perplexed by the nuances of discipline-specific writing styles. These students are referred to the Writing Center, which is conveniently located in the Miller Library building in keeping with the current trend of having libraries serve as multipurpose facilities (Lippincott 2004, 147). Whereas academic libraries of yesteryear cherished stand-alone facilities, modern libraries embrace a multipurpose approach that is conducive to harried student moms with time constraints.

It is not surprising that information overload is a stress factor for university students and faculty. Moreover, many students come to higher education without much preparation to search Web-based library resources, thereby elevating the importance of library instruction (Kent 2008, 19). The personalized instruction service allows Miller librarians to ascertain what gaps exist in the library user's repertoire of library skills and to determine the value the user is placing on the information retrieved. The importance of "just for you" instruction is best illustrated anecdotally by Wayne Wiegand's efforts to have his mother perform information-seeking techniques. These techniques, it turns out, reflected his, not her, assessment of the value of the information she sought, and, upon reflection, he concluded that "certain kinds of information are valued differently because personal values themselves are radically contingent on multiple factors unique to each person's life" (1998, 57).

In addition, academic libraries' space utilization is evolving to accommodate women's needs. Fortunately for the Miller Library, the renovation completed in 1997 by James B. Redford of ASA Architects provides flexibility. The open-space design facilitates the rearranging of modular furniture. Rather than incorporating space for a linear arrangement of individual study carrels that was designed for the Rodin Perplex male patron, the space allows for collaborative inquiry and interactivity, the preferred atmosphere for women's transformative learning. Many women are "connected" scholars who thrive in cooperative endeavors (Brooks 2000, 144–145). The Miller Library capitalizes on this preference by promoting the availability of rooms for group study and encourages the rearrangement of modular furniture on the first-floor open study area. I have observed that more women than men take advantage of the spatial opportunities for cooperative study and research. The Miller Library has designated the second floor as the Quiet Zone for library users who require or prefer privacy in studying or researching, which is still an important space to have.

The remodeling has allowed the Miller Library to continue its commitment to making use of the library a family affair. Diaper-changing stations have been installed in both the men's and the women's restrooms, which makes child care easier for fathers who are "hanging out" in the library while student moms are attending class or conducting research. Like most academic libraries, the Miller Library has a children's book collection to support the needs of students studying to be teachers. Plans are under way to convert underutilized space as a children's story-time area. Through collaboration with student groups, Friends of the Library, and the student teachers in the School of Education, the Miller Library will host story times on a regular schedule.

Also planned is the revival of an end-of-semester event aimed at student parents. Cookie Stolpe, a long-time employee, recollected in a conversation with me in 2009 that the Miller Library encouraged parents to bring their children in their sleepwear during extended hours in the week of finals. While parents studied for exams, library employees and volunteers engaged the children in learning activities in a designated area in the library. Just as Alison Bartlett (2006) appealed to higher education to allow mothers to bring their lives to the workplace (as opposed to taking work home), this end-of-semester event demonstrates how academic libraries have the opportunity to bring parents' lives into this academic space rather than strip student and faculty parents of their identities as parents. Stolpe remarked that as a bonus to ending the child-care quandary during finals week, parents in this context serve as positive role models for their children.

Academic libraries have an obligation to serve as professional and social advocates for the scholarly needs of women. As already noted, women now outnumber men as university and college students. Furthermore, studies are reflecting the reality that students are no longer postponing parenthood as they did in prior generations (Kennelly and Spalter-Roth 2006; Kuperberg 2009; Springer, Parker, and Deviten-Reid 2009). The time has arrived for libraries to welcome the maternal perspective, alongside the technological one, as a change agent in academia. Mothers now have the potential to be a dominant user group in academic libraries. Library administrators of both genders have the social and academic obligation to cease rendering them invisible.

14

REIMAGINING THE FAIRYTALE OF MOTHERHOOD IN THE ACADEMY

Barbara A. W. Eversole, Darlene M. Hantzis, and Mandy A. Reid

ACADEMIC WOMEN know that our presence in our profession evidences earlier acts of transgressive border crossing. Despite years of challenging borders and revising the profile of professors, however, women represent a minority of the newly hired and of professors in every legitimate rank. We are officially welcomed in the academic house, but the culture of the academy teaches us repeatedly that women are not (yet) "rightful residents" of our professional homes. The persistent discomfort of a problematic fit characterizes most academic women and rises significantly for academic mothers. Talking together about our lives as "momprofs," we recognized the powerful pedagogy of mothering in the academy; it is never just right and always transgressive of normative institutional culture. Our reflective analysis recognizes that transgressions of social identity can elicit punitive consequences, subtle and explicit, despite official policies or practices established to remedy injustice. This chapter features experiences from each of the three authors regarding the challenges we face(d) as mothers and professors at different career stages and in different professional roles. Our experiences are specific but not unique; we preserve echoes and resonances between and among our stories to demonstrate the common ground of academic mothers while honoring the importance of time and place in experience.

We locate "momprof" as a stigmatized social identity. Erving Goffman posited the power of stigma first by recognizing the sociality of subjectivity. The "self" is always already imbricated in a social structure that, in Goffman's terms, affords the "category of persons available for [one] to be" (1963, 3). Social identity categories ease social intercourse by prescribing characters that inhabit each category, thus producing a set of appearances and actions as well as beliefs and attitudes that can be reasonably expected of each member of the category. Goffman significantly noted that such "normative expectations" transform "into righteously presented demands" that guarantee the stability of the social category by policing its borders (2). Individuals who manifest attributes that violate their social identity are stigmatized, which authorizes punitive responses from the obedient inhabitants of the violated social identity category and by others who recognize that licensed violation in one category threatens the structure itself.

The stigma of "academic mother" derives from multiple determinations of transgressions: the increased visibility mothering yields to the already stigmatized identity of woman professor; the potential suspicion of secrecy or deception surrounding the disclosure of pregnancy or motherhood to colleagues across the academy; the potential disruption in the normative timeline of professional success; and the multiple, disruptive time conflicts between the academic workday and the demands that accompany mothering. The stigma of academic mothers is bolstered by attributes that potentially stigmatize any mother, including (among other attributes) the mother's marital or partnership status, working status, and personal characteristics (e.g., age, race, class, perceived health). In addition, mothers are scrutinized based on the method by which one becomes a mother and the identity characteristics of one's child(ren). This essay does not rehearse the arguments that demonstrate the persistent social inequality of women or the ways in which that inequality marks every additional social identity inhabited by women, including the category of academic woman. Efforts to chronicle, document, and explain while resisting pervasive sexism and its consequences are ongoing and multiple. The experiences recounted here demonstrate our attempts as academic mothers to cope with and challenge Goffman's so-called spoiled identities—in this case, those of momprofs. Although Goffman's work on stigma makes it clear that those who inhabit stigmatized identities often act from that positionality and are acted upon based on the perception of their status as stigmatized, through this essay we want to offer a different point of view.

EXPERIENCES MANAGING "ACADEMIC MOTHER"

Through the sharing of our experiences as momprofs, a common language surfaced among us that characterized our understanding of the ways in which choosing to inhabit the social identity of "mother" while working and living the social identity of "professor" seemed to violate both catego-ries. For instance, through conversations with each other it became clear that our academic mothering transgressed the temporal logic of our profes-sion in specific and varied ways. In addition, our interactions with formal and informal policies and practices of "academic culture" meant we were constantly negotiating concepts of faculty "work" (labor) and confronting the policed border that marks the personal and the public. Ultimately, in one form or another, we all insistently worked toward transgressing the rules and, like Goffman, saw a lingering ambivalence about the normative attri-butes of social identities.

TRANSGRESSING TIME

We have learned that there is no right time or right way to become a mom-prof. Whether a woman is single or partnered, pre- or post-tenure, becom-ing an "academic mother" has historically violated the social identity of "professor" while stigmatizing motherhood. Researchers have suggested that the normal timeframe of completing the doctorate, postdoctoral fel-lowships, and the pretenure period competes with motherhood's biological clock. In some cases, women have chosen to defer motherhood to achieve job security, but for those of us who have chosen to combine the social identities of mother and professor during the pretenure period often experi-ence the censure that accompanies stigma, including the failure to earn ten-ure. The conflict between parenthood and professional success is cited as a factor in the persistent "tenure gap" that marks women as significantly less likely to progress toward tenure. Becoming a mother after tenure threatens professional success less obviously. It compromises no "clock," and tenure offers protection from some of the potentially punitive actions by colleagues who may doubt the momprof's commitment. However, reports that tenured professors are increasingly choosing to "stand still" rather than to pursue promotion to the rank of full professor suggests that female associate profes-sors are prioritizing parenting rather than extending their research agendas. Yet such simplistic analyses fail to consider how tenured women have his-torically carried the weight of departmental service and the ways in which academic policy and practices have unfairly gendered the promotion to full professor. Certainly, no official policies prohibit motherhood. Just as cer-tainly, however, policies can and do discourage the choice and forms of disclosure by creating unnecessary conflicts between professional success and parenting and by licensing an academic climate that, in turn, reveals the stigmatizing presence of prescripted expectations of professors that exclude motherhood. Here we each reflect on choices we made about disclosure of our stigmatizing narratives.

Barbara entered graduate school pregnant and let her pregnant body speak for her because that was the only disclosure she could not control. Passive disclosure in this way attempts to control others' commentary by forcing them into the difficult position of having to ask directly if a woman is pregnant. Despite Barbara's control of specific information, the consistent message conveyed through repeated commentary was that mothering violated the identity of a graduate student.

> I first felt that I was transgressing when I entered my graduate program six months pregnant with my first child. I knew it would be difficult to pursue my graduate education while pregnant and later, as a mother, but I couldn't bear to give up either my education or mothering. I suspected that if I asked for permission to do both, my future adviser would deny it. I reasoned I would never have to actually "'fess up" because my pregnant belly would speak for me. The first day of the term my adviser told my class that "we" had discussed delaying my entry into the program as a consequence of my pregnancy and that "we" decided against a delay. No such discussion oc curred. His disclosure of my pregnancy established my transgression to my peers and diminished my agency by claiming that he authorized my decision to begin graduate school. When I refused to participate in a class river-rafting trip because I was nursing my newborn, the same man inappropriately and intrusively commented that I could pump while encamped along the river. He assigned an A minus in a later course because, he said, "I noticed that you have become more stressed since having the baby." Not playing by the rules, it seems, warrants punishment.

Mandy chose motherhood at what is generally acknowledged as the wrong time to have children: on the tenure track. Expecting censure, she also practiced informational control as a strategic choice, keeping the knowledge to herself as long as she could. Once her body revealed her choice, she was surprised by the amount of commentary her pregnancy provoked. Mandy's pregnancy incited even more commentary because she chose motherhood not only pretenure, but also premaritally, as a single woman.

My body's disclosure of my pregnancy provoked similar, consistent commentary, censuring through apparent expressions of concern and condemnation of my decision. It's still not clear to me if becoming a single mother by choice or doing so while pretenure was the greater transgression. Both identities transgress time: pretenure and premarital. I was told that my decision was "the kiss of death for tenure," so I suppose the greater transgression was ostensibly my tenure status. Single mothering on the tenure track is damn hard. I don't have the luxury of spending time joining the discussions among my colleagues about whether my decision was courageous or foolhardy. I'm too busy grading papers, drawing elephants, and pursuing a research agenda. I understand that my pretenure colleagues and I have the same twenty-four hours in a day. I recognize that my colleagues also have life obligations in addition to work (spouses, partners, children, hobbies, etc.). The culture of commentary makes it clear that choosing to be a single mother comes with a penalty that is not applied to other choices.

Darlene entered motherhood at what some have claimed is the right time: after achieving tenure. However, for most women, waiting until after tenure also means waiting too late biologically. The commentary Darlene received suggested that waiting "too long" is expected and normative for academic mothers.

In the normative narrative of academic mothers (earn a Ph.D., earn tenure, birth a child if you are able), I am identified as one who "waited." I understand the assessment: when a well-past-tenure, midforty-year-old associate dean becomes a mother, the choice must be explained. The collegial discussions in which I did not participate generously explained and speculated that "she must have waited" because she prioritized her career, and it is harder to be a mother and a dean than to be a mother and a professor. It can appear logical for women to "delay" motherhood to ensure professorial success, which is timed by the tenure clock, and logical to conclude that administration further discourages motherhood. Although actually I simply changed my mind about motherhood, I frequently found myself cast in the role of "one who waited" and in the position of responding to critical commentary about the costs of my "delay." That commentary referenced adoptive mothering and my energy and stamina alongside an infant's needs and my capacity to continue to succeed professionally. Mothering is always a public text, visible and open to scrutiny. The public text of my mothering includes also the facts that I am single and my race differs from my child's. Certainly, the decision alone engendered comment among those few to whom I disclosed it. I was unsurprised by repeated queries from women colleagues reflecting a concern that I had not thought it through: "Are you sure?" "Are you nuts?" "At your age?" Their incredulity signaled my transgression of normative behavior.

TRANSGRESSING ACADEMIC CULTURE

Academic institutions are increasingly adopting policies and practices designed to respond to faculty's real-life needs that have been deemed unacknowledged by formal academic culture. These policies function as what Goffman (1963) might identify as "benevolent social actions" undertaken to soften and ameliorate responses to folks in stigmatized categories. Advocacy for such policies certainly minimizes the impact of stigma written into the academy's formal and informal culture. Policies such as "stopping the tenure clock," flextime, and professional development facilitate, encourage, and support faculty members who are attempting to negotiate the complex demands of work and life. Not surprisingly, stigmatized faculty members underuse policies that require them to make themselves highly visible. For example, women faculty do not use tenure-clock options or extended parental leave in significant numbers due to stigma and the lack of diverse practices that can address both official and unofficial culture. The academy's unofficial culture often discourages utilization of the accommodations by disparaging those who participate and by diminishing the merit of the work completed as a result of accommodation. According to Goffman, a stigmatized individual is expected "to act so as to imply neither that [his] burden is heavy nor that bearing it has made [him] different" (1963, 122) which can unfairly affect momprofs.

Mandy began motherhood on the tenure track, and her decision called into question her commitment to the job and more broadly to her career. Mandy's story highlights that choosing motherhood (or not) should not be a factor in the tenure-review process.

> Recognizing that our university does not offer paid maternity leave (through the institution or the Family Medical Leave Act), my chair assigned me an online teaching schedule for the semester following my son's birth. Full-time online teaching is not standard for faculty in my department, yet other faculty viewed

my accommodation as an extraordinary departure from institutional norms. However, everything my chair did for me was available under the institution's policies. Plus, he consistently makes accommodations for other faculty's life demands (elder care, commuting from other cities, and teaching assignments that align with school or day-care schedules). Even though my accommodations were allowed under university policy, some colleagues considered them suspect. A crucial and increasingly available form of institutional support is the opportunity to reset the tenure clock after the birth or adoption of a child. Choosing to reset my tenure clock, however, came with strings attached. The unspoken but understood terms of my "extra" year to tenure are that, although I do not deserve this extra time, my file would need to surpass the minimum expectations for tenure because my extra year should have produced superior achievement in research. Institutionally speaking in terms of policy, I have been supported. What has not been supported is my choice to become a single parent pretenure and without a partner. Despite colleagues' grumbling, my greatest ally within the university is my department chair. Without his willingness to support all faculty, my life as a momprof would be much more difficult.

Barbara's story, in contrast, illustrates what her institution did right in supporting her attempt to combine professing with mothering her school-age children when she first began a tenure-track career. Many of this institution's policies (such as networking support, the availability of child care, and flexible work and leave arrangements) helped not only academic mothers be successful, but all employees at the university, thus creating a positive environment in which folks can lead more productive and satisfying lives.

I never thought I would be hired into a tenure-track position as a forty-seven-year-old mom of two school-age children. I violated the social identity norms of an assistant professor on the tenure track: I was too old, I had children, and I was a woman. I was fortunate, however, that in my first tenure-track year I was able to participate in a very powerful networking experience: a pretenure women's Faculty Learning Community. Recognizing that it is difficult for women who are already stretched for time to be involved in professional development, participants in the learning community were given a stipend. I met women from all ranks of the university. Without these networks, I would have remained isolated in my male-majority college and would not have had the opportunity to work with female colleagues more senior than I am. Having access to women and mothers in all ranks and across the university has been invaluable in reducing the isolation that I felt. Compensated, recognized, and measured participation from faculty across campus is crucial to the success of these kinds of programs. However, other beneficial supports were absent at our institution, and their absence indicated the failure to understand the reality of balancing work and family responsibilities. Expectations of availability for meetings, formal or informal, on weekends or after 5:00 P.M. disregard the "second shift" of parenting. I cringed when a male professor spoke to new faculty and asserted that, to meet our research goals, "Saturday is your friend. Come into the office." Momprofs would find it impossible to routinely spend Saturdays at work in the office away from our children. A complex understanding of contemporary work–life issues would lead an institution to provide support such as broad access to child care (on site, full-time, drop-off, and willing to take slightly sick children). Policy recognition would come in revising sick leave to bank and donate sick time and allow flexible work arrangements (extended time to tenure; flexible work load and increased time to tenure; part-time tenure track). Yet a university is only as family-friendly as the department chair. Unlike Mandy's chair, my chair had no idea how to help me manage my mothering and professing. Chairs need to provide the support that mothers need to be able to combine mothering with professing, yet they often do not know how. It is also important that these institutional supports not be viewed as individual accommodations; this breeds charges of unfairness and favoritism, and could result in backlash against academic mothers. These supports need to be viewed as positive institutional interventions and good retention practice rather than as special accommodations for certain faculty.

Darlene's story further illustrates the need for the creation of academic work–life policies even for faculty in administrative positions. Choosing to begin her family "late in life" by normative standards, Darlene faced a workplace where policies recognized only the norm of being married with grown children and did not admit the possibility of an administrator who was the single parent of a school-age child.

At most academic institutions, including my own, the majority of academic deans and associate deans are married with grown or nearly grown children. In the twenty years I have been here, most deans have been men, and about half of the associate deans have been women. I worked for several years with one other associate dean who was mothering a small child; she was married and had an older child at home. I became a single mother while we worked in the dean's office. Together, we navigated the difficulties of parenting associated with the work of administration. Perhaps more than any other sector of the university, academic administration retains "traditional" expectations about the workday and the worker. The relatively minimal change in the demographics of academic administrators means that such expectations face few challenges. My colleague and I were unsuccessful by any measure in changing practices or the beliefs that underwrote those practices. Although the university benefitted from our efforts, we were forced to claim sick or leave time. Equally insulting and ironic is the university enforcement of the illusion of a 37.5-hour work week for administrators; we consistently (and with full knowledge of the institution) completed work at home and at the office late into evenings and during weekends without additional compensation. Furthermore, failing to appear at least some Saturday and Sunday mornings or afternoons in the office was a signal of slacking and proof that parenting and "deaning" don't mix well. Now, as a tenured full professor out of the dean's office, I find myself justifying why I (ordinarily) will not attend meetings outside reasonable work hours. When I fail to persuade colleagues to schedule our work during the week, between eight and five each day, I may find myself excluded from important service work or denied the opportunity to complete work for which I was elected (e.g., the College Promotion and Tenure Committee).

CONCLUSION: HAPPILY EVER AFTER?

According to the American Association of University Professors' (2001) "Statement of Principles on Family Responsibilities and Academic Work," "Transforming the academic workplace into one that supports family life requires substantial changes in policy and, more significantly, changes in academic culture. These changes require a thorough commitment from the leaders of educational institutions as well as from the faculty" (2001, para. 9).

A fully happy ending for momprofs requires the transformation not only of institutional cultures, but also of those cultures' influence on the social identity of professor. Eliminating the professional penalty that is often paid by women professors who become mothers moves us toward equity in our profession. For instance, becoming a father for a male faculty member actually increases his chances of achieving tenure (Mason and Goulden 2002). We need to work together to restructure the culture of our academic spaces by protesting those policies and practices that hinder the success of professors who parent and by advocating for those that do not. We need to insist that efforts to support women, especially those who are mothers, through their entire career trajectory, from tenure to promotion to full professor, be explicit and encouraged. Documented best practices should be assessed after implementation to ensure they meet the needs of a particular community and should be shared with others to inspire capacity building. Some of the practices that will help in the pursuit of professional excellence include flexible work times and tenure clocks; sick-day "banks"; opportunities for paid professional development; on-site or near-site child care; the designation of child and elder care as reimbursable expenses associated with professional travel; the elimination of derisive labels such as "mommy-tracked"; and the modeling of a language respectful of faculty work and lives. These policies and practices cannot be acts of benevolence to offset sustained stigmatizing of those who violate the social identity of professor; they must be part of the transformation of policy, culture, and politics.

Higher-education institutions can become leaders in the effort to transform work–life environments, developing models for other sectors to emulate rather than lagging behind in invention, adoption, and efficacy of policies and practices. By including our personal narratives in this chapter, we reaffirm our personal and political choice to enter the academy as professors, to fight against the stigmatization of mothers, and to remain unapologetically committed to pursuing scholarly excellence, while happily transgressing temporal, spatial, and cultural rules and expectations imposed upon us by academia. In bearing witness, we mark our lives and our institutions with hope.

15

TALES FROM THE TENURE TRACK

The Necessity of Social Support in Balancing the Challenges of Tenure and Motherhood

Sandra L. French and Lisa Baker-Webster

MORE WOMEN are enrolled in U.S. degree-granting colleges and universities as undergraduates, graduates, and professional students than at any other time in history (National Center for Education Statistics 2011). Yet despite the higher numbers of women entering the academy as students, full-time tenure-track and tenured women faculty make up only 34 percent of the academy (West and Curtis 2006). Several scholars argue that the explanation for these statistics lies in systemic inequities in the higher-education environment. For example, University of California–Berkeley emeritus education scholar Geraldine Clifford (1983) criticized the fact that traditional histories of higher education either ignore or minimize women's experience, linking women's access to higher education as a major feminist struggle involving educational, social, legal, and political reforms. Although women have reaped the benefits of three decades of federal, state, and local legislation and regulations to increase women's equity and advancement, a "chilly campus climate" continues for women in higher education. Bernice Sandler (1986), senior scholar at the Women's Research and Education Institute, focused her attention on women faculty, administrators, and graduate students, noting the subtle ways in which women continue to be treated differently from men within the academy. Yet more than twenty years after Sandler's study, a supercilious campus climate is still an issue for women in academia.

For example, women on the tenure track are 20 percent less likely to achieve the goal of tenure than their male colleagues. The news is even worse for working mothers in the academy. In 2003, the *Harvard Journal of*

Law & Gender published a study (Williams and Segal 2003) describing the "maternal wall" that women academics come up against once they become mothers. It further documents that women who have children soon after receiving their doctorate degree are much less likely to achieve tenure than their male counterparts who have children during the same time frame. University of California–Berkeley (2003) researchers have referred to this phenomenon, in which women complete doctoral programs but drop out of the running for tenure-track positions, as the "leaking pipeline" of women Ph.D.s. How can women who are also mothers balance the demands at home and at the academy? Several scholars have noted that one option for women academics is to opt out of the tenure-track route in favor of adjunct or "mommy-track" positions (Harper, Baldwin, and Gansneder 2001).

This chapter focuses on women who choose the tenure track and explores the role of supportive social networks in the lives of tenure-track mothers. We begin with a background on the environment that tenure-track mothers face in the academy and finish with suggestions and real-life examples of social support networks in action. Although women who work in higher-education administration or as adjuncts and lecturers also face many obstacles in balancing both their personal and their professional lives, this chapter focuses primarily on those who are on the tenure track because in many departments it is the tenure-track employee who fulfills the varied responsibilities such as doing research, writing publications, attending conferences, serving as academic advisers, and performing committee obligations. In addition, tenure-track employees have a set number of years to prove to the university that they will be an asset to the institution. The pressure to "publish or perish" can be much more intense on those who are on the tenure track, and thus some other area of their life such as motherhood may be impaired.

We decided to write this chapter together because we are women who started our professional careers in higher education at the same time we were getting married, working on dissertations, and having babies. For both of us, the "superwoman" soon became a laughable myth. Multiple conversations and online interactions with other women revealed this once-silenced subject; being a mother and working toward tenure are often a difficult journey. The drive and motivation to become the best teacher, scholar, and researcher in one's field often conflict with the same drive and motivation to be the best mother one can be. No one wants to be "that" colleague who is always late for meetings and unreliable to finish assigned tasks. In the same sense, no one wants to be "that" mother who forgets a play date or can never volunteer to help the Parent–Teacher Association. We want to do it all, be it all, and achieve it all. What we as women are discovering is that working full-time and being a mother is hard, and many do not want to admit that we oftentimes fall short of our own unattainable self-standards. Within a semester of each other, we arrived at our institution, a medium-size university in the South that has a liberal arts focus, each with two small children in tow, each on the tenure track and looking to prove our worth. What we have discovered is that our friendship and the friendships we carry on with other academic mothers have proven invaluable to whatever success we have attained. It is these experiences of social support that we seek to explore in this chapter.

THE ACADEMIC ENVIRONMENT

Women pursue academic careers for many reasons, such as intellectual engagement, flexible work life, and self-fulfillment. However, a *Chronicle of Higher Education* article suggests women are leaving academia in large numbers for jobs in industry (Fogg 2003). This trend is so disconcerting that the American Council on Education completed a project on models for flexible tenure-track faculty career pathways to investigate this exodus from higher education. According to the report, the traditional tenure career path is rooted in "societal norms from an earlier era" and thus "inhibits the success of many women with spouses and children" (2005). The patriarchal structure of higher education leads to inhospitable working conditions on the tenure track for women in general and for mothers in particular and makes it difficult for women to reenter tenure-line positions after an absence due to extended maternity leave, pregnancy complications, or deliberate career gaps to raise children.

LISA'S EXPERIENCE

Pregnant as a tenure-track professor, I was amazed at the number of women who approached me at regional and national conferences asking such questions as "Do you think this [nodding toward my huge belly] will hurt your chances for tenure?" "Is your department supportive?" and most often "Is this a 'surprise' pregnancy?" The latter question insinuated there was no way I would intentionally have a baby in the middle of an academic semester. Although I did receive many raised eyebrows, some women pulled me aside, often behind closed doors, and expressed their desire to start a family but were "too scared" of what it could mean for them professionally. Considering that there are laws against pregnancy discrimination in the workplace, that women in higher education are receiving (and to some degree promoting) the unwritten message that reproducing children during the tenure-track process is a major rule breaker.

Such difficult working conditions have likely contributed to academic women's decisions to limit the size of their families. According to the 2000 census, which tracks professions including academic faculty, physicians, lawyers, and CEOs between the ages of thirty-five and fifty, women in the academy reported having fewer children than women in all the other professional fields (Mason 2008). Joan Williams (2002), who directs the Program on Gender, Work, and Family at American University, writes that women professors are fighting back against their often hostile work environments at their institutions as they seek to balance work and family. She cites the June 2000 case of a University of Oregon assistant professor who sued for being denied tenure and received $495,000. This assistant professor had taken two maternity leaves while on the tenure track and was openly criticized by the university's provost for failing to teach classes while on maternity leave or present papers at conference while absent due to medical complications of her pregnancy. According to Williams, "Many female professors and staff members report that they felt treated like valued colleagues until they had children, and then they felt their colleagues' assessment of their competence start to plummet" (para. 6). Williams related another instance where one female professor recalled a meeting with her male dean during which she was told, "You know, my daughter tried to work and raise a family. She decided that her family was more important and left her job." It seems clear that most colleges and universities simply are not interested or at the very least are poorly equipped to assist tenure-tracks mothers. So how can mothers on the tenure track cope in these difficult environments? We argue that social networks can help offset the pressures and negative atmosphere that mothers often face.

SANDY'S EXPERIENCE

As a new faculty member, I was anxious to prove my value to my department and to seek guidance from those with more experience. I was thrilled when I found out another woman, Lisa, had started in our department the semester before me, in the spring, which I thought somewhat unusual. I was quickly informed she had been hired for the fall but allowed to start in January because she had been due to give birth during the fall semester. My first thought was excitement, then apprehension. Would I be in competition with this other mother? Was she handling the multitasking required of academic and motherhood more successfully than I would be able to? It is difficult enough for women who are mothers to make their mark in higher education, but I am an older mother. I took off several years between obtaining my master's and Ph.D. degrees and came to motherhood later as well. I had "high-risk" pregnancies, as they call it, having my first child at thirty-four and my second at thirty-five. How would my new colleague and I manage? Would she see me as an ally or a rival?

My fears were quickly put to rest as we were introduced and hit it off easily. In the years since, we have leaned on one another for guidance on how to handle the balancing act we have chosen—academia and motherhood. My coauthor was recently pregnant with her third child, due toward the end of the spring semester. After many conversations, we pitched the idea to our supervisor that we team-teach so as to retain continuity in her class as she left for maternity leave, which we were allowed to do. This combining of the personal and professional was truly collaborative, truly enjoyable, and reflective of the type of social support few female faculty members receive.

SOCIAL SUPPORT NETWORKS

In a national study of U.S. women faculty, Nadya Aisenberg, who taught women's studies courses at Brandeis University, and Mona Harrington, current program director of the Massachusetts Institute of Technology (MIT) Workplace Center, considered the difficulties women encounter as "informed outsiders" attempting to combine personal and professional responsibilities, expectations, and aspirations in the face of inadequate resources and the lack of a general career strategy (Aisenberg and Harrington 1998). By helping to create social support networks, colleges and universities can better serve the needs of tenure-track mothers, improve employee relations, and retain effective and efficient professors. But what types of social support networks should be available to working mothers in academia? We argue that women and the institutions that employ them would benefit from both internal and external networks.

INTERNAL NETWORKS

Approximately 160 institutions of higher learning currently have some type of center for work and family life, such as the University of California–Berkeley, which was given a $420,000 grant to develop a package of family-friendly policies, which could include such support as on campus day care and flexibility in scheduling for tenured faculty (Fogg 2003). Other schools, such as MIT, offer a part-time tenure track, an extended tenure clock, and even a reduced teaching load at full pay for brand-new parents (Fogg 2003). As stated in the MIT policy regarding faculty family: "The goal of this policy is to take away the career disadvantage that women currently face from pregnancy, childbearing, and nursing an infant. For example, travel is restricted by all of these aspects of a woman's biological role just at the time that attendance at conferences may be particularly important. Or, another example, women who work in areas near hazardous material may be hampered in carrying out their research" (2003, 2).

One important aspect of this policy is that it also extends to adoptive parents (both male and female) and a faculty member whose partner has borne a child. The institution does not view this policy as "mommy tracking," but rather as creating a supportive working environment for both mothers and fathers. The school clearly states, "The goal of these policies is to help MIT faculty have productive careers and still meet their family responsibilities" (1).

However, even when institutions have family-friendly policies, professors are often hesitant to take advantage of them. Research conducted at Pennsylvania State University's main campus in University Park suggests that 30 percent of those surveyed did not ask for the offered parental leave due to fear of career reprisals. The general feeling of the report is that professors who are parents sought to minimize or even hide their family commitments for fear they would be perceived as less dedicated than their childless counterparts (Wilson 2004a). Research also suggests that tenure-track fathers are even less likely than mothers to find father-friendly benefits and policies and, if they do find them, to take advantage of them (Mason 2009c). This tendency not to utilize such policies seems evident from a review of other types of internal support networks offered by several colleges and universities to female faculty. At first glance, one might applaud these schools' efforts to provide a place for women professors to network and collaborate. One such group, Texas A&M's Women's Faculty Network, describes itself as "an organization committed to encouraging and promoting the professional development of women faculty through both formal programming and informal networking opportunities" (Texas A&M University n.d., para. 1). The Association of Women Faculty at Washington University in St. Louis indicates a desire to "promote professional and social interactions among women faculty and to advocate for the interests of women faculty at [the university]" (Washington University Louis 2009, para. 1). Interestingly, however, a closer examination of the descriptions of these organizations indicates that although their overall goals revolve around helping women, they clearly see the women they are targeting as single, with most of their networking opportunities and research symposia being scheduled in the evenings, but no mention is made of women as mothers, nor are there any indications of family-friendly networking. The organizations seem focused on helping women navigate the masculine world of higher education, with seminars on the importance of diversity and the finer points of employment law as well as presentations of female-authored faculty research. Although these practices should be lauded, their focus seems to reinforce the assumption of faculty women's childlessness that is still alive and well in collegiate internal social networks (Timmers, Willemsen, and Tijdens 2010).

We argue that internal collegiate social networks would benefit from reframing their focus to better work with tenure-track mothers. It is generally acknowledged that faculty rewards are directly related to research productivity. Even at institutions traditionally known as teaching colleges, the competition for professors to publish, establish a name in their academic field, and obtain grant money for that institution is becoming more prevalent. With recent budget cuts affecting the financial situation at many higher-education institutions, both public and private colleges, research and comprehensive, are now vying for grant money and scholarly notoriety. Also, from a student-recruitment standpoint, the more faculty members an institution has who are nationally and internationally known and admired in their discipline, the stronger the marketing points for that college or university. Encouraging colleagues to publish and attend conferences with each other can ultimately help a college or university's image. Although this practice may already be the case in several disciplines, such as the sciences, a more universal acceptance of it by all academic areas would be helpful. Given the need for all faculty to engage in substantive research programs, higher-education institutions should encourage collaborative research opportunities not only among tenure-track mothers in the same discipline, but also in cross-disciplinary studies.

For example, our university has a division called the Center for Innovative Teaching and Learning that works in cooperation with Academic Technologies and the university library and provides an opportunity for faculty and staff to learn from each other and share expertise and knowledge. Also, the Center for Gendered Studies facilitates interdisciplinary dialogues about how faculty experience stereotyping, harassment, wage inequity, and other gendered issues in the workplace. Finally, to raise awareness about women's history month in the academic community, Her-Story Listserv at Radford University was designed so "each day in March subscribers would receive an essay, character sketch, photo, journal, or poem submitted by a community member contemplating the women or aspects of womanhood that have had an important impact upon, or been a source of inspiration for, the writer. This celebration is unique in that each day's tribute was composed by a student, staff, or faculty member" (Radford University 2010, para. 2).

In addition, internal support networks should recognize that the type of scholarship created by tenure-track feminist scholars (both with and without children) is likely to be different than that of their male colleagues. Patricia Gumport (1990), current director of the Stanford Institute for Higher Education Research, suggests that feminist scholars operate in a different context from male faculty engaged in traditional forms of inquiry in that they seek to transform not only the discipline but also the very premises of scholarly inquiry and to explore the intersection of personal, political, and intellectual interest. Feminist scholars encounter problematic philosophical issues of wanting to share experiences and ideas yet have to evaluate the boundaries that exist within each classroom, each departmental committee, each conference they attend, and each publication they submit. Colleges and universities, with the support of administrators, should encourage tenure-track female professors, including mothers, to explore new research areas and methodologies.

Second, colleges and universities should strive to create a supportive and congenial working environment that values family. Tenure-track women who become mothers are oftentimes perceived as less productive or a burden to their department from the moment they announce their pregnancy. Such projections do not come only from male coworkers. One professor recounted to us, under the promise of anonymity, that when she told a tenured female coworker that she was pregnant, the coworker responded by saying she had "just ruined her chances at tenure." A few weeks later, during a department faculty meeting, a tenured male colleague stated that her pregnancy was "creating problems" with the teaching schedule. Adding insult to injury, another tenured male coworker mistakenly informed graduate students that he would no longer be offering an upcoming graduate course because he had to teach the classes the female faculty member would not be able to teach during her maternity leave. At no point during these conversations did any faculty member (tenured or untenured) or administrator correct the inappropriate comments. Failing to sanction such inappropriate statements facilitates a work environment that encourages discrimination. Laura Skandera-Trombley, writing for the *Chronicle of Higher Education*, describes a similar experience:

> There was public support for my newly achieved maternal status. An office baby shower was thrown for me, attended by all the administrators, yet my darling domestic quality was deemed inverse to my competency as a professional. When it came to professional advancement and my administrative future at the college, clearly pregnancy and motherhood were liabilities. I discovered that during my pregnancy and in the first few months after my son was born, people appeared to automatically assume that I was not working full time, not working as hard as I once did, as hard as I ought to be. My reaction to my lack of promotion, quite understandably, was to look for another job. But I found that while my vita attracted positive attention, my motherhood did not. (2003, 12)

A department's overall atmosphere and its receptiveness to the inclusion of both the public and private spaces of professors' lives can help reduce discrimination and increase individuals' productivity. Such inclusion helps create a context that encourages colleagues to rethink assumptions about motherhood and professional life. However, although the support of its employees should be an essential component of any organization, the responsibility to offer assistance and interpersonal connections does not lie solely with the organization.

EXTERNAL NETWORKS

Tenure-track mothers must also seek out and even sometimes create their own social support networks on and off campus. According to Harvard

Business School professor Mikolaj Jan Piskorski, social networks "are most useful when they address real failures in the operation of offline networks" (quoted in Silverthorne 2009, para. 3). Sites such as Facebook and LinkedIn can help tenure-track moms connect with women from their graduate school days and form powerful online support systems. Higher education is an organization, and it is good to know that those of us who work in such an organization have the same frustrations, successes, and failures. When working with young adults, we often must find humor in some of the daily events that occur and excuses we hear from students. Electronic social networks give us a way to connect with others whom we may not know personally or see often but can relate to through shared comparable encounters.

Topic-driven online communities also offer social support. One of the most popular external support systems noted by respondents in a study by Clare Madge and Henrietta O'Connor (2005) are the online "parenting" communities. These communities can offer tenure-track mothers the opportunity to meet and correspond with other mothers throughout the globe and provide a sense of freedom of expression not founded in face-to-face communication. For example, the online publication *Inside Higher Ed* has the "Mama Ph.D." blog and the *Chronicle of Higher Education* has a topic-specific discussion forum on mothering. Expressing emotions and feelings with coworkers can sometimes be awkward and viewed as unprofessional. Online mommy communities, in contrast, grant a tenure track mother the space to express her more personal side without fear of being judged by colleagues.

Additional sources of external social support are community programs such as Mommy and Me classes, Mommy's Day Out, and church- and civic-sponsored events. Tenure-track mothers should look for opportunities to step away from professional connections and embrace the more personal side of their lives. The flexibility of scheduling offered by a career in higher education is rarely exercised, with professors instead constantly working both in the office and at home. Opportunities to engage in social occasions outside of the workplace with our children should not instigate feelings of guilt but rather help working mothers feel more balanced. Most tenure-track mothers echo a common sentiment: we are not giving enough to one area or another in our lives.

Is there a magical formula waiting to be discovered that will give tenure-track mothers the ability to balance successfully and equally both professional and personal obligations? Unfortunately, no. However, social support networks, both internal and external, can assist mightily in reducing burnout, enhancing productivity, and restoring the enjoyment of being both professor and mother. Just knowing that others have been in similar situations and have dealt with the many negative and isolating emotions of being a working mother in academia can help with the feelings of loneliness and exhaustion. Seeking internal and external support structures is a key to navigating the many paths traveled by working parents. Also, it is important to remember to embrace the positive elements that come from working for a college or university. Flexible scheduling, the ability to work from home, and the opportunity to take your family to conferences in great cities or overseas for teaching abroad opportunities makes higher-education institutions different than other workplace environments. Finally and most important, we implore readers not to hide or be ashamed of being a tenure-track mother in academia. A former colleague who now teaches communication at a small private university, speaking on condition of anonymity, relayed to us how being a professor and mother can help one to feel fulfilled: "My world is more balanced as a result of being a mother and a professional. Spending time with my daughter brings life back to what really matters—love, relationships, the present moment—and pushes me to be a better, more selfless person. Spending time at work keeps my mind alive and allows me to build professional relationships where I'm an adult and not a mommy."

Together we can help others to see that tenure-track mothers are not asking to be exceptions in job responsibilities, but we are seeking work environments that reject negativity toward working parents, offer more opportunities to interact and connect with other tenure-track mothers. By creating more hospitable work environments through internal and external social support networks, we may be able to plug the leak in the female tenure-track pipeline. Our own experiences reinforce this idea, yet we still long for the days when encouragement and support are received not only from other academic mothers, but from all academic colleagues.

16

HOW HIGHER EDUCATION BECAME ACCESSIBLE TO SINGLE MOTHERS

An Unfinished Story

Summer R. Cunningham

THE NEW Graduate Student Orientation at my university seems to be quite a well attended event. After sitting through a two-hour presentation in the student union's filled-to-capacity, seven-hundred-seat theater, we have adjourned to one of the neighboring ballrooms, where several colleges, student services representatives, and community interest groups have set up informational booths. The Graduate School has provided lunch, and I can't help but wonder if the free food is part of the draw for most of the students present. Admittedly, it is for me. I grab a veggie burger and a bottle of water and head over to a table where two women stand chatting over their meal.

"Mind if I join you?" I ask.

"Of course not," says the woman to my right. "We were just discussing our programs. It turns out we're both in the College of Education."

"Oh, how nice to already know one of your colleagues before classes start," I reply.

"What about you?" the woman on my left asks.

"I'm in the Department of Communication. I'm currently working on a couple of essays about maternity; one is about reproductive choice, and the other is about being a single mom and a graduate student. I hope to expand some of my research in this area while I'm here."

"Wow, you're a single mom?" the woman to my left asks rhetorically. "Good for you."

"It's nice to see a single mom actively pursuing an education," says the woman on my right. "I swear, all I usually hear are excuses from single moms about how everything is impossible and it's just too difficult to go to school."

"Yeah, good for you for not letting it get in your way."

"Yep, single moms," I reply, "are inherently lazy. Can you believe we're not all doctors already, what with the free educations they're just throwing at us? Not only do we get to go to school at no cost, but the government has this new program where they pay for all your child care while you're in class, they send you a private nanny to get up with your child in the middle of the night when she's sick so you can get an uninterrupted eight hours of sleep, and they even pay someone to do all your homework for you so that you don't miss out on quality bonding time with your child."

OK, I don't really make that last comment. At first, I just stare, dumbfounded and infuriated at these comments made by these women. I wonder if they might want children of their own someday. Or perhaps they, like so many other academic women, are putting off maternity until they finish their doctoral degrees and obtain tenure. Perhaps they are destined to join the two-thirds of tenured women in the humanities and social sciences who, ten years after obtaining a Ph.D., still do not have any children or the 43 percent of academic women who do not have children at all (Mason and Goulden 2002; Townsley and Broadfoot 2008). In the end, I simply replied, "That's exactly why I want to do this kind of research."

WELCOME TO THE STORY

As I reflect on my experiences as a single mom pursuing a higher education, I find myself contemplating the best way to frame this narrative. Motherhood, especially single motherhood, is difficult; obtaining a higher education, in particular a graduate degree, is challenging and sometimes alienating, and attempting the two simultaneously often seems impossible. But the endeavor shouldn't actually be impossible. Many scholars have addressed the obstacles that (single) mothers face when completing a higher education (see, e.g., Van Stone, Nelson, and Niemann 1994; Silva 1996; Hofferth, Reid, and Mott 2001; Haleman 2004; Lynch 2008; Mottarella 2009). Those obstacles include prejudice, problematic departmental and institutional practices, financial precarity, time poverty, child care, scheduling dilemmas, conflicting responsibilities, and academic conventions that are not conducive to (single) mothering. Yet simply listing these challenges is not enough to illustrate the complexities that (single) mothers face in their pursuit of a higher education. Moreover, these studies and the accompanying list of obstacles do not illuminate the various ways in which other members of the academic community play a pivotal role in a student mother's ability to complete her degrees. The purpose of sharing my story of obtaining a higher education as a single mom is to ask readers to consider the ways in which they are part of this story. If more single mothers are going to return to school and succeed, things will need to change. We will need to work together to change them.

BECOMING A SINGLE MOTHER AND A STUDENT

I found out I was pregnant three days before my eighteenth birthday, July 1998, the summer before I was to begin my freshman year in college. The decision to continue the pregnancy and keep the baby was not made lightly. As many women who have found themselves in similar situations know, maternal decisions are complex. I cannot begin to account for them all here, but I will foreground a particular set of considerations that was foundational to my decision-making process. I decided I could not ethically become a mother at this point in my life unless I was confident of two things: (1) I would not allow myself to fulfill the negative stereotypes associated with teenage single mothers, and (2) I would not allow my child's overall well-being (economic, emotional, social, physical, psychological, and so forth) to be threatened because I was young, single, and unable to provide for him as easily as a parent who was a bit older, perhaps with a career or a steady income or a partner. After much contemplation and soul searching, I decided I could do it. I could transcend stereotypes. I could be a good mother to my child without forsaking my own future or my son's. Indeed, our futures were now intertwined. In order to be a good mother, I would need to invest in my future, which meant attending college.

My freshman year of college was awkward to say the least. I tried to hide my growing belly under baggy T-shirts and pants, but after a while it became obvious. I was an adult, but I was still a teenager. My body with its protruding middle and swollen feet marked me as different from my freshman contemporaries, and I felt myself become the object of chastising stares. They say that pregnant woman have a glow about them; I wasn't feeling it. I felt awkward and ashamed, trapped in a body that told my story for me whether

I wanted it to be known or not. I mostly didn't want it known. I didn't talk openly about my situation unless I had to. The beginning of my second semester was unfortunately one of those times that I had to talk about it; I was scheduled to give birth to my son midsemester.

On the first day of classes, I spoke with each of my professors, assuring them that I would keep up with all my assignments and that I would miss only as many classes as was absolutely necessary. Most of my instructors were very understanding and even accommodating, but my English professor was not. He had a very strict attendance policy: absences—excused or not—resulted in a significant point deduction from one's overall grade. I approached him after the first class, nervous but hopeful he might be able to make an exception considering that an absence was going to be unavoidable for me.

"No exceptions," he said. This made me a little angry, but I respected the fact that he made everyone play by the same rules. I nevertheless felt that I had a compelling argument, and I continued to plead with him: "A low grade could possibly jeopardize my scholarship. I promise I will keep up with the work. I just want the opportunity to obtain a good grade in your class." But he insisted, "No exceptions."

He made his point and could have left it at that, but he didn't. This English professor felt he had the right to tell me that there were other alternatives for "girls like me" and that it wasn't appropriate for me to be physically present at school during my pregnancy. He was surprised that I didn't have the foresight to "take some time off" to handle my "condition" or simply "drop out," but he was appalled that I didn't at least have the decency to pursue my curriculum via correspondence classes. Inside of me a voice screamed, "I have the right to be pregnant! I have the right to pursue an education without being penalized or discriminated against for my decision to have a child." But my words, stifled and shamed, remained trapped in my body, undeliverable.

Research indicates that student mothers consider positive, supportive interaction with faculty members regarding their familial constraints to be critical in their academic success (Medved and Heisler 2002). Student parents interact with faculty members as a way of managing the school–life balance, seeking support or assistance in the form of deadline extensions or excused absences. Studies have found that faculty members often refuse such requests for accommodation, reasoning that it would not be fair to make exceptions for certain students over others. Some students report that they perceived their only alternatives in such situations were to fail assignments or tests or to drop the class (Medved and Heisler 2002). In my situation, I fell into the latter category. I ended up dropping the English class, resuming it later with a different instructor. I refused to allow my former professor's personal ideology to impede my progress, and I continued to pursue my studies tenaciously, albeit slowly. Looking back now, it frustrates me that I believed dropping the class was my only option for success, and it frustrates me more that the professor felt perfectly justified in speaking to me that way.

SUCCESS AND STRUGGLE

It took me eight and a half years to complete my bachelor's degree as a single mom, working full-time, taking classes any way I could, and sleeping infrequently. But I did it, graduating in spring 2006 in the top one percent of my class and with my college's highest honors. Due to my successful undergraduate career, several of my professors encouraged me to apply to graduate school, and I did. Yet as a graduate student, I continue to face issues with respect to work–life balance, social support, financial obligation, and university policies in an academic culture that frequently does not seem conducive to (single) motherhood. I often question my decision to pursue this path. I wonder if it is really the best choice for my family (my son, our cat, and me). I question it not because I don't enjoy school, but because the pursuit of a higher education has taken a toll on my family in ways that I couldn't have possibly imagined. And at times, being a good mom seems at odds with being a good graduate student. Research indicates that motherhood and academia are not solely at odds in my life, but rather that the structural norms and conventions of academe make it a difficult place to succeed for any woman who has children (see "Heeding the Calls" 2008). The following incident provides just one glimpse of this conflict.

It's 10:18 A.M., and I get a call from the school nurse at my son Benjamin's school. He is in her office. Coughing, sick, tired. Probably just a cold, but he wants to come home. He told me this morning that he didn't feel well. I sent him to school anyway. Not because I'm cruel, but because I thought maybe he would feel better after he started moving around. He had no fever and didn't seem to be in a dire state of illness.

"If you feel worse by second or third period, call me, and I'll come get you," I said, crossing my fingers, hoping he wouldn't call.

I have a lot to do today. I have a graduate class at 2:00 P.M. I still have to finish reading the three-hundred-page book that was assigned for this week and write a relevant intervention question. I'm trying to organize a panel for the Southern States Communication Association's annual convention, and the deadline is tomorrow. I know none of this will get done if Benjamin is home sick. If I go home, this will be the second class I will have missed as a result of single-parent-related obligations; it's only the third week of the semester. I imagine what my cohort and professor must think: "Oh, there she goes, pulling the single-mom card again."

It's not like that at all. I wish I could be in class. I wish that my son were well. I also wish that I could be home caring for him without feeling guilty about it. But I do feel guilty. Almost daily I find myself making decisions where I must choose between being a good student and being a good mom, usually to the detriment of one or the other role. My options at other times are even more constrained, the conflict between obligations irresolvable because the conditions are created within a system not intended for people with my particular circumstances. A recent conversation with a campus administrator illustrates this point.

(UN)SUPPORTING CHARACTERS

"I am glad you were able to stop by so that I could meet you, Summer," begins the associate dean. "I wanted to congratulate you in person, and let you know that this fellowship is the most prestigious that our university offers. You should also know that this honor comes with much responsibility and high expectations."

I nod, inviting him to continue.

"The Graduate School has a number of events geared toward improving the experience and success of our students. We expect that as a Presidential Fellow you will be in attendance at these events. Here is a list of the workshops we offered this past semester; we anticipate adding even more by the time you join us next fall."

He hands me a list of nearly a dozen seminars, each of them from two to four hours long. Many are held on the weekend or in the evening. I wonder what to do about child care, and I wonder how often I will actually see my son. Like many student parents, I worry about the lack of affordable access to child care on campus, which is critical for mothers to successfully pursue an education with a family in tow (Haleman 2004). Studies indicate that many institutions unfortunately do not provide on-site child-care facilities, and if or when facilities exist on site, they are often not affordable for students or not available during evening or weekend hours, when some mothers are required to be in class (Medved and Heisler 2002; A. F. Pearson 2010; Vancour and Sherman 2010).

"We also expect our fellows," the associate dean continues, "to actively engage in research, participate in disciplinary conferences, and eventually publish work in scholarly journals. We are endowing you with these funds with the expectation that you will represent us in the field."

"Do you offer any additional funding in the form of research or travel grants?" I ask, mentally calculating the expense of buying not just my way but also my eleven-year-old son's to all the conferences I'll be expected to attend. I also contemplate the cost to my son's educational experience when he misses time from school as I further my education.

The associate dean responds, "Well, I think the Graduate Student Association offers a little funding, and sometimes individual departments have funding for their students."

The scarcity of funding for travel doesn't surprise me, but I guess I was hoping that the expectation to travel and represent my school at various conferences might somehow come with the financial means to do so.

Finally, the associate dean concludes, "What do you think? We'd really like to see you undertake your doctoral studies here. Are you up for this challenge?"

"Of course I want to tell you that I am," I respond, "but I cannot give you my decision today because this decision impacts more than just me." I nod toward my son, who sits in the chair next to me. "Look," I continue, "I want to participate in as many of the Graduate School's activities as possible. I want to immerse myself in my research and share those discoveries at forums with other scholars in my field. However, if I sign that paper, it means that I am committing to doing the very best that I can in light of all my responsibilities, my commitments, and my situation. But I can't guarantee that my 'best' will deliver the kind of performance you have in mind. How will that be viewed in the eyes of the Graduate School? Should I still sign on?"

"You've made it this far; I'm sure you've got what it takes to see this through." He does not pause to consider that the Graduate School or he as the associate dean, for that matter, might need to offer different kinds of support for students with nontraditional needs. He does not acknowledge the ways in which my success might be contingent on the practices of others, but instead he leaves it all up to me.

WORKING TOWARD A HAPPY ENDING

After I accepted the position as a Presidential Fellow, my son and I moved across the country last August. Despite my apprehension about some of the graduate school's expectations and the difficulty of moving away from our entire support network of friends and family to a place where we knew no one, I still felt this award promised the best chance of actually completing a doctoral degree while also supporting and raising a child on my own. I figured the accompanying stipend would be enough to provide for us financially while simultaneously alleviating my teaching duties, thus giving me more time with my son.

The first year of my Ph.D. program unfortunately didn't go as smoothly as I had hoped. Due to lack of available child care, my son spent several nights each week sitting alone in my office for hours so that I could attend graduate classes that finished well after his regular bedtime. He also missed an unprecedented amount of school, most of which was related to my academic choices and obligations. Some of his missed school days were the result of traveling with me to conferences, and although he presented with me, I will not see any reimbursement for his travel costs because they do not qualify as legitimate expenses. In fact, the cost of providing for another person while attending college does not seem to factor in anywhere, including the federally regulated financial aid formulas that universities are required to use when estimating students' cost of attendance. Finally, the prestigious and generous fellowship offered by my university did not provide enough financial support to cover all of our living expenses. By the end of my fall semester, I was a month behind on my rent, I had to borrow money from another graduate student for groceries, and my son attended the last couple weeks of the semester with a piece of duct tape holding together the sole of his shoe. As a consequence, after receiving special approval from the dean of the Graduate School, I resumed teaching as a means of bridging the gap between the fellowship and financial aid I was receiving and our actual cost of living. Although the teaching helped financially, it also meant I would be spending even less time with my son.

However, my son and I discovered an abundance of new opportunities and amazing experiences over the last year as a direct result of relocating for my doctoral program. One of the journeys we have recently embarked upon together is initiating a collaborative research project about graduate student single mothers and their children. When I say "collaborative," I mean Benjamin is my coresearcher; he interviews the children, and I interview the moms. We are interested in investigating how other single-mother-headed families are impacted by a mother's pursuit of a graduate education. What obstacles do they face? How do they negotiate them?

So far our research has led to two major realizations. First of all, it is extremely difficult to find participants. We chalk that up to the fact that it is extremely rare to find single mothers who are completing a graduate degree. Second, there are limits to our study because research alone will not produce change. Policy changes must also be pursued. In the interim, the possibility for change can happen in the space(s) between the individual and the institution, in day-to-day relational interactions and negotiations between different individuals at and within institutions. This change requires the awareness and participation of various members of academia, not just single mothers. It means that women entering universities as new graduate students who meet single mothers at campus events and professors with young pregnant women in their classes need to realize that ways in which they perpetuate, unconsciously or not, negative stereotypes about single mothers. It means that deans of graduate programs who bestow single mothers with fellowship awards need to listen when recipients speak of their unique constraints and to reevaluate the institution's expectations accordingly. It means that members of the academic community need to realize that the way we do things presently often has a way of precluding the participation of nontraditional students such as single mothers. This unfinished story is in need of collaborative revision.

HOW HIGHER EDUCATION CAN BECOME ACCESSIBLE TO SINGLE MOTHERS

In a recent conversation about the challenges I have faced as a single mother pursuing a higher education, my friend said to me, "You are not the first, you are not alone." It is true: I'm not the first single mom to pursue an advanced degree; there were women before me, and there are other single moms doing it right now. I know some of them. I am, however, the only single mother among the graduate students in my large department at a Research I university. In this sense, I am alone.

Yet I am also part of a local community of students and professors and part of a larger community of scholars. I contribute even though it is often difficult to do so in a system that wasn't designed for "girls like me." When I began pursuing my college education as a single mother, I wanted to prove that it can be done despite the stereotypes and cultural narratives that say otherwise and despite the very real material constraints that threaten success on an almost daily basis. However, there are many days when I honestly do not believe I will reach my goal — not because I'm not smart enough or because I lack the drive or desire, but because so many of the challenges and obstacles that single mothers face when pursuing a graduate degree reside in circumstances that we simply cannot change on our own.

This essay ends here, but I hope it is not the end of the story. I hope to finish my education. I hope to see more single mothers do the same thing. Won't you join me in finishing this story?

17

MAKING IT WORK

Success Strategies for Graduate Student Mothers

Erynn Masi de Casanova and Tamara Mose Brown

SEVERAL YEARS AGO the American Sociological Association (2004) published a research brief in response to sociology graduate students' and early career academics' commonly asked question, "When is the best time to have a baby?" The answer: there is no "best time" to have a baby because any combination of childbearing/child rearing and academic pursuits involves challenges and sacrifices. Yet given the disproportionate involvement of women in caregiving because of gender roles in our society, women's careers are more affected by parenthood than are men's (Hays 1996; Kennelly and Spalter-Roth 2006; Stone 2007a). In terms of the distribution of housework and child-care duties, little has changed since sociologist Arlie Hochschild first wrote about women's "second shift" (see, e.g., Hochschild and Machung [1989] 2003). As many social scientists now argue, it makes sense to think of "care work" as including care for elderly or disabled family members as well as the raising of children (Folbre 1994; England 2005); this definition becomes especially important as the U.S. population ages. Despite the possibility of viewing "mothering" as a practice rather than a role that only women can perform (Rothman 2005), and despite many academics' personal commitments to equality and feminist beliefs, in practice it is usually women who take on these caregiving roles in our families (Home 1998; Lynch 2008). The trade-offs required by academic careers are common to all disciplines, though the examples and advice presented in this chapter come from our experience in the social sciences.

This chapter outlines six steps that graduate students can follow in order to negotiate mothering while in school and negotiate school while mothering. Our suggestions also apply to graduate student fathers who are their children's primary caregivers, although the sexism in academia and unrealistic ideals of motherhood target women more directly (Thierry et al. 2007). We are careful not to generalize from our experience to that of all graduate student mothers and recognize that what worked for us might not work for everyone, given the varying levels of stigma attached to motherhood in different academic institutions (Thierry et al. 2007; Lynch 2008). Yet we feel confident that these strategies can help graduate students manage their studies, research, and roles as mothers despite the negative attitudes and practical obstacles that can make doing it all seem impossible. Before discussing our experiences, we want to make one thing clear. We are in favor of changes in social structures, norms, and institutions that would make graduate student mothers' lives easier. The advice in this chapter, however, is geared toward working within existing constraints (e.g., expensive or inaccessible child care or both), which can differ somewhat from person to person.

We begin with the following question: How can the demands of parenting and academia be reconciled? Doing coursework and dissertation research and at the same time working to pay the bills in graduate school are difficult even for nonparents. In addition, graduate school is not always a welcoming forum for discussions of parenting, especially for mothers (Kennelly and Spalter-Roth 2006). As recent Ph.D.s and mothers of two young children each, we are often asked—by fellow students, friends, and professors—how we managed to get through our doctoral program in five years. From the beginning of our graduate studies, we saw ourselves as being on a "turbo plan": with mouths to feed, we didn't have time, as some students did, to use graduate school to "find ourselves." We needed to find ourselves some jobs! When one child became two children, the motivation to finish grew even stronger. The logic seems counterintuitive, but having children made us more focused, efficient, and strategic in our approach to the intellectual and practical challenges of graduate school. We describe here some of the lessons we learned through trial and error on the path to the Ph.D.

DON'T MAKE EXCUSES

The ability to make excuses sometimes spares individuals from contending with life's demands. People make excuses for why something has not been finished on time, why they haven't achieved more in life, and why they can't manage both a career and family. Balancing a career in academia (which begins in graduate school) and family is not easy; it is often one of the most challenging aspects of a graduate student mother's life. After successfully finishing our own graduate program in five years while having children to care for, we feel that the less graduate student mothers turn to making excuses (despite the real challenges they face), the more they will gain the confidence needed to accomplish their goals.

As graduate students, we had to negotiate the everyday monotony of going to classes, attending colloquia and conferences, working as research assistants, teaching courses, completing research papers, and attempting to publish, which became incrementally more challenging once we added pregnancy, feeding, day care, and the time-consuming task of raising children. We are not claiming that all situations are alike; in fact, they are not because some graduate student mothers have partners to help them, whereas others are raising children on their own, but there are definite ways to negotiate completing graduate school and having children, especially for mothers, who have the added challenge of going through pregnancy.

In our sociology department, we heard a variety of excuses from graduate students. Students in our department (at a public university) were not usually fully funded and had to contend with the high cost of living in New York City, so most worked long hours to make ends meet. These graduate students often had to teach each semester to handle their living and academic expenses. In addition to hearing all students' complaints about the workload, we would hear mothers say: "The baby didn't sleep last night, so I couldn't get any work done," or "I am waiting for my family to come and help me so that I can get back to my work," or "I will postpone my graduation another year until the baby starts sleeping through the night." We often felt the same way but soon decided that we were not going to allow ourselves to fall into the trap of making excuses despite visible constraints. We are not proposing a strategy of what Karen Lynch (2008) calls "maternal invisibility": hiding the fact that we are mothers from professors and fellow students. We are suggesting that being seen as someone who is a mother and also an excellent and diligent student can benefit your reputation in grad school and beyond.

The truth is that no set of excuses will help us as students move forward, so the first suggestion for scaling this obstacle is to prepare ourselves mentally for the challenge during the months of pregnancy or the adoption process. Getting into the mindset of accepting that having children while in graduate school is what we planned for (or not) and that our life must now accommodate this new family structure was one of the first steps we took as graduate students, although we also realize that there are valid financial and social constraints for some student mothers. However, simply understanding this broader context helped us make a commitment that we would not make excuses for why we weren't getting the academic work done. As a consequence, we began to reshape our goals and outlook, but we didn't do it alone and sought help from others.

DON'T BE AFRAID TO ASK

Many times academics appear to have it all under control. After all, many of us have A-type personalities and feel as if we need to work at an absurd level of competence in solitude. What we didn't see as graduate students but now see as faculty members is the potential for partnership occurring behind the scenes. Graduate students often feel that they should know how to manage their academic life and parental roles, so they fear asking for help from those who have gone through the same process. However, graduate mothers should understand that others are willing to give advice and many want to help them achieve their goals. In addition, we have resources in our lives that may be able to help us such as other peers, partners, family members, neighbors, professors, and support groups found through university-based psychologists or counselors.

Tamara recalls asking her professors who had children how they navigated their careers, how they timed their children's births (though she didn't take their advice; her two children are thirteen and a half months apart), and how they coped with writing and child care. Although their extensive publishing record while raising children set the bar high, they advised her to see the dissertation as a process and not as one's life's work. The best advice she received was to wait until getting a tenure-track job to begin her life's work because at least she would be getting paid well to do it. Simply knowing that the dissertation was a process and an exercise in writing original research made it seem more manageable.

Remember all those times when someone said to you, "Oh, I will babysit for you," when you were pregnant? Well, now is your chance to take them up on it. Ask a neighbor to take the kids for a couple of hours, or find out if other parents participate in cooperative child care (swapping babysitting duties). If family members are willing to give you some of their time, let them help out. Explain to your partner, if you have one, what needs to happen in order to complete your coursework and dissertation and ask him or her to help you find the time to be productive at school and at home. After Tamara told her husband what she needed in order to complete her dissertation, which included long stretches of silence, he would take both kids to the park, go for a jog with them in the stroller, or take them to a museum. They would be out of the house for six hours on both Saturday and Sunday. For those who may not have weekends to write, there is still an opportunity to carve out blocks of time during which someone can help with child care. Asking for advice, help, or patience from the people in your life will help you complete your goals as an academic and a parent. Explaining clearly what it takes to finish your dissertation or other work is the first step, and then you can ask for what you need. It may not always work in your favor, but as one of our mothers said, "It never hurts to ask." Plus, once you're working as a faculty member, there is always the adage that gets repeated constantly: "If you don't ask, you don't get."

CULTIVATE A SUPPORT NETWORK

In planning ahead for the changes that will come about with your newly added family members, you should not only ask for help with child care but also cultivate a support network that is career focused. Graduate students and junior faculty can benefit from working with people with similar goals (e.g., completing projects or writing for publication). So many students get stuck in the ABD (all but dissertation) abyss because they attempt to work alone on their dissertations. This experience is not unique to parents, but it's easier for us to fall into this trap because we have the best reason in the world for not completing the degree: children.

Added support in the form of a writing group that meets regularly to discuss writing, research, and goal setting will help those attempting to complete a degree in a timely fashion. Pamela Richards's chapter in Howard Becker's *Writing for Social Scientists* (2007) helped us understand that all students go through moments of anxiety while writing, which is why it becomes critical to have multiple readers of your work. You simply cannot work in a vacuum. This support network will push you forward and give you the confidence needed to finish the dissertation.

Once ABD, we formed a dissertation writing group with our classmate Andrea Siegel, and we met every two weeks for five months with a low-stakes writing goal of five pages for every meeting. We often would produce a whole chapter, though, because five pages would get us into a writing groove that moved us past the original required number of pages. By the end of five months, we had written entire chapters and complete drafts of dissertations. Thus, we highly recommend finding fellow students on whom you can depend for maintaining consistency and who will actually read your work and give you critical feedback. By doing this, you will make the task of writing much easier. If you need to bring your child/children to a meeting, prepare your writing group ahead of time and negotiate that you go first so that when the children become agitated, you can leave early. If this happens, be sure to write an extensive email or follow up in person with added comments on others' work.

The support network does not need to end there. Graduate mothers can also find this type of support through campus organizations, parent groups, and even good relationships with faculty who understand the struggles of parenting while being an academic. Students need to surround themselves with people who will be positive, give them critical feedback, and work in a true partnership that will carry them through their career. Just remember that you should return the favor.

MAKE A SCHEDULE AND PLAN AHEAD

During her first semester of grad school, Erynn mapped out how she would progress through the doctorate program in sociology under ideal conditions (passing exams and courses on the first try, funding my research, progressing quickly). She set goals for each year, planning not only the "what" but also the "when." Below the timeline, she listed five to eight potential dissertation topics. As time went on, she ruled out unfeasible or uninteresting dissertation ideas and added new ones. Nothing was written in stone: if she hit a snag, she would make adjustments. Because of her commitment to finish in a timely fashion, she ultimately had to give up on finding external funding for her dissertation project. This meant dipping into her savings, getting bigger student loans, and spending less time in the research field. Knowing where she was headed, however, was useful, and she felt a sense of accomplishment each time she checked off one of her goals. This is just one way to approach short-

and long-term planning. Those of us with children have to be more organized and clearer about our progress through our graduate programs because it is easy to get bogged down in the everyday details of parenting.

Students often enter graduate school with no idea of their interests and no ideas for dissertation topics. Graduate student moms do not have this luxury! It is a good idea to develop a handful of potential topics by at least the second year. As Tamara was advised, the dissertation is a step toward a goal (graduating and obtaining a professional position), and although you should try to make it as good as possible, however "good" is defined in your discipline, you don't have to think of the dissertation as your life's work. If the research project develops into a lifelong passion, that is a wonderful by-product of the dissertation process, but not necessary for career success. Likewise, "progress, not perfection" is a great motto for moving forward and not getting stuck as you write your thesis.

BECOME A "CONNECTOR"

In *The Tipping Point*, author Malcolm Gladwell (2000) describes "connectors," people who make it their business to know people and who act as the "hubs" of social networks. If you try to become a "connector" while in graduate school, you will learn valuable networking skills and build the foundation for a future professional network. While in graduate school, we organized a range of informal student activities: pub outings, backyard barbeques, study groups, and writing groups. Being seen as an active member of the department can help compensate for times when you have to miss events because of a sick baby or rush out five minutes before class ends to relieve your babysitter. For instance, Tamara introduced Erynn to students who worked on topics similar to Erynn's, one of whom spoke in a course she was teaching and is now organizing a conference panel with her. Seek out other mothers in your graduate program or those who are students at other schools; you will sometimes find them to be equally motivated and eager to share their experiences and advice.

Honing those "connecting skills" can also be beneficial beyond your department and institution. If you see someone whose work interests you, send that person an email message or introduce acquaintances who work on the same issues. This is how academics find coauthors and create meaningful intellectual dialogue. It can also help once you enter the job market. And being a mother in academia can make you a special kind of "connector": seeking the wisdom of other mothers who have made it work (or are trying to do so) in your quest to create fulfilling career and home lives is helpful and a great way to build community as well.

THINK OF CREATIVE WAYS TO COMBINE RESEARCH AND PARENTING

This piece of advice is related to our experience as graduate students doing qualitative research in sociology; it would certainly be more difficult to incorporate children into research on nuclear physics or infectious diseases. But in the social sciences, mothers (and increasingly fathers) sometimes combine research and parenting: anthropologists take their children into fieldwork settings, linguists study their children's speech development, and psychologists gain insights into child development through spending time with their children. We were able to find ways to make research and parenting simultaneous and compatible, resulting in publishable work (de Casanova 2007, 2011; Brown and de Casanova 2009; T. Brown 2011).

For example, after countless hours of trying to ignore her son's favorite television shows (so she could get some work done already!), Erynn realized that she could put that time to good use. She noticed that children's programs that featured Spanish-speaking characters were an unexplored goldmine of data about different versions of multiculturalism in the media. She was soon taking notes on the ways the Spanish language was used and tied to ethnicity, and the result was a peer-reviewed article (de Casanova 2007). This form of research and publication is not always possible, but if there are ways to overlap aspects of our home lives with our academic lives, then we should identify these opportunities.

Trying to get out of the house with her fussy baby, Tamara discovered parks near her Brooklyn home and stumbled onto a fascinating social world. As she got to know some of the babysitters who visited the parks with the children they cared for, Tamara became interested in the work that these women—many of them immigrants—did and the ways their caregiving took place in both public and private spaces. She was able to gain access to this group and ended up combining caring for her child with fieldwork for her dissertation-turned-book about West Indian childcare providers in Brooklyn, New York (Brown 2011).

Becoming parents opened us up to new social settings and cultural products, which can become the source of research topics in the social sciences. We need to learn to take advantage of opportunities to combine parenting and research. Parenting can often produce insights that help us understand our world, which we can then share with others through our teaching, service, and research.

There are no perfect strategies and no "best" time to have a baby (although some do intentionally time the births of children), but, in reflecting on our experiences, we have identified some steps that graduate student mothers can use to "make it work." Despite the prevalence of negative attitudes toward students with children and the practical challenges of managing studies and research, graduate parents can devise useful strategies that they can continue to use throughout an academic career. Going against the odds outlined in the literature (Kennelly and Spalter-Roth 2006), both of us obtained tenure-track faculty positions straight out of graduate school, one at a doctorate-granting program and the other at a four-year institution. Our strategies have expanded beyond graduate school, and on the path toward tenure we now coauthor some of our work, such as this essay, taking turns on first authorship. This approach works because our research interests are related, and we know each other's strengths, weaknesses, and work ethic. We organize conference panels together instead of tackling such tasks alone, and we regularly read and comment on each other's writing.

It shouldn't be surprising that two mothers would bond over the shared experience of having children, but academic work tends to be seen as a solitary pursuit. Mothers have often organized collectively to improve their daily lives at home and work (Stephen 1997; Pardo 1998), and they can bring this sociability into the academic workplace. Strategies for success do not have to end with the suggestions made in this chapter. These six steps are only the beginning of what might easily be a hundred-point list; our aim here is to give graduate student mothers the confidence to make it work in graduate school and beyond.

18

ACADEMIC MOTHERS ON LEAVE (BUT ON THE CLOCK), ON THE LINE (AND OFF THE RECORD)

Toward Improving Parental-Leave Policies and Practices

Colleen S. Conley and Devin C. Carey

ACHIEVING A work–life balance is particularly challenging for women; mothers spend substantially more time than fathers engaged in caregiving, even when accounting for hours of paid employment (Bond et al. 2003; Hochschild and Machung 2003; O'Laughlin and Bischoff 2005). Because academic work is so pervasive, boundless, and demanding, often to the exclusion or detriment of family responsibilities, the challenges of the work–life balance are particularly salient for academic women (Drago and Williams 2000; American Association of University Professors [AAUP] 2001; Wolf-Wendel and Ward 2006). Despite increased rates of earning doctoral degrees, women are drastically underrepresented in tenured and administrative positions (Ottinger and Sikula 1993; AAUP 2001; Mason and Goulden 2002; Wilson 2004b). Among women who attain academic positions, more than half of those with children consider leaving academia, and turnover—including tenure denial—is higher among women, in particular those with children (McElrath 1992; Brown and Woodbury 1995; Mason and Goulden 2002; Yoest and Rhoads 2002). This problem is likely two directional: academic women are less likely to have children in the first place, even though they might want to, and those who do have children are less likely to survive in such a demanding career (Mason and Goulden 2002). Many have connected these problems to insufficient family-leave policies, such that academic women do not receive adequate resources—namely, paid, protected time—for establishing a manageable balance between work and family responsibilities (Finkel and Olswang 1995; Drago and Williams 2000; AAUP 2001; Comer and Stites-Doe 2006).

In response, some academic institutions have worked to develop family-friendly policies and benefits that promote the work–life balance for faculty. Although a wide variety of family-friendly policies and practices affects women in academia, this chapter focuses specifically on parental leave, which we define as a designated release from work time and obligations to adjust to a newly born, adopted, or fostered child. Furthermore, although family leave and work–life balance are important for women at all stages of an academic career, here we focus on policies and practices for faculty members. Finally, we concentrate on higher-education institutions in the United States, where family-leave policies are in particular need of improvement.

Academic institutions' parental-leave policies vary widely, and actual practices often deviate from official policies. Policies at U.S. institutions range from no paid leave to two academic terms at full pay, which if timed just so within a nine-month appointment can yield nine months or more "off." Without clear, consistent, mandated policies, women are often left to work out their individual leave situations with chairs and deans, which can bring about either supportive flexibility or an inequitable burden. Although some of their professional peers in other fields enjoy months of uninterrupted time to bond with a new child and adjust to the demands of parenthood, many academic women who are "on leave" are in fact still "on the clock"—teaching classes, mentoring students, and scrambling to meet scholarly deadlines and tenure expectations—while they juggle the constant responsibilities of nurturing a newborn. Even when leaves are available, many women fear stigma and career repercussions and thus avoid taking full advantage of leave policies by shortening their allowed leave, having summer babies, or delaying mothering until after tenure, which brings health and infertility risks (Ward and Wolf-Wendel 2004). Drawing on broad samples from academic institutions ranging from small teaching-oriented colleges to large research-oriented universities, this chapter explores the issues academic mothers face in negotiating parental leave by interweaving (1) a multidisciplinary body of theory and research on parental-leave policies and practices as well as their effects on academic women and institutions; and (2) personal accounts of navigating parental leave, which we gathered from more than fifty interviews and surveys of academic mothers and administrators. This synthesis, in turn, has generated recommendations for supportive policies that nurture the work–life balance to the benefit of both faculty and their institutions.

ON THE LINE AND OFF THE RECORD: PROBLEMS WITH FORMAL AND INFORMAL POLICIES

The United States lags far behind the majority of the developed world in paid family leave. Out of 173 countries studied by Jody Heymann, Alison Earle, and Jeffrey Hayes (2005), the majority provided fourteen weeks or more of paid family leave; the United States was one of only four countries that had no federally funded paid family leave. On the other end of the spectrum, Swedish parental leave includes up to sixty-eight weeks paid and an additional eighteen weeks unpaid for each child (Chronholm, Haas, and Hwang 2007). The U.S. Family Medical Leave Act of 1993 (FMLA), which provides up to twelve weeks unpaid leave per year, is inadequate as *parental* leave because it is unpaid, is not offered to all employees at all institutions, and does not cover nonbirth parents in domestic partnerships. Furthermore, it covers such a wide range of circumstances that can arise in the same year, such as health issues or elderly care, that women who have to use this leave when they encounter these other issues may be disqualified from taking time off after the arrival of a new child. Due to the federal Pregnancy Discrimination Act of 1978 (amended in 2005), institutions with paid disability leave might offer six weeks of paid leave following childbirth if authorized by a physician. However, some disability-leave policies do not take effect until after six weeks of disability, thus essentially excluding childbirth (Hollenshead, Sullivan, and Smith 2005). Even when disability or sick leave is paid, it is still inadequate as a parental-leave policy because it addresses the medical recovery of childbirth but not the personal needs of adjusting to parenthood and thus does not provide time off for nonbirth parents. One mother recalled: "[My university] had no official maternity leave policy, but I was eligible for disability leave. When asked to 'please describe what is wrong with you,' I had to write, 'I'm pregnant.' Classifying maternity as a medical disability was insulting to me and unfair to my nonbirth parent colleagues who were thus ineligible for leave." Addressing the lack of sufficient federal policies, some individual states and employers have worked to offer their own more generous paid parental-leave policies. However, the Center for the Education of Women's (CEW) 2007 national survey of higher-education institutions found that most have their employees take unpaid time off (as required by FMLA) or use sick, vacation, or disability leave (if they are eligible) to cover parental leave; only 18 percent offer distinct, paid, dependent-care leave (including parental leave), and 10 percent report no policy or accepted practice for maternity leave (3, 17).

Complicating the picture further, many institutions have ad hoc, informal, unspecified policies and practices, resulting in inconsistent and inequitable treatment. For example, one national survey revealed that leave beyond FMLA was "negotiable" at 60 percent of institutions (Hollenshead, Sullivan, and Smith 2005), and another reported that 23 percent of schools that do not offer paid leave have informal policies (Yoest 2004). One faculty mother noted that at her institution, "there are no set policies beyond FLMA. This is a huge problem [because] each mother-to-be has to negotiate, from a low-power position typically, for her accommodation, and the person she's negotiating with doesn't know what's reasonable." Another shared, "The college HR [human resources department] prefers to keep the policy unwritten. . . . [T]his really [tripped] me up because I couldn't learn what the policy actually was when I needed to know." Without clearly established and enforced institutionwide policies, individual leave situations fluctuate with the structure and resources of departments as well as with the personalities and negotiation styles of chairs, deans, and faculty members: some faculty members scrape by with the bare minimum or even less, and others make off with much more (Yoest 2004). Even administrators we interviewed noted great problems with "lack of consistency" and "inequity" due to informal or unclear policies at their institutions. Furthermore, despite knowing of colleagues who have negotiated additional benefits off the record, many women fear that their job status is on the line and thus hesitate to try to work out anything informally. One woman noted that in the absence of an official policy, "I have been afraid to ask for too much and only got what I needed when official people gave more generously." An astonishingly large proportion of women does not take advantage even of existing, formal policies often because they fear stigma or career repercussions, especially when they are pretenure (Finkel, Olswang, and She 1994; Finkel and Olswang 1995; Yoest and Rhoads 2002; Drago et al. 2006). Interestingly, interviews with higher-education administrators indicate that there may indeed be stigma attached to faculty's utilization of formal and informal policies (Yoest 2004). This contradiction between seemingly supportive work–family policies and actual workplace climate surrounding use of these policies is similar to trends found in other work settings (Kirby and Krone 2002). In addition, our own interviews revealed both stigmas and penalties for taking parental leave. One woman said she "was told by a tenured female faculty member on my first day on the job to not have children before tenure." When she had her second child in June, "I was told by my department chair that 'I had the summer off,' but to make sure that I was highly productive or the pregnancy would count against me toward tenure." Another aptly noted: "A lack of clarity about procedures can be a stressful experience for a woman who is trying to negotiate for herself and her family needs at a time when she may be feeling vulnerable, and may be . . . judged as a less serious academic." In sum, the ambiguity and inconsistency of parental-leave policies and practices make it difficult for both faculty and administrators to understand the rules, often resulting in inequality and resentment (Hollenshead, Sullivan, and Smith 2005).

ON LEAVE BUT ON THE CLOCK: STANDARD LEAVE POLICIES DO NOT FIT WELL WITH ACADEMIC WORK

The most common types of leave policies offered for raising children simply do not fit with the nature of academic positions and academic work. Because many academics do not receive sick or vacation time, they are not eligible for these paid-leave options for which staffs are often eligible (CEW 2005; Hollenshead, Sullivan, and Smith 2005). Furthermore, the highly specified, pervasive, and demanding nature of academic work typically means that faculty members still have several of their job responsibilities even while on leave, and thus unpaid FMLA and medical disability leave do not make sense in this context. Finally, the academic calendar, which commonly entails nine-month faculty contracts but expectations for year-round (and often unpaid) work on scholarly endeavors, poses specific challenges for faculty responsibilities, which family-leave policies must address.

The touted flexibility of academic work has been called an illusion, even a gilded cage: although some academic work is portable, its volume and nature are extremely demanding, thus posing great challenges for the work–life balance (Sorcinelli and Near 1989; Bailyn 1993; Ward and Wolf-Wendel 2004). As one woman put it, "I get to choose whatever sixty to eighty hours of the week I want to work!" Much of academic work—pursuing ongoing scholarly projects, running a research lab, presenting at conferences, writing grants and articles, meeting publication deadlines, mentoring student theses and dissertations—is so specialized and time sensitive that it cannot be put on hold or performed by a substitute during a leave of absence. In fact, many faculty-specific family-leave policies address only teaching responsibilities and omit scholarly, service, and administrative responsibilities from the leave provisions. Thus, even when leave is offered, faculty members often receive only a partial reduction in their workload.

A common theme in academic mothers' stories is that of being "on leave" but still "on the clock," both in terms of the big picture (the tenure clock) and on a smaller scale in the daily details of being an academic: "I did work at home throughout most of my leave"; "I worked until the night I went into labor. I returned to work part time . . . when [my baby] was two weeks old." Just as academic work bleeds into personal life at other times, academic mothers on parental leave commonly report spending hours a day engaged in work correspondence and meetings (phone, online, or face to face), student mentoring, scholarly projects, and service responsibilities in the early weeks following the arrival of a new child. One woman shared: "Out of a sense of obligation . . . I continued to read drafts of theses and dissertations and to have regular email contact with graduate students. I also had some phone and face-to-face meetings with them. My goal was to be sure that their progress was not held up by my leave." Another woman gave scholarly presentations at two national conferences during her maternity leave, noting, "I couldn't afford to have such a gap in my [curriculum vitae]." Yet another explained, "I had a substantial research program at the time I became pregnant. My department had no interest at all in how I was going to meet my research grant obligations. The granting bodies did not seem to have any policies or provisions for this circumstance. They simply expected the research to be delivered as promised. I felt pressured by colleagues and collaborators not to make a fuss about this. At the same time, none of my collaborators could take over my roles on the research projects, so I went on working on projects during my maternity leave." Just days after giving birth, another mother received reviews on a scholarly article that required her to spend hours a day holding her newborn as she sat in front of the computer, working to meet this deadline: "I had already invested five years into this project, so I couldn't just give it up now. There's no such thing as being on leave with this type of work." Indeed, even when faculty members are on leave, they are still expected to publish (Yoest and Rhoads 2002; Fothergill and Fetley 2003; Ward and Wolf-Wendel 2004). Being "on leave but on the clock" seems to be a pervasive problem for academic mothers due to universities' unspoken expectations. It deprives mothers of the opportunity to focus on essential parenting responsibilities, and in some cases it means that women are working without pay or against medical orders or both. One mother noted, "Toward the end of my leave,

I was told by HR [human resources] that I was not authorized to do any work, even from home, until my doctor signed my return-to-work papers. If only they had known how much I had worked during my 'leave.' They just didn't seem to get what academic work is like." These stories collectively speak to a pervasive struggle for balance among the equally consuming identities of being a mother and being an academic; integrating such "dualities" successfully seems to be a core tension for academic women (Gawelek, Mulqueen, and Tarule 1994, 196). Indeed, our own experiences and interactions with other academic mothers reinforce the tension of this balancing act.

Although much of an academic's scholarly work cannot be put on hold or performed by another person while he or she is on leave, teaching is one part of the job that might be covered most easily during a leave of absence. Faculty members get released from teaching for various reasons, such as scholarly leaves, for an entire academic term or more. However, parental leaves at U.S. institutions are typically for periods shorter than a semester, and, given the unreliability of due dates, faculty who need to take parental leave often encounter complicated logistical challenges in their teaching responsibilities. We heard from several women who taught right up until their children arrived—continually adjusting plans to transfer courses to colleagues—and then jumped back into teaching at the end of the semester, after being out of touch with the students and the flow of course material for several weeks. Some had to make their own arrangements to cover their teaching, sometimes piecing together colleagues to cover classes, which poses an unfair burden to all involved and may foster resentment among colleagues. We also encountered examples of women continuing to teach even when officially on leave: teaching class from home (in person, by phone, by Web cast), recording lectures to be played in class, or returning to the classroom after a few short weeks or even days. One woman recounted: "My graduate student covered my lectures for only three weeks. I was still required to answer emails, attend to students, and help with the grading. . . . It was made clear that my duties would not change because I gave birth." The 2005 CEW report highlights the discrepancy between traditional leave policies and academic teaching responsibilities. It notes, "If departmental coverage of term-long teaching responsibilities is not adequately addressed, traditional sick leave policies may require or pressure women to return to the classroom sooner than the six to eight weeks following childbirth that is considered to be good medical practice" (9). Aside from the burden to the faculty member "on leave," these shifts in who is teaching a class are incredibly disruptive for students' learning, as reflected in course evaluations (Baker and Copp 1997). In addition, such piecemeal arrangements pose challenges for substitute instructors, department chairs, and other administrators. Two administrators in our sample noted that it cost their universities the same to hire a replacement instructor for part or all of a semester as it does to arrange for substitutes; thus, it seems to make most sense—for all involved—to replace a faculty member in her courses for an entire term. By providing semester-long replacements for teaching in their parental-leave policies, academic institutions not only help faculty and administrators strike an equitable workload balance but also, as the University of Nebraska–Lincoln policy states, "assure continuity of instruction of students" (2009, para. 5).

The unique nature of faculty positions and academic work has prompted many institutions to offer family-leave policies specifically designed to accommodate faculty work. For example, Knox College's faculty handbook states: "The College's health plan allows six weeks of sick leave with pay. In interpreting this policy as it affects academic obligations, the College recognizes the special nature of faculty obligations on the term system by granting . . . one term of leave with pay" (2011, para. 13). In cases where parental leave does not cover an entire term, many institutions provide an additional modified-duties policy for faculty that releases or reduces their "teaching, research, or service load for a temporary period (usually a term or two) without commensurate reduction in pay," following the arrival of a new child (Hollenshead, Sullivan, and Smith 2005, 44). Besides addressing the logistical and teaching-continuity issues that affect administrators, replacement instructors, and students, these policies offer a fair workload for faculty members, who typically perform other aspects of their work while officially on parental leave.

ON THE BALL: RECOMMENDATIONS FOR SUPPORTIVE PARENTAL-LEAVE POLICIES

The American Psychological Association recently launched an initiative on work and families, offering suggestions for employers and policymakers that include paid family and maternity leave, noting that "implementing family friendly policies . . . is good business" (2004, 8). Similarly, the

AAUP advises, "The development and implementation of institutional policies that enable the healthy integration of work responsibilities with family life in academe require renewed attention" (2001, 220). Offering such policies not only improves faculty morale but is also likely to bring institutional benefits in recruiting and retaining quality faculty, which ultimately is most cost effective (Friedman, Rimsky, and Johnson 1996; University of Colorado–Boulder 2001; Williams and Norton 2008). Based on our review of theory and research on parental-leave policies and practices as well as on discussions we have had with faculty and administrators, the following recommendations may improve the work–life balance, with a cascade of positive effects for faculty and academic institutions. (For additional policy recommendations, see Drago and Williams 2000; AAUP 2001; Mason and Goulden 2002, 2004a; Ward and Wolf-Wendel 2004; Hollenshead, Sullivan, and Smith 2005; Smith and Waltman 2006; Williams and Norton 2008. For general work–life policy recommendations, see American Psychological Association 2004 and Halpern 2005b).

1. *Establish principles and practices that promote a work–life balance.* Being on leave but on the clock, not taking full advantage of leave policies for fear of career repercussions or stigma, and allowing a disconnect between policy and practice are deeply entrenched, pervasive problems in academia. These problems engender an incompatibility between academia and motherhood (Armenti 2004). Thus, an important first step in providing supportive parental-leave policies is to establish and promote a culture that supports a work–life balance and reduces the stigma of needing, wanting, and taking leave to tend to essential parenting responsibilities.

A work–life balance might broadly be defined as "sufficient time to meet commitments at both home and work," but it also includes one's perceptions of balancing roles and demands from work and home life (Guest 2002, 263) and of being supported at work as a person with a personal, family life (O'Laughlin and Bischoff 2005). Whether from objective, instrumental support or subjective, perceived support, work–life balance contributes to an employee's performance in both roles. Therefore, being sensitive to such role demands and conflicts creates an environment where women faculty members have the flexibility to realize themselves as mothers and academics equally.

The most supportive parental-leave policies have a guiding philosophy that focuses not on the medically or legally mandated business of providing benefits, but rather on the best practices of nurturing employees as whole people. For example, Harvard University's *Guidelines for Faculty Maternity and Paternity Leave* articulately states:

> The years during which scholars are under the most pressure to produce work of extraordinarily high quality are often the same years those individuals are, or wish to be, starting families. A system where academic success is incompatible with family life is undesirable because it discourages talented scholars from pursuing academic careers, and particularly because it disadvantages women, who often bear a larger share of parenting responsibility than do their male colleagues. To the maximum extent possible, Harvard University seeks to support faculty parents as they welcome new children into their families, whether by birth or adoption, by providing them with paid time off and opportunities for relief from their teaching duties. (2006, 1)

It is notable that even such a supportive statement as this specifically addresses only faculty teaching duties, which typically compose only 40 percent of a faculty member's responsibilities (Mancing 1991).

Faculty and administrators we spoke with at institutions with similarly supportive philosophies reported a positive work climate, a healthy balance between work and family, and better retention of faculty. One administrator noted that her institution is working to improve the policies and the culture of family leave by communicating such messages as the following: "Leave is not lost time; there is nothing to make up for. You're on leave; don't try to get work done; it will only make you crazy, and it's not fair." A more direct way to promote a culture of work–life balance is to take organizational measures to protect faculty leave time, such as by ensuring that teaching, advising, and service responsibilities are transferred over completely during parental leave and by removing parents on leave from all but the most essential institutional communications.

Institutions also can provide a tenure-clock stop automatically, not by request, and enforce evaluation standards to ensure that this practice is not adversely weighted in tenure and promotion decisions (Hollenshead, Sullivan, and Smith 2005; Smith and Waltman 2006). Other examples of parental-leave provisions that promote a supportive culture include Grinnell College's statement that "the College will provide staff for course replacements; . . . the College, not the parent, is responsible for finding a faculty member to teach these courses" (2009, 61). The Stanford School of Medicine has a paid, two-term teaching-reduction policy that states, "[Faculty] should not be required to assume extra burdens of teaching when they resume full-time work" (2000, para. 19). Such policies take concrete steps to ensure that faculty members get the leave to which they are entitled, without an actual or implicit burden to make up for these accommodations. The University of Maine's policy captures this message with the explicit promise that "no faculty member will be penalized for making use of this policy" (2009, para. 2). In sum, such messages and policy measures create and on some level mandate a supportive culture of work–life balance, reduce the stigma of taking leave, and ensure that faculty members receive a full and fair leave.

2. *Provide specific leave for parenting in its diverse arrangements.* At a minimum, institutions should offer specific parental-leave policies beyond sick, medical, and disability leave. Such policies regard the transition to parenthood as a unique life event—not as an illness, a medical procedure, or a disability—and ensure that faculty parents remain eligible for the same general benefits as their nonparent colleagues. Supportive, nondiscriminatory policies cover birth, adoption, and foster placements and include primary or coequal caregivers regardless of birthing status, gender, or marital and domestic partnership arrangements. For example, Massachusetts Institute of Technology's *Policy for Family Care for Faculty* states, "Faculty members, regardless of gender, who wish to spend the majority of their academic time on the care of and responsibility for a newborn child or a child newly placed with them for adoption or foster care will be released from teaching and administrative duties for one semester at full pay" (2006, para. 23). Such inclusive policies afford all faculty parents the opportunity to adjust to their new roles and increased responsibilities at home without jeopardizing their roles and responsibilities at work (see also Smith and Waltman 2006; Ecklund and Lincoln 2011).

3. *Provide paid leave or modified duties or both for at least a full academic term.* The majority of higher-education institutions offering paid parental leave do so under sick or disability leave and for birth mothers only (CEW 2005), and such policies typically apply to all employees at the institution. A more appropriate approach is to offer a faculty-specific paid parental-leave policy that accounts for the nature of faculty appointments (e.g., nine-month contracts, no vacation or sick time) and responsibilities (e.g., teaching on a semester system and performing service and scholarship as well, frequently outside of a nine-month appointment). The most fair and facilitative policies include paid leave for a certain period of time (most commonly twelve weeks or a full academic term, though sometimes up to

six months) as well as modified duties (e.g., no teaching, specifically for faculty) for an entire academic term or two. Other parental-leave policies, such as Vanderbilt University's, relieve faculty of all of their work obligations for a full semester, with full pay and benefits: "The faculty member shall be relieved of the obligation to teach . . . , relieved of research and scholarship expectations . . . , [and] relieved of all faculty service responsibilities, including committee work and student advising, for one semester" (2009, 145). The most supportive policies also allow the parent to choose the academic term during which to take the leave. Santa Clara University's policy states that leave can be taken anytime "within the first year following [childbirth,] adoption, or foster care placement" (2011, para. 3). Because faculty contracts vary from nine- to twelve-month terms, this policy makes leave equitable regardless of the time of year in which a faculty member welcomes a new child. We have encountered similar long-term paid leave or modified-duties policies at numerous institutions spanning the range from small to large and teaching to research oriented.

4. *Make policies and practices formal yet flexible.* Unless policies are clearly specified and consistently applied, inequities will persist within academic institutions, affecting morale and turnover, especially of faculty who are mothers. At the same time, it is important for institutions to provide some flexibility—in an overt, formalized way—to help individual faculty members achieve balance and optimize their potential as people and academics. One administrator we interviewed stated that "good policies must be malleable to individual circumstances," and another noted that even generous policies should be regarded as "minimum standards" to be applied more thoroughly on an individual basis. Recognizing that faculty—for a variety of personal, professional, medical, and familial needs—"benefit from the temporary opportunity to focus more attention on their personal lives," several institutions offer additional unpaid time off, reduced appointments or workloads, job-share appointments, or part-time accommodations that range from a semester to five years, or all of these options (Smith and Waltman 2006, 5).

Many of these changes cost nothing or very little to implement, and the initial costs of some changes pale in comparison to the price of recruiting and hiring new faculty (Friedman, Rimsky, and Johnson 1996; Davis et al. 2001; Jackson 2008). Indeed, on a broader scale across workplace settings, there is compelling evidence in favor of offering more family-friendly policies to the benefit of employees as well as employers (Halpern 2005a). Quality faculty ranks are worth investing in, as universities routinely do with start-up packages and other funding. Investing in family-friendly policies has a substantial payoff in terms of improving institutional climate as well as recruiting and retaining quality faculty who seek to balance their professional and personal lives (Williams and Norton 2008).

Improving parental-leave policies and practices can have a substantial impact on helping academic women achieve work–life integration. One woman summed up, "I did it. I did it all. The career, the babies, tenure, grants, conferences, committees, advising/mentoring students. . . . But the cost to me was huge. I have very little memory of my daughter [at some points], only pictures. . . . What I never achieved was a sense of balance. Perhaps that is too elusive in an academic career, at least for women. . . . It is possible, but it isn't easy, and it isn't for everyone." Academic institutions have an opportunity and a responsibility to invest in their faculty as academics and as people so that their faculty can progress as scholars while also thriving as parents. More important, universities and colleges become models for work environments at large. Well-balanced and satisfied employees succeed both at work and at home, and, as a result, their institutions succeed as well.

19

SUPPORTING ACADEMIC MOTHERS

Creating a Work Environment with Choices

Brenda K. Bushouse

AT AN ACADEMIC conference in 2009, I participated on a panel in which faculty described their career trajectories to aspiring graduate students and recent Ph.D.s. Until that day, I had not realized that I had a story to tell, but as I saw the reactions from the young, female graduate students and assistant professors and answered their questions, I realized that these women were aspiring to have my life. From their vantage point, I had attained the "holy grail" of tenure while mothering, with the added feature that my husband also attained tenure at the same institution. These women wanted to become mothers, they wanted tenure-track positions, and some of them also wanted tenure-track positions for their partners, but the goal that I had achieved seemed out of reach to them. As I reflected on my experience, I realized that it was not that long ago that I, too, thought the goal was unattainable. In this chapter, I intermix my personal history with the growing literature on tenure-track mothers in academia (Fox 2000; Gatta and Roos 2004; American Council on Education 2005; Wolf-Wendel and Ward 2006; Center for the Education of Women [CEW] 2007; O'Meara 2007; Jackson 2008; Mason 2009b; Misra, Templer, and Hickes-Lundquist 2010). After reviewing family-leave policies, I turn to the challenges of returning to work to discuss the range of options for modifying tenure-track appointments and the concomitant perils that accompany those choices. The chapter concludes with a discussion about the need for advocates to support successful implementation of family-leave policies and continued support throughout the tenure process.

My academic career began in 1998 with a tenure-track position at the University of Massachusetts–Amherst. I initially began as a lecturer but was promoted to assistant professor in 1999 when I completed my dissertation. The position was a joint appointment between the Department of Political Science and the newly created Center for Public Policy and Administration (CPPA), with teaching and service split between the two offices, although my tenure line is wholly within the Department of Political Science. When I began at the University of Massachusetts, there was not a spousal-hiring policy, but my husband fortunately had a postdoctoral fellowship at Indiana University and was able to telecommute from Amherst.

In 1998, I was in the enviable position of having a tenure-track position but faced an all too common thirty-something biological alarm clock. Because of my age, delaying childbirth until after tenure was not an option. Both my husband and I wanted children, and in 2001, two years into my tenure clock, we became the parents of twins we named Sophia and Maxwell. Three months after their birth, my husband began a tenure-track position at University of Massachusetts. My path to tenure was not assured, nor was it one that I would choose to traverse again. But for those attempting to travel the tenure track and at the same time mothering young children, supportive family-leave policies and the option for modified duties are critical to successfully attaining tenure. Those policies must be supported by an organization culture that recognizes such policies as "normal" rather than exceptions or unfair extensions to the six-year tenure clock.

I place my experience in a larger context of support policies for academic mothers. At the time, I thought that I was alone in my struggles and was unaware of the literature documenting that my experience was typical of mothers in rigid bureaucracies. Women who are both academics and mothers often feel that it is an individual "problem" rather than a structural problem, but the reality is that the university tenure system is not structured in such a way to be anything other than difficult for mothers and active fathers who strive to build their careers *and* care for children. The important work by Joan Acker (1990, 2006) makes it clear that structural inequality in organizations occurs across work environments. In the context of the university, inequality is built into the bureaucracies created with a long-standing male-centered model that make it tremendously difficult to achieve both motherhood and academic success. Yet if universities want to retain faculty and students who are also mothers, they must make policy changes to support these women. Just as important as the policy change is the shift in organization culture that must accompany those changes so that women have confidence that they can utilize the policies without sacrificing their career advancement.

Because universities run on semesters or quarters, parental leaves need to reflect that cycle. Six-week leaves make no sense in the middle of the semester, and not everyone can time their pregnancies so that they deliver in the summer, although many of us try. But even with parental leave tied to semesters or quarters, women returning to work need support during the intensive early parenting period, in particular women who are also on the tenure track. In order for this support to be given, there needs to be a modification of duties as an alternative to the six-year, cookie-cutter mold for tenure.

FAMILY-LEAVE POLICIES

In 2001, the University of Massachusetts implemented a broadly inclusive, far-reaching parental-leave policy for the Massachusetts Society of Professors (MSP), the union representing faculty and librarians. Prior to the family-leave policy, expectant mothers had to negotiate on a case-by-case basis with their department chairs, who in turn had to cover courses without any funding from the administration to hire temporary replacement faculty. A woman could use accrued sick leave and vacation time or could apply for unpaid leave under the federal Family Medical Leave Act, which provides for twelve weeks of unpaid leave. But if her accrued leave ran out or she was unable to forgo pay, she had to return to work. The MSP had been advocating for parental leave for several years, but in the 2001 collective-bargaining process faculty and department chairs testified at a daylong event in support of family-leave policy, which then became a catalyst to advance change. When I testified, I was very pregnant with twins, and I made the argument that without a delay in the tenure decision year it would be impossible for me to remain in a tenure-track position. My department chair was a sixty-five-year-old bachelor who also testified about the difficulty he had just experienced in negotiating maternity leaves for two assistant professors in my department due to the absence of a standard policy. Listening to the testimony throughout the day, I was struck by the inequity: some women had negotiated a full-semester leave, whereas one woman had returned to the classroom a mere two weeks after giving birth. The testimony was a pivotal moment in which the administration first "heard" the extreme inequality across the campus. The administration soon afterward agreed to include a maternity-leave policy in the MSP contract. Better yet, the union pushed for and won the inclusion of both fathers and mothers in the policy (Page and Clawson 2009). Those efforts resulted in a family-leave policy that provided tenure-track faculty (and contract faculty with a minimum of six years at the university) with one semester of paid leave and a one-year delay in the tenure decision year for the birth or adoption of a child (MPS 2010).

The University of Massachusetts family-leave policy is unusual in that it provides one paid semester of leave and a one-year tenure delay for both academic mothers and fathers. Recent survey data from the University of Michigan finds that tenure-clock extensions are now prevalent in "doctoral extensive" higher-education institutions. In fact, the survey data indicate that between 2002 and 2007, tenure extensions had the highest growth in family-friendly policies across all types of higher-education institutions. For "doctoral extensive" institutions, stopping the clock is available in 92 percent of the survey respondents, with other institutions ranging between 44 to 69 percent (CEW 2007, 8). However, it is important to note that the circumstances that produce eligibility and the frequency of use are not standard, and some institutions offer the policy on an ad hoc basis rather than as a formal policy.

Far less common is a paid semester of leave. In the 2007 CEW survey, only 29 percent of higher-education institutions (across the varying types) provided paid leave beyond the disability period (17). The term *disability period* stems from the 1978 Pregnancy Discrimination Act, which requires that women affected by pregnancy, childbirth, and related conditions receive benefits equivalent to those of other employees who are unable to work for other medical reasons. If a university provides less paid time off for pregnancy than for other medical conditions, it is an illegal practice. The minimum amount of leave is six weeks for an uncomplicated birth. But academics' lives revolve around the academic calendar. Having six weeks of leave and yet having to return to complete the term does not absolve the faculty member from designing the course and coordinating with the substitute instructor. Researchers at the University of Virginia found that they had to develop a broader definition of leave policies to capture the range of policies that exist in academia. For a 2004 survey of 168 randomly selected universities by the Family, Gender, and Tenure Project at the University of Virginia, the definition of paid parental leave was "more than 6 weeks of full relief of the faculty member's teaching duties with full pay, or half relief of teaching for one full semester or quarter, or full relief with half pay for a semester or quarter" (Yoest 2004, 6). The survey results for the 153 universities responding indicated that 35 percent of the sample provided no parental leave, and only 18 percent provided a full semester, with the rest providing less than a semester of leave. The remaining universities provided a range of policies: 25 percent allowed faculty to use accrued sick leave, 8 percent provided six weeks or less, 9 percent provided between eight and twelve weeks leave, 5 percent provided half pay or reduced teaching (Yoest 2004, 7).

In my personal experience, the tenure-clock extension and paid leave were absolutely crucial for me to return to my tenure-track position, but the birth of my twins occurred eighteen days shy of the policy start date. However, I petitioned the administration, and on June 12, 2001, I became the first MSP member to receive one paid semester of leave and a one-year delay in my tenure clock. The leave was necessary to bond with my children, but it was also a medical necessity. I had severe post partum complications and was quite weak when the fall semester started. Had I been required to return to teaching, I would have resigned. My husband began his tenure-track position that fall and was technically eligible to take a parental leave, but he did not feel comfortable taking it, particularly because he was starting a new position. His experience is mirrored by a University of Massachusetts survey in which it was found that only about half of the eligible parents took parental leave (O'Meara 2007). At the University of Massachusetts and other universities, data indicate that the main factor in an individual's decision to take leave or stop the clock is department culture (Drago et al. 2001; Mason 2005; O'Meara 2007; Misra, Templer, and Hickes-Lundquist 2010). Although I did take a parental leave, it was thus not without cost.

RETURNING TO WORK: THE NEED FOR MODIFIED DUTIES AND CULTURAL SHIFTS

When I returned to campus for the spring semester, a senior male colleague complained that my maternity leave had provided me with a "sabbatical" that was unfair to the other assistant professors. Exactly when I could have conducted research during the newborn months was beyond my comprehension; I remember having to choose between eating, sleeping, and showering in the forty-five minutes between feedings. I have heard mothers talk about working on research during naptimes, but there were no downtimes for me to squeeze in academic work given that I had twins. Unfortunately, my experience in returning to work was not unlike that of prior generations of academic mothers. Similar to women in Mary Gatta and Patricia Roos's (2004) study, I felt marginalized due to a department culture in which I was compelled to separate public and private spheres and therefore forced to view the family–work tension as an individual problem rather than as something to be addressed collectively.

The university has an important role to play in creating an environment in which academic mothers have the support they need to succeed. Such a call for change occurred in 2001 when the American Association for University Professors (AAUP) published its revised Statement of Principles on Family Responsibilities and Academic Work. The new version called for "substantial changes in policy and, more significantly, changes in academic culture" to transform the academic workplace into one that supports family life (2001, para. 8).

Yet to transform the academic workplace, there must be funding for research to determine which changes will be effective. In 1994, the Sloan Foundation created the Workplace, Work Force, and Working Families Giving program, which was related to its Economic Performance and Quality of Life program area. Since its inception, the foundation has awarded funding for six academic Centers on Working Families at the University of California (both Berkeley and Los Angeles), Cornell University, the University of Michigan, and Emory University, as well as for a combined center between the University of Chicago and Michigan State University. Sloan funded grants for other types of institutions and more than one hundred research projects related to work and family. The foundation's funding enabled the collection of basic data on the lives of working parents that has since informed policy development.

To address the challenges of recruitment and retention of women in science and engineering, the National Science Foundation and the National Academies also began new funding programs. The National Science Foundation created the ADVANCE grant program in 2004 to fund research aimed to positively impact universities' ability to recruit and retain women in science and engineering. In addition, the National Academies funded the project Women in Science and Engineering: A Guide to Maximizing Their Potential. Completed in 2006, the project generated two reports focusing on the necessary components for women to succeed in science and engineering. Both of these funding programs brought resources and attention to the work environment of women in the sciences with the aim of eliminating barriers and raising the profile of the need for family-friendly policies.

The University of California drew much attention to the need to change university policies and culture with the publication of its Sloan-funded 2002–2003 Faculty Work and Family Survey. The survey of 4,400 tenure-track faculty revealed, among other findings, that women between the ages of thirty and fifty put in the longest combined hours of professional, care-giving, and household responsibilities. The research led to the creation of the University of California Faculty Family Friend Edge to advance poli-cies, programs, services, and benefits to improve the work–family environ-ment. The University of California now leads the country with its adoption of family-friendly policies.

Since the passage of family-leave policies at the University of Massachu-setts, attention has shifted to creating an environment that allows faculty to attain a work family balance. The Joint Administration–MSP Work–Life Committee conducted a campuswide study funded by MSP, the Provost's Office, and the Office of Faculty Development. The study led to recom-mendations for policy changes including modified duties, the extension of paid parental leave to all faculty (it is currently restricted to tenure-track and senior lecturers), and the expansion of on-campus child care (Lundquist et al. 2010). The study also addressed the need for cultural change so that participation in these policies becomes the norm rather than the exception. Strategies for culture change include educating deans, chairs, and person-nel committees about family-friendly policies, publicly recognizing depart-ments with faculty who utilize the policies, making tenure extensions for new parents automatic so that junior faculty are not forced to request them, normalizing parental leave by adding a category in the annual review that all faculty members submit, and featuring the university's family-friendly environment in recruiting efforts (Lundquist et al. 2010). These recommen-dations are spot on for reducing the stress on families and on women faculty in particular, who are balancing work and family responsibilities.

When new mothers return to the workplace, they may have physically healed from childbirth, but they are still experiencing the intense demands of caring for infants. Many need a reprieve from a full academic research, teaching, and service load. There are some promising developments in the direction of creating "modified duties," which can be permanent or tempo-rary arrangements and include reduced teaching or part-time tenure-track appointments. The CEW survey found that all respondents with modified-leave policies provide them for tenured and tenure-track faculty and that 69 to 100 percent also provide the benefit for non-tenure-track faculty (2007, 13). Leading the country, the University of California allows part-time appointments on a temporary or permanent basis (Mason 2009b).

In the early years of my children's lives and my tenure-track appointment, there were no options for part-time work or reduced teaching loads at the University of Massachusetts. If there had been a part-time option, it would have been the best choice for me. Trying to fulfill tenure expectation and motherhood pushed me to my breaking point. Part of the challenge for me was that I needed to start new research projects. Yet due to the complexities of child care, I was not able to attend academic conferences or undertake fieldwork to start a new research project. Without the networking required to launch my career, I missed a window of opportunity to build connections that could have led to collaborations, publication opportunities, and research projects, yet all of these things are crucial for career success (Prpic 2002; McBrier 2003). For me, the dual pressures of tenure track and motherhood were too much, and I needed to step away from the tenure process.

In the summer of 2003, when my children were two, I became acting director of the CPPA. In the fall, an opportunity arose for me to continue in an administrative capacity when the CPPA's associate director took an extended medical leave. The CPPA needed the help, and I found that I needed the administrative position to stop the tenure clock and relieve me from the pressure to publish. The "administrative leave" essentially bought out one course per semester from the Department of Political Science, which effectively reduced my teaching load from the standard two–two to a one–one. In exchange, I provided administrative support and developed new programs. Even though I was still working full time, the administrative work allowed me to achieve some balance between work and home because it removed the nagging pressure to publish. During this time period, I fully engaged in the administrative work and seriously considered leaving my tenure-track position. It is important to note that I was still formally on the tenure track and that my department was not aware that I was considering leaving my appointment. It was not until the third semester of administrative leave, when the associate director returned to CPPA, that I needed to make a choice. By that time, my children were three, and I decided to restart my tenure clock.

The modified duties included in the CEW survey and other published sources do not encompass the type of administrative leave that I was able to utilize to stop and resume the tenure clock again. For many academic mothers, an administrative leave might not be desirable because it would reduce time available for their research. For me, it was a lifeline that allowed me space to breathe and regain perspective on my academic career.

THE CATCH-22 OF MODIFIED DUTIES

The challenge for a pretenure faculty member in taking a part-time option or other modified-duty arrangement is the risk to her tenure portfolio and its assessment. Pretenure faculty who choose a modified-duty option may be regarded as less committed to their research agendas. Because these policies are relatively unchartered territory, there are no comprehensive data on the number of tenure-track faculty who work part-time, but there is some evidence that pretenure faculty are reluctant to participate. A 2002–2003 University of California survey found that 75 percent of female professors with children said they were interested in part-time options; however, the reality was that few actually took the option after it became available in 2006 (Wilson 2008). Although assistant professors with children may need part-time appointments or other modified-duty arrangements, risk-averse faculty may not want to pioneer new paths to tenure (Mason 2009b).

The challenge for me when I returned from modified duties to a full-time faculty position was the belief among some of my department colleagues that my tenure clock had "gone long." My administrative leave for CPPA, despite technically providing a release from research expectations, created a perception that I was not a committed scholar, as evidenced by my willingness to do administrative work and the gaps in my publishing record. It was unclear to me at the time whether my department would support my tenure case even if I managed to publish at a level expected for tenure. Because my trajectory did not mirror any other faculty in the department, and I would exceed the standard six-year tenure time frame, I felt considerable stress about my prospects. My experience of high stress levels in trying to balance tenure pressures and family responsibilities mirrors findings in published studies (Acker and Armenti 2004).

My tenure stress increased exponentially when I underwent my pretenure review in 2004 (in the fourth year of my tenure clock, but my sixth year at the university). The general guidance from the department was to shift from publishing articles to writing a book. Prior to that time, I had planned to publish only articles because my dissertation was not appropriate for a book. Yet colleagues who supported my case strongly encouraged me to acquiesce to department norms and publish a book. Based on their advice, I made the decision to shift to a new book project; this decision was particularly challenging because it would involve extensive field research and a tight deadline.

One of the reasons I undertook such an ambitious project was that I felt particularly passionate about the topic: the creation of state universal preschool policies. My passion for the topic was in direct response to the choices I faced as a parent. I was fortunate to have the income to purchase high-quality preschool for my children, but I knew that others did not, and I strongly believe that all children should have access to high-quality early education and care regardless of family income. Several states had passed legislation creating universal preschool programs, and I wanted to understand how they succeeded. With renewed enthusiasm for research, I was able to secure two internal grants that funded my fieldwork in six states (Georgia, Illinois, New York, Oklahoma, Tennessee, and West Virginia). Although I had a full two–two teaching load, my department allowed me to experiment with a two-and-a-half-hour undergraduate course that met only once per week. Combined with my graduate CPPA course, I taught 2 two-and-a-half-hour courses on the same day, which provided flexibility for fieldwork, travel, and writing.

On the home front, several developments helped me focus my energy on my book project. My children were now in preschool, potty trained, and moving out of the constant-care phase of the infant and toddler years. The intense pull factors I felt when they were infants and toddlers were giving way to an appreciation of their need for socialization and education. I still felt tremendous guilt being separated from them, as so many working mothers do, but the feeling was less pervasive. My experience is mirrored by research by Mary Fox (2000) on the high productivity levels of women with pre-school-age children. Second, my husband had been awarded tenure, which both reduced the general household stress level and had an unexpected positive impact on my motivation to achieve tenure. Our dream since graduate school had been to achieve two tenured faculty positions in the same geographic location, and now the "holy grail" was within reach. I found myself invigorated and excited about my new research project and fully focused my energy on that goal. What had once seemed unattainable now seemed possible. Third, I had important support from family. My parents accompanied me on research trips to help with child care or came to my home when I traveled. While I worked late into the night for more nights than I care to remember, my husband took care of the children. My mother-in-law supported me extensively by reading drafts and providing moral support. With their assistance, I was able to concentrate my energy on completing the book project. But it is important to note that even with research funding, a concentrated teaching schedule, and supportive family, I sacrificed considerable sleep (and my health) to complete the project. Sandra Acker and Carmen Armenti's (2004) study aptly titled "Sleepless in Academia" clearly indicates that I was not alone in this pattern. For the women surveyed in their study, sacrificing sleep was their main strategy to achieve their goals, as it was for me.

By my tenure decision year in 2006–2007, I was on track to complete the book and had secured an advance contract for publication with a good university press. However, in the course of my research, I realized that if I could have an additional year, I would be able to extend the analysis to include the role of foundation funding in advancing universal preschool policies. I knew this inclusion would significantly strengthen the book and wanted to pursue it, but the challenge was how to do it and not risk tenure. With the exception of my parental leave, I had been working full-time at the University of Massachusetts since 1998, which meant that I was technically due for sabbatical (applications for sabbatical may be filed every six years at the university). However, I was concerned about negative perceptions in my department if I took a sabbatical prior to tenure. It would have been the best option had the policy been in place and the culture been supportive.

Through a combination of serendipity and overt support from the CPPA director, I was granted a one-year administrative leave to assist CPPA in the transition to a new director. The founding director stepped down to become the chair of the Political Science Department, and the incoming director was relatively new to the university and agreed that additional administrative support would ease the transition. I was granted a one-course release in exchange for the administrative work. Because this release was counted as "administrative leave," my tenure clock was stopped for the year.

During that same year, I was awarded a Center for Research on Families Faculty Fellowship that helped to launch my post-tenure research program.

The fellowship provided a one-course reduction to enable the faculty member who received it to apply for grants. As part of that fellowship, I applied for several awards and was successful in two of my applications. One of the awards funded sabbatical research in New Zealand, and the other was a two-year, nonresidential fellowship that led to the development of a new research project. When I came up for tenure in 2007–2008, my book *Universal Preschool: Policy Change, Stability, and the Pew Charitable Trusts* was forthcoming with the State University of New York Press (Bushouse 2009); several of my articles had been published, and more were in the pipeline; and I had a new funded sabbatical research project and a fellowship that would lead to developing my second major research project.

Yet even with my research accomplishments, my tenure case could have turned out differently if I had not had advocates who could explain why my tenure-track appointment started in 1999 but my tenure decision year was not until 2007. Senior faculty in my department and in CPPA who provided a supporting tenure letter framed the additional time on the tenure clock as a positive rather than negative. They were able to do this in part because of published research on women faculty's career trajectories that demonstrated the long-run productivity of women who become mothers. An example of research that was fundamental in making this case is John Long's (1992) longitudinal study of scientific productivity differences between men and women professors, in which he found that whereas men start their careers with higher rates of productivity than women, the reverse occurs at the end of careers, with women's productivity outpacing men's.

In addition, my department had changed significantly in the years leading up to my tenure decision year. The generation of white males with wives at home and 1950s attitudes about women had largely retired and were replaced with junior faculty with small children and senior female faculty who fully understood the intense pressures that assistant professors who are mothers of young children experience. My department also had a chair that actively supported junior faculty, especially new parents. These changes and the additional support made all the difference in my tenure case. The reality is that my curriculum vitae did not look like the typical Research I university assistant professor's CV. As Mary Ann Mason (2009b) persuasively argues, if we are committed to supporting women in academia, then we must be willing to accept that there are gaps in CVs, allow for tenure clocks to "go long" and be flexible with modified duties. The difficult task ahead is to alter university culture so that these changes are not interpreted as individual failings but rather expected accommodations for faculty with family responsibilities.

As academics, we move for jobs, and that often takes us far from extended family. Every working woman has to develop her support structure. Some hire college student babysitters, a nanny, or au pair; others have a stay-at-home spouse; and still others piece together a patchwork of arrangements (Jackson 2008). These fundamental structures in our lives allow us to function on a daily basis. However, although support outside of work is crucial, it is insufficient if the workplace does not allow us to succeed by creating policies that support parental leave and modified duties. Even with those policies in place, if the work culture does not welcome participation in those policies, mothers will be hesitant to use them to get the support they need.

Now that I have tenure, I am thankful to have been able to see my way through to the other side. My children are now nine years old, and I find that I can balance work and family much better at this stage of my career and their stage of development. I love my children, I love my work, and I am thankful for having both in my life. Yet at many points during those early years, I did not think I would get to this place. Without the family-leave policy at the University of Massachusetts, I could not have continued in a tenure-track position. But it is important to note that the family-leave policy was just the beginning of the support I needed to succeed. The administrative leaves with the CPPA were crucial in allowing me a reprieve from the pressure to publish. Without the option of an administrative leave, I have no doubt that I would have left my tenure-track position. And finally, when my case for tenure was presented, it was critically important that senior faculty who understood the dual demands of academia and motherhood presented my case to my department and to higher levels in the university to counteract negative perceptions of gaps in my publishing record, modified duties, and "going long." Mothers need parental leave, but they also need support throughout their pretenure years to help them cope with the intense dual demands of academia and child rearing; otherwise, we will lose far too many of them to the "leaky pipeline" (Jackson 2008), and the academy will be the poorer for it.

EPILOGUE

Final Reflections

Mari Castañeda and Kirsten Isgro

A DECADE into the twenty-first century, the ideals of a stable job market and family-friendly policies are in disarray due to the near U.S. economic meltdown and the dismantling of public-policy initiatives birthed during the civil rights movement. Over the three years we have been working on this book project, large grassroots uprisings have taken place around the world, and people are justifiably upset about the deep inequities in society. Much of the current financial crisis we see on Wall Street is reverberating in our academic halls as well (Ross 2009). It is statistically complicated to compare senior executive and chief functional officers at public and private colleges and universities with the various ranks of professors, lecturers, staff, and students across disciplines. However, the average presidential pay rose faster than full-time faculty salaries from 2007 to 2011, with the average increase being 11.5 percent for the former compared to 5.4 percent for the latter (American Association of University Professors [AAUP] 2011). According to a 2010–2011 survey conducted by the College and University Professional Association for Human Resources, median base salary for a president/CEO at a single institution ranged from $167,895 at community colleges to $385,000 at doctorate-granting institutions (2). The average annual salary of full-time faculty members in 2010–2011 across institutions and academic rank was one-quarter or less of administrative salaries (AAUP 2011). Staff salaries are unfortunately also low.

Long-time scholar and commentator on higher education and activism Cary Nelson has noted that the increasingly bloated salaries of higher-education administrators is at the expense and exploitation of part-timers, grad-uate employees, and campus support staff. He notes, "Higher education has adopted the robber baron values of late nineteenth-century capitalism: treat workers as disposable and do everything possible to maximize profits; be-have like nothing else matters" (1997, 252). As AAUP president, Nelson is well aware of how such exploitation erodes higher education's moral status. At a time when unions in general are in decline in the United States and academic unions in particular are under attack (as witnessed in the state of Wisconsin in 2011), there is undoubtedly concern for many of us working and studying at colleges and universities across the country. As some of the authors in this book discussed, academic unions have played an important role in addressing some of the inequities that parents (mothers in particu-lar) face in the academy. The decline of unions and limited collective-bar-gaining capabilities should be a significant concern for faculty. In 2011, the Chronicle of Higher Education ran a special forum on the future of faculty unions ("Forum" 2011), suggesting that this period is a historical moment of state and local economic downturns and large-scale corporatization. Inter-estingly, absent from this forum was any discussion as to how the assault on unions and public education is not only classed, but also highly gendered and racialized. In short, it is a critical time for mothers in the academy to speak up—hence the need for this book.

The statistics shared throughout this book refer to the fact that many women (and mothers) make up a larger portion of the contingent and part-time workforce in academia, even at a time when more women and stu-dents of color are entering college. In many ways, this trend is a sign of per-haps the larger restructuring of education within a global marketplace. In this context, learning is treated as an undersold commodity and students as consumers of a weightless product. As the mothers' narratives in this collec-tion attest, we are living with multiple and contradictory relations of power in the policies and practices of higher education. Some of these practices are of our own making, but others are deeply embedded in our institutions' academic structures and organizational cultures. In fact, many of the in-stitutional biases and injustices shared by the authors here reveal that the "power of dominant ideological systems lies in the ability to *construct the very terms upon which we stake our resistance*" (Cotera 2010, 335, emphasis in original). The personal stories of mothers working in academia allow us to see "schooling relationally" (Apple 1996, 4). That is, we bear witness to how education is fundamentally connected to the struggles and compromises related to the domination of and resistance to bureaucratization as well as to the ill treatment that exists in the larger society (Tuchman 2009; Cotera 2010).

The struggles faced by women in the academy manifest themselves in the chapter authors' discourses. Although it may be perceived that a "rhetoric of choice" is present in the chapters, to situate each of the women's narratives in this anthology as involving "private choices" is to miss the larger neoliberal ideals and values that focus so much on the individual as a way to divert larger oppressive structures. Choice can certainly operate as a strategy for women to maintain a feeling of being independent and liberated agents free of gender constraints of prior generations, but it also has detrimental effects (McCarver 2011). Our choices do not occur in isolation because we often make them accompanied by social pressures and judgments as well as by institutional rules. As Virginia McCarver notes in her analysis of discourses about career, motherhood, and family, "Choice rhetoric can be dangerous to women because it obscures a reality of limited choices, assigns blame and individual responsibility to women alone for the outcome of their choices" (2011, 33). In the context of faculty members' finding their departments threatened with downsizing or closure or having limited parental-leave policies or child-care options or being denied tenure or earning less than their male colleagues, it becomes apparent that "choice" may simply be a way to guise a series of poor alternatives and double-binds that working mothers find themselves facing in academia and beyond. Rather than discuss some of the choices women have made as mothers working in academia, some of the authors in this volume have employed what can be viewed as a "rhetoric of sacrifice," which addresses what these women forfeited as a result of gender inequity beyond their control. And although the rhetoric of sacrifice may be considered as less empowering, it can be a useful concept for exposing the structural absence of good choices (McCarver 2011). Cultural narratives that highly value individual freedom and personal autonomy are laden with narrow scripts of gendered experiences of work and family, and women who embody motherhood have a series of limiting alternatives, especially when the latter are compared to the choices available to men. The rhetoric of choice is held in tension with recognition of barriers and oppression that many mothers experience in academia. Thus, when we as parents discuss the partial choices, the institutional and social limitations, and the career paths and opportunities we may forfeit as a result of child rearing, we as contributors to this anthology are calling into question and are resisting how "sacrifices" are often expected and lauded by institutionalized motherhood. As communication scholars and editors of this anthology, we want to challenge the sacrifice of perfect motherhood and would rather heed to Virginia McCarver's call to turn on its head the "rhetoric of sacrifice[,] [which] may serve to address issues of gender inequity concerning family and work as well as possible additional alternatives to the rhetoric of choice" (2011, 37).

Beyond the rhetoric of choice and sacrifice, what this collection's *testimonios* reveal is the larger project of making "campuses moral workplaces" (Nelson 1997, 258). There have been stories in these pages about women who refuse to be isolated from their colleagues or to act as agents of oppression toward their students, staff, or other faculty. There are other stories where women have experienced overt hostility from other academic women. Some women have successfully created alternative networks and space within the academy where they can share their learning, teaching, and coping strategies. Some women have figured out how to find allies for the task of balancing the intersectional identity "mother in the academy." Social transformation is slow, yet the stories shared by the fierce female scholars in this anthology reveal the hope as well as the diversity of the struggles and triumphs surrounding motherhood in academia.

REFERENCES

Acevedo, L. D. A. 2001. Daughter of bootstrap. In Latina Feminist Group, ed., *Telling to live: Latina feminist testimonios*, 139–147. Durham: Duke University Press.

Acker, J. 1990. Hierarchies, jobs, bodies: A theory of gendered organizations. *Gender and Society* 4 (2): 139–158.

——. 2004. Gender, capitalism, and globalization. *Critical Sociology* 30 (1): 17–41.

——. 2006. Inequality regimes: Gender, class, and race in organizations. *Gender and Society* 20 (4): 441–464.

Acker, S. and C. Armenti. 2004. Sleepless in academia. *Gender and Education* 16 (1): 3–24.

Adair, V. C. and S. L. Dahlberg. 2003. *Reclaiming Class: Women, poverty, and the promise of higher education in America*. Philadelphia: Temple University Press.

Airini, [no initial], S. Collings, L. Conner, K. McPherson, B. Midson, and C. Wilson. 2011. Learning to be leaders in higher education: What helps or hinders women's advancement as leaders in universities. *Education Management Administration & Leadership* 39 (1): 44–62.

Aisenberg, N. and M. Harrington. 1998. *Women of academe: Outsiders in the sacred grove*. Amherst: University of Massachusetts Press.

Alicea, M. 1997. "A chambered nautilus": The contradictory nature of Puerto Rican women's role in the social construction of a transnational community. *Gender & Society* 11 (5): 597–626.

Allison, J. 2007. Composing a life in twenty-first century academe: Reflections on a mother's challenge. *NWSA Journal* 19 (3): 23–46.

American Association of University Professors (AAUP). 2001. Statement of principles on family responsibilities and academic work. Retrieved from http://www.aaup.org/AAUP/pubsres/policydocs/contents/workfam-stmt.htm.

——. 2006. *AAUP Faculty Gender Equity Indicators*. Washington, D.C.: AAUP. Retrieved from http://www.aaup.org/NR/rdonlyres/63396944-44BE-4ABA-9815-5792D93856F1/o/AAUPGenderEquityIndicators2006.pdf.

——. 2010. *No refuge: The annual report on the economic status of the profession 2009–2010*. Washington, D.C.: AAUP. Retrieved from http://www.aaup.org/NR/rdonlyres/AFB34202-2D42-48B6-9C3B-52EC3D86F605/o/zreport.pdf.

——. 2011. Faculty salaries vary by institution type, discipline. *Chronicle of Higher Education*, April 11. Retrieved from http://chronicle.com/article/Faculty-Salaries-Vary-by/127073.

American Council on Education. 2005. *An agenda for excellence: Creating flexibility in tenure-track faculty careers: Executive summary*. Washington, D.C.: American Council on Education. Retrieved from http://www.acenet.edu/bookstore/pdf/2005_tenure_flex_summary.pdf.

——. 2007. *The unifying voice for education annual report 2008*. Washington, D.C.: American Council on Education. Retrieved from http://staging.acenet.edu/Content/NavigationMenu/About/AnnualReport/2007AnnualReport.pdf.

American Federation of Teachers (AFT). 2011. *Promoting gender diversity in the faculty: What higher education unions can do*. Washington, D.C.: AFT. Retrieved from http://www.aft.org/pdfs/highered/genderdiversity0511.pdf.

American Psychological Association. 2004. *Public policy, work, and families: The report of the APA presidential initiative on work and families*. Washington, D.C.: American Psychological Association. Retrieved from www.apa.org/work-family.

American Sociological Association. 2004. *The best time to have a baby: Institutional resources and family strategies among early career sociologists*. Washington, D.C.: American Sociological Association. Retrieved from http://www.asanet.org/galleries/default-file/RBbaby.pdf.

Amnesty International. 2010. *Deadly delivery: The maternal health care crisis in the USA*. London: Amnesty International Secretariat.

Andrade, R. and H. L. González Le Denmant. 1999. The formation of a code of ethics for Latina/Chicana scholars: The experience of melding personal lessons into professional ethics. *Frontiers: A Journal of Women Studies* 20:151–160.

Anzaldúa, G., ed. 1995. *Making faces, making soul / Haciendo caras*. San Francisco: Aunt Lute Books.

——. 2007. *Borderlands / La frontera: The new mestiza*. 3rd ed. San Francisco: Aunt Lute Books.

Apple, M. 1996. *Cultural politics and education*. New York: Teachers College Press.

Aranda, E. M. 2007. *Emotional bridges to Puerto Rico: Migration, return migration, and the struggles of incorporation*. Lanham, Md.: Rowman and Littlefield.

Archer, L. 2010. "We raised it with the head": The educational practices of minority ethnic, middle-class families. *British Journal of Sociology of Education* 31 (4): 449–469.

Armenti, C. 2004. Women faculty seeking tenure and parenthood: Lessons from previous generations. *Cambridge Journal of Education* 34 (1): 65–83.

Bailey, T. M. and W. J. Hussar. 2009. *Projections of education statistics to 2018.* Washington, D.C.: National Center for Education Statistics, U.S. Department of Education. Retrieved from http://nces.ed.gov/pubs2009/2009062.pdf.

Bailyn, L. 1993. *Breaking the mold: Women, men, and time in the new corporate world.* New York: Free Press.

Baker, P. and M. Copp. 1997. Gender matters most: The interaction of gendered expectations, feminist course content, and pregnancy in student course evaluations. *Teaching Sociology* 25 (1): 29–43.

Bannerji, H. 1995. *Thinking through: Essays on feminism, marxism, and anti-racism.* Toronto: Women's Press.

Bartlett, A. 2006. Theory, desire, and maternity: At work in academia. *Hecate* 32 (2): 21–33.

Bassett, R. H., ed. 2005. *Parenting and professing: Balancing family work with an academic career.* Nashville: Vanderbilt University Press.

Bazillion, R. J. and C. L. Braun. 2001. *Academic libraries as high-tech gateways: A guide to design and space decisions.* 2nd ed. Chicago: American Library Association.

Becker, H. S. 2007. *Writing for social scientists: How to start and finish your thesis, book, or article.* 2nd ed. With a chapter by P. Richards. Chicago: University of Chicago Press.

Belcastro, A. and V. Purslow. 2006. An integrative framework: Meeting the needs of the new-traditional student. Paper presented at the Meeting of the Association of American Colleges and Universities, Chicago, November 9–11.

Belkin, L. 2003. The opt-out revolution. *New York Times*, October 26. Retrieved from http://www.nytimes.com/2003/10/26/magazine/26WOMEN.html?pagewanted=all.

Benjamin, L., ed. 1997. *Black women in the academy: Promises and perils.* Gainesville: University Press of Florida.

Bennetts, L. 2007. *The feminine mistake: Are we giving up too much?* New York: Hyperion Press.

Benson, P. L., A. R. Sharma, and E. C. Roehlkepartain. 1994. *Growing up adopted: A portrait of adolescents and their families.* Minneapolis: Search Institute.

Berry, T. and N. Mizelle. 2006. *From oppression to grace: Women of color and their dilemmas within the academy.* Sterling, Va.: Stylus.

Beverley, J. 2005. Testimonio, subalternity, and narrative authority. In N. Denzin and Y. Lincoln, eds., *The Sage handbook of qualitative research*, 3rd ed., 547–557. Thousand Oaks, Calif.: Sage.

Block, J. 2007. *Pushed: The painful truth about childbirth and modern maternity care*. New York: DaCapo Press.

Bond, J. T., C. Thompson, E. Galinsky, and D. Protas. 2003. *The 2002 national study of the changing workforce*. New York: Families and Work Institute.

Bonner, F. 2001. Addressing gender issues in the historically black college and university community: A challenge and call to action. *Journal of Negro Education* 70 (3): 176–191.

Bose, C. and E. Acosta-Belen. 1995. *Women in the Latin American development process*. Philadelphia: Temple University Press.

Boyd, R. L. 2007. Historically black colleges and universities and the black business elite. *Sociological Perspectives* 50 (4): 545–560.

Brooks, A. K. 2000. Transformative learning in the lives of women. In E. Hayes and D. D. Flannery, eds., *Women as learners: The significance of gender in adult learning*, 139–154. San Francisco: Jossey-Bass.

Brooks, D. and R. P. Barth. 1999. Adult transracial and in-racial adoptees: Effects of race, gender, adoptive family structure, and placement history on adjustment outcomes. *American Journal of Orthopsychiatry* 69:87–99.

Brophy, P. 2005. *The academic library*. 2nd ed. London: Facet.

Brown, B. W. and S. A. Woodbury. 1995. Gender differences in faculty turnover. *Upjohn Institute Staff Working Paper* 95 (34): 1–9.

Brown, R. L. and A. A. Amankwaa. 2007. College females as mothers: Balancing the roles of student and motherhood. *ABNF Journal* 18 (1): 25–29.

Brown, R. and A. Perlesz. 2008. In search of a name for lesbians who mother their non-biological children. *Journal of GLBT Family Studies* 4:453–467.

Brown, T. M. 2011. *Raising Brooklyn: Nannies, childcare, and Caribbeans creating community*. New York: New York University Press.

Brown, T. M. and E. M. de Casanova. 2009. Mothers in the field: How motherhood shapes fieldwork and researcher–subject relations. *Women's Studies Quarterly* 37 (3–4): 42–57.

Brown-Claude, W., ed. 2009. *Doing diversity in higher education: Faculty leaders share challenges and strategies*. New Brunswick, N.J.: Rutgers University Press.

Bryant, E. 2008. European nations offer incentives to have kids. *San Francisco Chronicle*, August 10. Retrieved from http://www.sfgate.com/cgi-bin/article.cgi?f=/c/a/2008/08/10/MNTQ11UVLJ.DTL&type=moms.

Budig, M. J. and P. England. 2001. The wage penalty for motherhood. *American Sociological Review* 66:204–225.

Burrelli, J. 2008. *InfoBrief SRS: Thirty-three years of women in S&E faculty positions*. NSF08-308. Arlington, Va.: National Science Foundation.

Burnham, L. 1985. Has poverty been feminized in black America? *Black Scholar* 16 (2): 14–24.

Büscher, A., B. Sivertsen, and J. White. 2010. *Nurses and midwives: A force for health*. Geneva: World Health Organization.

Bushouse, B. 2009. *Universal preschool: Policy change, stability, and the Pew Charitable Trusts*. Albany: State University of New York Press.

The business of being born. 2008. DVD. Burbank, CA: New Line Home Entertainment.

Castañeda, M. and M. Hames-Garcia. Forthcoming. Breaking the associate professor glass ceiling. In S. Fryberg and E. Martinez, eds., *Engaging our faculties: Faculty of color and university administrators on diversity and excellence in higher education*. New York: Palgrave Macmillan.

Center for Disease Control and Prevention. 2005. QuickStats: Mean gestational age, by plurality, United States. MMWR 2008;57:09(238). Retrieved from http://www.cdc.gov/Features/dsAvgPregnancyDuration.

Center for the Education of Women (CEW). 2005. *Family-friendly policies in higher education: Where do we stand?* Ann Arbor: University of Michigan. Retrieved from http://www.cew.umich.edu/sites/default/files/wherestand.pdf.

——. 2007. *Family friendly policies in higher education: A five-year report*. Ann Arbor: University of Michigan. Retrieved from http://www.cew.umich.edu/sites/default/files/ReduxBriefFinal5-1.pdf.

Chang, G. 2000. *Disposable domestics: Immigrant women workers in the global economy*. Cambridge, Mass.: South End Press.

Chávez, M. 2012. Autoethnography, a Chicana's methodological research tool: The role of storytelling for those who have no choice but to do critical race theory. *Equity & Excellence in Education* 45 (2): 334–348.

Chodorow, N. 1978. *The reproduction of mothering: Psychoanalysis and the sociology of gender*. Berkeley: University of California Press.

Choo, H. Y. and M. M. Ferree. 2010. Practicing intersectionality in sociological research: A critical analysis of inclusions, interactions, and institutions in the study of inequalities. *Sociological Theory* 28 (2): 129–149.

Christian, B. 1989. *Black feminist criticism, perspectives on black women writers*. New York: Pergamon.

Chronholm, A., L. Hass, and P. Hwang. 2007. *Sweden*. London: International Network on Leave Policy and Research. Retrieved from http://www.leavenetwork.org/lp_and_r_reports/country_notes/Sweden.published.aug_2007.pdf.

Clark, J. 1970. Motherhood. In T. C. Bambara, ed., *The Black Woman*, 75–86. New York: Washington Square Press.

Clawson, D. and N. Gerstel. 2002. Caring for young children: Child care in Europe and the United States. *Contexts* 1 (4): 28–35.

Clifford, G. J. 1983. Shaking dangerous questions from the crease: Gender and American higher education. In J. S. Glazer, E. M. Bensimon, and B. K.

Townsend, eds., *Women in higher education: A feminist perspective*, 135–174. Needham Heights, Mass.: Ginn Press.

Coiner, C. and D. H. George, eds. 1998. *The family track: Keeping your faculties while you mentor, nurture, teach, and serve.* Urbana: University of Illinois Press.

Colbeck, C. L., A. F. Cabrera, and P. T. Terenzini. 2001. Learning professional confidence: Linking teaching practices, students' self-perceptions, and gender. *Review of Higher Education* 24 (2): 173–191.

Cole, J. B. and B. Guy-Sheftall. 2003. *Gender talk: The struggle for women's equality in African American communities.* New York: Ballantine Books.

Collay, M. 2002. Balancing work and family. In J. M. Cooper and D. D. Stevens, eds., *Tenure in the sacred grove: Issues and strategies for women and minority faculty*, 89–106. New York: State University of New York Press.

College and University Professional Association for Human Resources. 2011. CUPA-HR salary survey finds 1.4 percent increase over last year in overall median base salary for senior-level administrative positions in higher education. Press release. Retrieved from http://www.cupahr.org/surveys/files/salary2011/NFSS11ExecutiveSummary.pdf.

College and University Work/Family Association. n.d. Mission. Retrieved from http://www.cuwfa.org/mc/page.do?sitePageId=23837&orgId=cuwfa.

Collins, P. H. 1994. Shifting the center: Race, class, and feminist theorizing about motherhood. In E. N. Glenn, G. Chang, and L. R. Forcey, eds., *Mothering: Ideology, experience, and agency*, 45–65. New York: Routledge.

——. 2000. *Black feminist thought knowledge, consciousness, and the politics of empowerment.* New York: Routledge.

——. 2002. Toward a new vision: Race, class, and gender as categories of analysis and connection. In M. Kimmel and A. Ferber, eds., *Privilege: A reader*, 332–348. Boulder: Westview Press.

——. 2005. *Black sexual politics: African Americans, gender, and the new racism.* New York: Routledge.

Colón, A., M. Mulero, L. Santiago, and N. Burgos. 2008. *Estirando el peso: Acciones del ajuste y relaciones de genero ante el cierre de fabricas en Puerto Rico.* Puerto Rico: Centro de Investigaciones Sociales, Universidad de Puerto Rico.

Colón-Warren, A. and I. Alegria-Ortega. 1998. Shattering the illusion of development: The changing status of women and challenges for the feminist movement in Puerto Rico. *Feminist Review* 59 (Summer): 101–117.

Combahee River Collective. 1982. A black feminist statement. In G. T. Hull, P. B. Scott, and B. Smith, eds., *But some of us are brave*, 13–22. New York: Feminist Press.

Comer, D. R. and S. Stites-Doe. 2006. Antecedents and consequences of faculty women's academic–parental role balancing. *Journal of Family Economy Issues* 27:495–512.

Correll, S. J., S. Benard, and I. Paik. 2007. Getting a job: Is there a motherhood penalty? *American Journal of Sociology* 112 (5): 1297–1338.

Cotera, M. 2010. Women of color, tenure, and the neoliberal university. In A. Nocella, S. Best, and P. McLaren, eds., *Academic repression: Reflections from the academic industrial complex*, 328–336. Oakland, Calif.: AK Press.

Crenshaw, K. 1994. Mapping the margins: Intersectionality, identity politics, and violence against women of color. In M. A. Fineman and R. Mykitiuk, eds., *The public nature of private violence*, 93–118. New York: Routledge.

Crittenden, A. 2001. *The price of motherhood: Why the most important job in the world is still the least valued.* New York: Henry Holt.

——. 2007. The mommy tax. In S. J. Ferguson, ed., *Shifting the center: Understanding contemporary families*, 698–708. New York: McGraw Hill.

Crittenden, D. 1999. *What our mothers didn't tell us: Why happiness eludes the modern woman.* New York: Simon and Schuster.

Crosby, F. 1991. *Juggling: The unexpected advantages of balancing career and home for women and their families.* New York: Free Press.

Crowley, J. and S. Curenton. 2011. Organizational social support and parenting challenges among mothers of color: The case of mocha moms. *Family Relations* 60 (1): 1–14.

Dallow, J. 2004. Reclaiming histories: Betye and Alison Saar, feminism, and the representation of black womanhood. *Feminist Studies* 30 (1): 74–113.

Davies, C. B. 2007. "Con-di-fi-cation": Black women, leadership, and political power. In S. M. James, F. S. Foster, and B. Guy-Sheftall, eds., *Still brave: The evolution of black women's studies*, 392–412. New York: Feminist Press.

Davis, A. 1981. *Women, race, and class.* New York: Random.

——. [1971] 1995. Reflections on the black woman's role in the community of slaves. In B. Guy-Sheftall, ed., *Words of fire: An anthology of black feminist thought*, 200–218. New York: New Press.

Davis, R. H., T. Gleeson, E. Hu-DeHart, W. Kintsch, W. Liston, D. Norman, and J. Wescoat. 2001. *Faculty recruitment and retention task force report.* Boulder: University of Colorado. Retrieved from http://www.colorado.edu/academicaffairs/pdf/fac_recruit_task_force_2001.pdf.

DeBerry, K. M., S. Scarr, and R. Weinberg. 1996. Family racial socialization and ecological competence: Longitudinal assessments of African-American transracial adoptees. *Child Development* 67:2375–2399.

De Casanova, E. M. 2007. Spanish language and Latino ethnicity in children's television programs. *Latino Studies* 5 (4): 455–477.

——. 2011. *Making up the difference: Women, beauty, and direct selling in Ecuador.* Austin: University of Texas Press.

Delgado, R. 1989. Storytelling for oppositionists and others: A plea for narrative. *Michigan Law Review* 87 (8): 2411–2441.

Delgado Bernal, D. 1998. Using a Chicana feminist epistemology in educational research. *Harvard Educational Review* 68 (4): 555–582.

——. 2001. Learning and living pedagogies of the home: The mestiza consciousness of Chicana students. *Qualitative Studies in Education* 14 (5): 623–639.

——. 2002. Critical race theory, Latino critical theory, and critical raced–gendered epistemologies: Recognizing students of color as holders and creators of knowledge. *Qualitative Inquiry* 8 (1): 105–126.

Delgado Bernal, D. and O. Villalpando. 2002. An apartheid of knowledge in academia: The struggle over "legitimate" knowledge of faculty of color. *Equity and Excellence in Education* 35 (2): 169–180.

Demichelis, S. and J. W. Weibull. 2008. Language, meaning, and games: A model of communication, coordination, and evolution. *American Economic Review* 98 (4): 1292–1311.

Deresiewicz, W. 2011. Faulty towers: The crisis in higher education. *The Nation*, May 23.

Dewey, K. G. 2001. Nutrition, growth, and complementary feeding of the breastfed infant. *Pediatric Clinics of North America* 48 (1): 87–104.

Dominguez, V. R. 1994a. Differentiating women/bodies of knowledge. *American Anthropologist* 96:127–130.

——. 1994b. A taste for "the other": Intellectual complicity in racializing practices. *Current Anthropology* 35:333–348.

Douglas, S. and M. Michaels. 2004. *The mommy myth: The idealization of motherhood and how it has undermined all women.* New York: Free Press.

Dowd, N. E. 2010. Asking the man question: Masculinities analysis and feminist theory. *Harvard Journal of Law & Gender* 33 (2): 415–430.

Drago, R. and C. L. Colbeck. 2004. Research on the workplace: A focus on academia. *Network News from Sloan Work and Family Research Network* 6.1. Retrieved from http://wfnetwork.bc.edu/The_Network_News/6-/TNN6-1_Drago.pdf.

Drago, R., C. L. Colbeck, K. D. Stauffer, A. Pirretti, K. Burkum, J. Fazioli, G. Lazzaro, and T. Habasevich. 2006. The avoidance of bias against caregiving: The case of academic faculty. *American Behavioral Scientist* 49: 1222–1247.

Drago, R., A. C. Crouter, M. Wardell, and B. S. Willits. 2001. *Final report to the Alfred P. Sloan Foundation for the Faculty and Families Project.* Working Paper no. 01-02. University Park: Pennsylvania State University, March 14.

Drago, R. and J. C. Williams. 2000. A half-time tenure track proposal. *Change* 32 (6): 46–51.

Duany, J. 2010. Reconstructing racial identity: Ethnicity, color, and class among Dominicans in the United States and Puerto Rico. In P. W. Scher, ed., *Perspectives on the Caribbean: A reader in culture, history, and representation*, 94–110. Chichester, U.K: Wiley-Blackwell.

Duquaine-Watson, J. M. 2007. "Pretty darned cold": Single mother students and the community college climate in post–welfare reform America. *Equity & Excellence in Education* 40:229–240.

Ecklund, E. H. and A. E. Lincoln. 2011. Scientists want more children. *PLoS ONE* 6 (8): 1–4.

Elenes, C. A., F. E. González, D. Delgado Bernal, and S. Villenas. 2001. Introduction: Chicana/Mexicana feminist pedagogies: *Consejos, respeto y educación* in everyday life. *International Journal of Qualitative Studies in Education* 14 (5): 595–602.

Ellis, C. and A. Bochner. 2000. Autoethnography, personal narrative, reflexivity: Researcher as subject. In N. Denzin and Y. Lincoln, eds., *The Sage handbook of qualitative research*, 2nd ed., 733–768. Thousand Oaks, Calif.: Sage.

Ellis, E. 2001. The impact of race and gender on graduate school socialization, satisfaction with doctoral study, and commitment to degree completion. *Western Journal of Black Studies* 25 (1): 30–45.

Ellison, K. 2005. *The mommy brain: How motherhood makes you smarter.* New York: Basic Books.

England, P. 2005. Emerging theories of care work. *Annual Review of Sociology* 31:381–399.

Epstein, A. 2007. *The business of being born.* New York: Barranca Productions.

Espiritu, Y. L. 2003. *Home bound: Filipino American lives across cultures, communities, and Countries.* Berkeley: University of California Press.

Evans, E. and C. Grant, eds. 2008. *Mama, PhD: Women write about motherhood and academic life.* New Brunswick, N J: Rutgers University Press.

Feinbloom, R. 2000. *Pregnancy, birth, and the early months: The thinking woman's guide.* 3rd ed. New York: Perseus.

Fernandez-Kelly, M. P. 1983. *For we are sold, I and my people: Women and industry in Mexico's frontier.* Albany: State University of New York Press.

Feyrer, J. and B. Sacerdote. 2008. Will the stork return to Europe and Japan? Understanding fertility within developed nations. *Journal of Economic Perspectives* 22 (3): 3–22.

Finkel, S. K. and S. G. Olswang. 1995. Child rearing as a career impediment to women assistant professors. *Review of Higher Education* 19 (2): 123–139.

Finkel, S. K., S. G. Olswang, and N. She. 1994. Childbirth, tenure, and promotion for women faculty. *Review of Higher Education* 17 (3): 259–270.

Fisher, G. 2007. "You need tits to get on round here": Gender and sexuality in the entrepreneurial university of the 21st century. *Ethnography* 8 (4): 503–517.

Flanagan, C. 2006. *To hell with all that: Loving and loathing our inner housewife.* New York: Little, Brown.

Flores, J. and S. Garcia. 2009. Latina *testimonios*: A reflexive, critical analysis of a "Latina space" at a predominately white campus. *Race, Ethnicity, and Education* 12 (2): 155–172.

Fogg, P. 2003. Why some women quit their coveted tenure-track jobs. *Chronicle of Higher Education*, June 13. Retrieved from http://chronicle.com/article/Family-Time/5114.

Folbre, N. 1994. *Who pays for the kids? Gender and the structures of constraint.* New York: Routledge.

———. 2001. *The invisible heart: Economics and family values.* New York: New Press.

Fordham, S. 1993. Those loud black girls: (Black) women, silence, and gender "passing" in the academy. *Anthropology & Education Quarterly* 24 (1): 3–32.

Forum: The future of faculty unions. 2011. *Chronicle of Higher Education*, July 24. Retrieved from http://chronicle.com/article/Forum-The-Future-of-Faculty/128305.

Fothergill, A. and K. Feltey. 2003. "I've worked very hard and slept very little": Mothers on the tenure track in academia. *Journal of the Association for Research on Mothering* 5 (2): 7–19.

Fox, M. F. 2000. Gender, family characteristics, and publication productivity among scientists. *Social Studies of Science* 35 (January 1): 131–150.

Freeman, C. 2001. Global as feminine:masculine? Rethinking the gender of globalization. *Signs* 26 (4): 1008–1037.

Freeman, C. and R. T. Cohen. 2001. Bridging the gap between economic development and cultural empowerment: HBCUs' challenges for the future. *Urban Education* 36:585–596.

Friedan, B. [1963] 1997. *The feminine mystique.* New York: Norton.

Friedman, D. E., C. Rimsky, and A. A. Johnson. 1996. *The college and university reference guide to work–family programs.* New York: Families and Work Institute.

Furstenberg, F. 2010. Diverging development: The not-so-invisible hand of social class in the United States. In B. Risman, ed., *Families as they really are*, 276–294. New York: Norton.

García, A. 2005. Counter stories of race and gender: Situating experiences of Latinas in the academy. *Latino Studies* 3 (2): 261–273.

Garey, A. 1999. *Weaving work and motherhood.* Philadelphia: Temple University Press.

Gaskin, I. M. 2003. *Ina May's guide to childbirth.* New York: Bantam Books.

Gasman, M. 2007. Swept under the rug? A historiography of gender and black colleges. *American Educational Research Journal* 44 (4): 760–805.

Gatta, M. L. and P. A. Roos. 2004. Balancing without a net in academia: Integrating family and work lives. *Equal Opportunities International* 23:124–142.

Gawelek, M. A., M. Mulqueen, and J. M. Tarule. 1994. Woman to woman: Understanding the needs of our female students. In S. M. Deats and L. T. Lenker, eds., *Gender and academe: Feminist pedagogy and politics*, 179–198. Lanham, Md.: Rowman & Littlefield.

Gee, M. and S. M. Norton. 2009. Improving the status of women in the academy. *Thought and Action* 25:163–170.

Gerson, K. 1985. *Hard choices: How women decide about work, career, and motherhood.* Berkeley: University of California Press.

Gerson, K. and J. A. Jacobs. 2007. The work–home crunch. In S. J. Ferguson, ed., *Shifting the center: Understanding contemporary families,* 678–682. New York: McGraw Hill.

Gerstel, N. 2011. Rethinking families and community: The color, class, and centrality of extended kin ties. *Sociological Forum* 26 (1): 1–20.

Gewirth, A. 1998. *Self-fulfillment.* Princeton, N.J.: Princeton University Press.

Gibbons, L., J. M. Belizean, J. A. Lauer, A. P. Betrán, M. Merialdi, and F. Althabe. 2010. *The global numbers and costs of additionally needed and unnecessary cesarean sections performed per year: Overuse as a barrier to universal coverage.* Geneva: World Health Organization.

Gilbert, N. 2008. *A mother's work: How feminism, the market, and policy shape family life.* New Haven, Conn.: Yale University Press.

Gildersleeve, R. E., A. M. Kuntz, P. A. Pasque, and R. Carducci. 2010. The role of critical inquiry in (re)constructing the public agenda for higher education: Confronting the conservative modernization. *Review of Higher Education* 34 (1): 85–121.

Gladwell, M. 2000. *The tipping point: How little things can make a big difference.* New York: Little, Brown.

Glass, J. and S. B. Estes. 1997. The family responsive workplace. *Annual Review of Sociology* 13:289–313.

Goeke, J., E. J. Klein, P. Garcia-Reid, A. S. Birnbaum, T. L. Brown, and D. Degennaro. 2011. Deepening roots: Building a task-centered peer mentoring community. *Feminist Formations* 23 (1): 212–234.

Goffman, E. 1963. *Stigma: Notes on the management of spoiled identity.* New York: Simon and Schuster.

González, J. C. 2007. Surviving the doctorate and thriving as faculty: Latina junior faculty reflecting on their doctoral studies experiences. *Equity and Excellence in Education* 40 (4): 291–300.

Grinnell College, Academic Affairs and Dean of the College. 2009. *Grinnell College faculty handbook.* Grinnell, Iowa: Grinnell College. Retrieved from http://web.grinnell.edu/dean/Handbook/FacultyHandbook.pdf.

Guest, D. E. 2002. Perspectives on the study of work–life balance. *Social Science Information* 41:255–279.

Gumport, P. 1990. Feminist scholarship as a vocation. *Higher Education* 20 (3): 231–243.

Guy-Sheftall, B., ed. 1995. *Words of fire: An anthologist of black feminist thought.* New York: New Press.

Gyure, D. A. 2008. The heart of the university. *Winterthur Portfolio* 42 (2–3): 107–132.

Haleman, D. L. 2004. Great expectations: Single mothers in higher education. *International Journal of Qualitative Studies in Education* 17 (6): 769–784.

Halpern, D. F. 2005a. How time-flexible work policies can reduce stress, improve health, and save money. *Stress and Health* 21 (3): 157–168.

——. 2005b. Psychology at the intersection of work and family: Recommendations for employers, working families, and policymakers. *American Psychologist* 60 (5): 397–409.

Hamilton, B. E., J. A. Martin, and S. J. Ventura. 2009. Births: Preliminary data for 2007. *National Vital Statistics Reports* 57 (12): 1–23.

Harper, E., R. Baldwin, and B. Gansneder. 2001. Full-time women faculty off the tenure track: Profile and practice. *Review of Higher Education* 24 (3): 237–257.

Hartmann, K., M. Viswanathan, R. Palmieri, G. Gartlehner, J. Thorp, and K. N. Lohr. 2005. Outcomes of routine episiotomy. *Journal of the American Medical Association* 293:2141–2148.

Harvard University, Office of the Senior Vice Provost for Faculty Development and Diversity. 2006. *Guidelines for faculty maternity and paternity leave.* Cambridge, Mass.: Harvard University. Retrieved from http://www.provost.harvard.edu/policies_guidelines/Maternity_and_Parental_Leave_Guidelines.pdf.

Hausman, B. L. 2003. *Mother's milk: Breastfeeding controversies in American culture.* New York: Routledge.

Hayes, E. 2000. Social contexts. In E. Hayes and D. D. Flannery, eds., *Women as learners: The significance of gender in adult learning,* 23–52. San Francisco: Jossey-Bass.

Hays, S. 1996. *The cultural contradictions of motherhood.* New Haven, Conn.: Yale University Press.

Heeding the calls of a new professoriate. 2008. Special issue of *Women's Studies in Communication* 31 (2).

Henry, A. 1995. Growing up black, female, and working class: A teacher's narrative. *Anthropology & Education Quarterly* 26:279–305.

Hequembourg, A. L. 2007. Becoming lesbian mothers. *Journal of Homosexuality* 53 (3): 153–180.

Hewlett, S. 2002. *Creating a life: Professional women and their quest for children.* New York: Hyperion.

Heymann, J. 2000. *The widening gap: Why America's working families are in jeopardy and what can be done about it.* New York: Basic Books.

Heymann, J., A. Earle, and J. Hayes. 2005. *The work, family, and equity index: How does the United States measure up?* Montreal: Project on Global Working Families.

Hicks, S. 2006. Genealogy's desire: Practices of kinship amongst lesbian and gay foster-carers and adopters. *British Journal of Social Work* 36:761–776.

Hirshman, L. 2006. *Get to work: A manifesto for women of the world.* New York: Viking Press.

Hochschild, A. 1997. *The time bind: When work becomes home and home becomes work.* New York: Holt Paperbacks.

——. 2007. The emotional geography of work and family life. In S. J. Ferguson, ed., *Shifting the Center: Understanding Contemporary Families,* 683–697. New York: McGraw Hill.

Hochschild, A. R. and A. Machung. [1989] 2003. *The second shift.* New York: Penguin Books.

Hofferth, S. L., L. Reid, and F. L. Mott. 2001. The effects of early childbearing on schooling over time. *Family Planning Perspectives* 33 (6): 259–267.

Hollenshead, C. S., B. Sullivan, and G. C. Smith. 2005. Work/family policies in higher education: Survey data and case studies of policy implementation. *New Directions in Higher Education* 130:41–65.

Hollingsworth, L. D. 1997. Effect of transracial/transethnic adoption on children's racial and ethnic identity and self-esteem: A meta analytic review. *Marriage & Family Review* 25:99–130.

——. 2000. Adoption policy in the United States: A word of caution. *Social Work* 45:183–186.

Home, A. M. 1998. Predicting role conflict, overload, and contagion in adult women university students with families and jobs. *Adult Education Quarterly* 48 (2): 85–97.

Hondagneu Sotelo, P. 1992. Overcoming patriarchal constraints: The reconstruction of gender relations among Mexican immigrant women and men. *Gender and Society* 6 (3): 393–415.

hooks, b. 1981. *Ain't I a woman: Black women and feminism.* Boston: South End Press.

——. 1995. *Killing rage. Ending racism.* New York: Henry Holt.

——. 2003. *Teaching community: A pedagogy of hope.* New York: Routledge.

Hornig, L., ed. 2003. *Equal rites, unequal outcomes: Women in American research universities.* New York: Kluwer Academic/Plenum.

Huh, N. S. and W. K. Reid. 2000. Intercountry, transracial adoption, and ethnic identity. *International Social Work* 43:75–87.

Ingold, C. and S. E. Searing, eds. 2007. Gender issues in information needs and services. Special issue of *Library Trends* 56.

Jackson, L. D. 2008. Reflections on obstacles and opportunities: Suggestions for improving the retention of female faculty. *Women's Studies in Communication* 31 (2): 226–232.

Jacobs, J. A. 2004. The faculty time divide. *Sociological Forum* 19 (1): 3–27.

Jaggar, A. 2001. Is globalization good for women? *Comparative Literature* 53 (4): 298–314.

Johnson, R. G. and G. L. A. Harris, eds. 2010. *Women of color in leadership: Taking their rightful place.* San Diego: Birkdale.

Johnson, V. D. 2003. A comparison of European and African-based psychologies and their implications for African American college student development. *Journal of Black Studies* 33 (6): 817–829.

Jordan-Zachery, J. 2008. *Black women, cultural images, and social policy.* New York: Routledge.

Kartik, N. 2009. Strategic communication with lying costs. *Review of Economic Studies* 76:1359–1395.

Kendall-Tackett, K. A. and M. Sugarman. 1995. The social consequences of long-term breastfeeding. *Journal of Human Lactation* 11 (3): 179–183.

Kennelly, I. and R. M. Spalter-Roth. 2006. Parents on the job market: Resources and strategies that help sociologists attain tenure-track jobs. *American Sociologist* 37 (4): 29–49.

Kent, D. 2008. Student search skills using library online resources: A small study. *Alki: The Washington Library Association Journal* 24 (3): 19–21.

Kinser, A. 2008. Embracing the tensions of a maternal erotic. In A. Kinser, ed., *Mothering in the third wave*, 119–125. Toronto: Demeter Press.

Kirby, E. L. and K. J. Krone. 2002. "The policy exists but you can't really use it": Communication and the structuration of work–family policies. *Journal of Applied Communication Research* 30 (1): 50–77.

Kirmeyer, S., J. Martin, M. Osterman, and R. A. Sheperd. 2009. Born a bit too early: Recent trends in late preterm births. *National Center for Health Statistics Data Brief* 24:1–8.

Knox College. 2011. Leave policies. Retrieved from http://www.knox.edu/offices-and-services/academic-affairs/faculty-handbook/iii-faculty-personnel-policies/i-leave-policies.html.

Koro-Ljungberg, M. and S. Hayes. 2006. The relational selves of female graduate students during academic mentoring: From dialogue to transformation. *Mentoring & Tutoring* 14 (4): 389–407.

Korosec, T. 2003. 1-hour arrest: When does a snapshot of a mother breast-feeding her child become kiddie porn? Ask the Richardson police. *Dallas Observer News*, April 17. Retrieved from http://www.dallasobserver.com/2003-04-17/news/1-hour-arrest.

Kuperberg, A. 2009. Motherhood and graduate education: 1970–2000. *Population Research Policy Review* 28:473–504.

Kurtz-Costes, B., L. A. Helmke, and B. Ülkü-Steiner. 2006. Gender and doctoral studies: The perceptions of Ph.D. students in an American university. *Gender and Education* 18 (2): 137–155.

Lake, Ricki, and Abby Epstein. 2009. *Your Best Birth: Know All Your Options, Discover the Natural Choices, and Take Back the Birth Experience.* New York: Grand Central Life & Style.

Landry, B. 2007. *Race, gender, and class: Theory and methods of analysis.* Upper Saddle River, N.J.: Prentice Hall.

Lareau, A. 2003. *Unequal childhoods: Class, race, and family life.* Berkeley: University of California Press.

Latina Feminist Group. 2001. *Telling to live: Latina feminist testimonios.* Durham: Duke University Press.

Lee, R. M. 2003. The transracial adoption paradox: History, research, and counseling implications of cultural socialization. *The Counseling Psychologist* 31 (6): 711–734.

Lewis, H. 2001. *Universal mother: Transnational migration and the human rights of black women in the Americas.* Iowa City: University of Iowa College of Law.

Lippincott, J. 2004. New library facilities: Opportunities for collaboration. *Resource Sharing and Information Networks* 17 (1–2): 147–157.

Loder, T. L. 2005. Women administrators negotiate work–family conflicts in changing times: An intergenerational perspective. *Educational Administration Quarterly* 41 (5): 741–776.

Long, S. 1992. Measures of sex differences in scientific productivity. *Social Forces* 71 (1): 159–178.

Loomis, S. and J. Rodriguez. 2009. Institutional change and higher education. *Higher Education* 58 (4): 475–489.

Lorde, A. 1981. The master's tools will never dismantle the master's house. In C. Moraga and G. Anzaldúa, eds., *This bridge called my back,* 98–101. New York: Women of Color Press.

——. 1984. *Sister outsider: Essays and speeches by Audre Lorde.* Freedom, Pa.: Crossing Press.

Lundquist, J., J. Misra, E. Holmes, A. Templer, and S. Agiomavritis. 2010. Family benefits at the University of Massachusetts–Amherst: An assessment. Retrieved from http://people.umass.edu/misra/ Joya_Misra/Work-Life_Research_files/Benefits%20Report%203–4-2010final.pdf.

Lynch, K. D. 2008. Gender roles and the American academe: A case study of graduate student mothers. *Gender and Education* 20 (6): 585–605.

Madge, C. and H. O'Connor. 2005. Mothers in the making? Exploring liminality in cyber/space. *Transactions of the Institute of British Geographers* 30 (1): 83–97.

Mailick Seltzer, M., J. Greenberg, F. Floyd, Y. Pettee, and J. Hong. 2001. Life course impacts of parenting a child with a disability. *American Journal on Mental Retardation* 106 (3): 265–286.

Mancing, H. 1991. Teaching, research, service: The concept of faculty workload. *ADFL Bulletin* 22 (3): 44–50.

Maranto, C. L. and A. E. C. Griffin. 2011. The antecedents of a "chilly climate" for women in higher education. *Human Relations* 62 (2): 139–159.

Mason, M. A. 2008. Frozen eggs. *Chronicle of Higher Education,* November 21. Retrieved from http://chronicle.com/article/Frozen-Eggs/45842.

——. 2009a. A bad reputation. *Chronicle of Higher Education*, February 6. Retrieved from http://chronicle.com/article/A-Bad-Reputation/44843.

——. 2009b. Balancing act: Rethinking the tenure clock. *Chronicle of Higher Education*, May 29. Retrieved from http://chronicle.com/article/Rethinking-the-Tenure-Clock/44268.

——. 2009c. Men and mothering. *Chronicle of Higher Education*, February 24. Retrieved from http://chronicle.com/article/MenMothering/44863.

——. 2011. The pyramid problem. *Chronicle of Higher Education*, March 9. Retrieved from http://chronicle.com/article/The-Pyramid-Problem/126614.

Mason, M. A. and E. M. Ekman. 2007. *Mothers on the fast track: How a new generation can balance family and careers*. Oxford: Oxford University Press.

Mason, M. A. and M. Goulden. 2002. Do babies matter? The effect of family formation on the lifelong careers of academic men and women. *Academe* 88 (6): 21–27.

——. 2004a. Do babies matter (Part II)? Closing the baby gap. *Academe* 90 (6): 10–15.

——. 2004b. Marriage and baby blues: Redefining gender equity in the academy. *Annals of the American Academy of Political and Social Science* 596 (1): 86–103.

Mason, M., A. Stacy, M. Goulden, C. Hoffman, and K. Frasch. 2005. *University of California faculty family friendly edge: An initiative for tenure-track faculty at the University of California*. Berkeley: University of California. Retrieved from http://ucfamilyedge.berkeley.edu/ucfamilyedge.pdf.

Massachusetts Department of Elementary and Secondary Education. 2011. *METCO Program*. Boston: Massachusetts Department of Elementary and Secondary Education. Retrieved from http://www.doe.mass.edu/metco.

Massachusetts Institute of Technology. 2003. Faculty family policies. Retrieved from http://web.mit.edu/facfamily/policies/policies.pdf.

——. 2006. Policies for family care for faculty. Retrieved from http://web.mit.edu/faculty/benefits/familycare.pdf.

Massachusetts Society of Professors (MPS). 2010. Parental leave policy. Retrieved from http://www.umass.edu/msp/id94.htm.

McBrier, D. 2003. Gender and career dynamics within a segmented professional labor market: The case of law academia. *Social Forces* 81 (4): 1201.

McCarver, V. 2011. The rhetoric of choice and 21st-century feminism. *Women's Studies in Communication* 34:20–41.

McElrath, K. 1992. Gender, career disruption, and academic rewards. *Journal of Higher Education* 63 (3): 269–281.

McGuire, G. M. and J. Reger. 2003. Feminist co-mentoring: A model for academic professional development. *Feminist Formations* 15 (1): 54–72.

McLaren, P. 2000. *Che Guevara, Paulo Freire, and the pedagogy of revolution*. New York: Rowman & Littlefield.

Medved, C. E. and J. Heisler. 2002. A negotiated order exploration of critical student–faculty interactions: Student-parents manage multiple roles. *Communication Education* 51 (2): 105–120.

Michailidis, M. P. 2008. Gender-related work stressors in tertiary education. *Journal of Human Behavior in the Social Environment* 17 (1–2): 195–211.

Misra, J., A. Templer, and J. Hickes-Lundquist. 2010. *Work-time, housework, care-work, and work–life balance.* Report to the University of Massachusetts Joint Administration/MSP Work–Life Committee. Amherst: University of Massachusetts. Retrieved from http://people.umass.edu/misra/Joya_Misra/Work-Life_Research_files/Worktimefinal.pdf.

Moberg, K. and R. Francis. 2003. *The oxytocin factor: Tapping the hormone of calm, love, and feeling.* Cambridge, Mass.: Da Capo Press.

Modern Language Association (MLA). 2007. *Do's and don'ts for MLA convention interviews.* New York: MLA. Retrieved from http://www.mla.org/jil_jobseekers_dos.

Mohanty, C. T. 2003. *Feminism without borders: Decolonizing theory, practicing solidarity.* Durham: Duke University Press.

Monosson, E., ed. 2008. *Motherhood, the elephant in the laboratory: Women scientists speak out.* Ithaca: Cornell University Press.

Monroe, K., S. Ozyurt, T. Wrigley, and A. Alexander. 2008. Gender equality in academia: Bad news from the trenches and some possible solutions. *Perspectives on Politics* 6 (2): 215–233. Retrieved from http://www.apsanet.org/imgtest/Perspectives Jun08MonroeEtal.pdf.

Moody, J. 2004. *Faculty diversity: Problems and solutions.* New York: Routledge.

Moraga, C. 2000. *Loving in the war years: Lo que nunca pasó por sus labios.* 2nd ed. Boston: South End Press.

——. 2008. Still fighting in the still war years. Lecture, Wellesley College, November 8, audiorecorded.

Morton, P. 1991. *Disfigured images: The historical assault on Afro-American women.* Westport, Conn.: Praeger.

Mottarella, K. E., B. A. Fritzsche, S. N. Whitten, and D. Bedsole. 2009. Exploration of "good mother" stereotypes in the college environment. *Sex Roles* 60:223–231.

Nash, J. 2005. Women in between: Globalization and the new enlightenment. *Signs* 31 (1): 145–167.

National Center for Education Statistics. 2011. *The Condition of Education 2011.* Washington, D.C.: U.S. Department of Education.

Nelson, C. 1997. Between meltdown and community: Crisis and opportunity in higher education. *Minnesota Review* 48:249–258.

Nussbaum, M. 2006. *Frontiers of justice: Disability, nationality, species membership.* Cambridge, Mass.: Belknap Press.

O'Brien Hallstein, D. L. 2008. Silences and choice: The legacies of white second wave feminism in the new professoriate. *Women's Studies in Communication* 1 (2): 143–150.

O'Laughlin, E. M. and L. G. Bischoff. 2005. Balancing parenthood and academia: Work/family stress as influenced by gender and tenure status. *Journal of Family Issues* 26:79–106.

Olson, E. 2007. In reversal, student is given extra exam time to pump breast milk. *New York Times*, September 27. Retrieved from http://www.nytimes.com/2007/09/27/education/27exam.html.

O'Meara, K. 2007. *Balancing work and family: A study of parental leave and the experiences of academic parents at the University of Massachusetts, Amherst.* Amherst: Massachusetts Society of Professors' Work and Family Committee.

O'Reilly, A. 2010a. Introduction. In A. O'Reilly, ed., *21st century motherhood: Experience, identity, policy, agency*, 2–24. New York: Columbia University Press.

——. 2010b. Outlaw(ing) motherhood: A theory and politic of maternal empowerment for the twenty-first century. *Hecate* 36 (1–2): 17–29.

O'Rourke, M. 2011. *The long goodbye.* New York: Riverhead Books.

Ortiz, A., ed. 1996. *Puerto Rican women and work: Bridges in transnational labor.* Philadelphia: Temple University Press.

Osterman, M. J. K. and J. A. Martin. 2011. Epidural and spinal anesthesia use during labor. *National Vital Statistics Reports* 59 (5): 1–16.

Ottinger, C. and R. Sikula. 1993. Women in higher education: Where do we stand? *Research Briefs* 4 (2): 9–10.

Padilla, R. and R. Chávez, eds. 1993. *The leaning ivory tower: Latino professors in American universities.* Albany: State University of New York Press.

Page, M. and D. Clawson. 2009. Building an activist union: The Massachusetts Society of Professors. *Thought and Action* 25 (Fall): 127–139.

Panofsky, R. 2007. Professor/mother: The uneasy partnership. *FEMSPEC* 8 (1–2): 65–74.

Pardo, M. S. 1998. *Mexican American women activists: Identity and resistance in two Los Angeles communities.* Philadelphia: Temple University Press.

Parreñas, R. S. 2001. *Servants of globalization: Women, migration, and domestic work.* Stanford: Stanford University Press.

——. 2005. *Children of global migration: Transnational families and gendered woes.* Stanford: Stanford University Press.

Patterson, G. A. 2008. Managing motherhood and tenure. *Diverse: Issues in Higher Education* 25 (20): 16–18.

Patton, L. D. 2009. My sister's keeper: A qualitative examination of mentoring experiences among African American women in graduate and professional schools. *Journal of Higher Education* 80 (5): 510–537.

Patton, S. 2000. *Birth marks: Transracial adoption in contemporary America.* New York: New York University Press.

Pearson, A. 2003. *I don't know how she does it.* New York: Anchor Press.

Pearson, A. F. 2010. The erosion of college access for low-income mothers. In A. O'Reilly, ed., *21st century motherhood: Experience, identity, policy, agency*, 216–233. New York: Columbia University Press.

Pérez, E. 1999. *The decolonial imaginary: Writing Chicanas into history.* Bloomington: Indiana University Press.

Pérez, M. 2009. The cost of being born at home. *RH Reality Check: Reproductive & Sexual Health and Justice*, March 19. Retrieved from http://www.rhrealitycheck.org/blog/2009/03/19/the-cost-being-born-at-home.

—— 2011. Birth(ing) justice. *Radical Doula*, August 11. Retrieved from http://radical-doula.com/2011/08/11/birthing-justice.

Perlesz, A., J. Power, R. Brown, R. McNair, M. Schofield, M. Pitts, A. Barrett, and A. Bickerdike. 2010. Organizing work and home in same-sex parented families: Findings from the work love play study. *Australian and New Zealand Journal of Family Therapy* 31 (4): 374–391.

Perry-Jenkins, M., R. Repetti, and A. C. Crouter. 2000. Work and family in the 1990s. *Journal of Marriage and the Family* 62 (4): 981–998.

Pew Hispanic Center. 2004. *National survey of Latinos: Education.* Washington, D.C.: Pew Research Center. Retrieved from http://pewhispanic.org/reports/report.php?ReportID=25.

Philipsen, M. I. 2008. *Challenges of the faculty career for women: Success and sacrifice.* San Francisco: Jossey-Bass.

Porpora, T. n.d. Breaking the glass: Working mothers attack the glass ceiling. Retrieved rom http://workingmoms.about.com/od/yourcareer/a/Breaking-The-Glass-Ceiling.htm.

Powell, K. A. and K. Wilson. 2000. *Living Miracles: Stories of Hope from Parents of Premature Babies.* New York: St. Martin's.

Probert, B. 2005. "I just couldn't fit it in": Gender and unequal outcomes in academic careers. *Gender, Work, and Organization* 12 (1): 50–72.

Prpic, K. 2002. Gender and productivity differentials in science. *Scientometrics* 55 (1): 27–58.

Pugh, L. 2005. *Managing 21st century libraries.* Lanham, Md.: Scarecrow Press.

Putnam, R. 2001. *Bowling alone: The collapse and revival of American community.* New York: Simon & Schuster.

Raddon, A. 2002. Mothers in the academy: Positioned and positioning within discourses of the "successful academic" and the "good mother." *Studies in Higher Education* 27:387–403.

Radford University. 2010. The "her-story" listserv project. Retrieved from http://www.radford.edu/~ewebster2/Her-Story.htm.

Record, A. and R. Green. 2008. Examining gender issues and trends in library management from the male perspective. *Library and Administration Management* 22 (4): 193–198.

Reviere, R. and A. Nahal. 2005. Finding our place: Women's studies at Howard University. *NWSA Journal* 17 (2): 150–155.

Richards, A. 2007. *Opting in: Having a child without losing yourself.* New York: Farrar, Strauss, and Giroux.

Richards, P. 2007. Risk. In H. S. Becker, *Writing for social scientists: How to start and finish your thesis, book, or article,* 2nd ed., 108–120. Chicago: University of Chicago Press.

Ricigliano, L. and R. Houston. 2003. Men's work, women's work: The social shaping of technology in academic libraries. Paper presented at the Association of College and Research Libraries Eleventh National Conference, Charlotte, N.C., April 10–13. Retrieved from http://www.pla.org/ala/mgrps/divs/acrl/events/pdf/ricigliano.pdf.

Ríos, P. N. 1990. Export-oriented industrialization and the demand for female labor: Puerto Rican women in the manufacturing sector, 1952–1980. *Gender and Society* 4 (3): 321–337.

Romack, K. 2011. Women's studies in the "post-feminist" university. *Feminist Formations* 23 (1): 235–256.

Roos, P. 2010. Not so separate spheres. *Contexts* 9 (4): 58–60.

Ropers-Huilman, B., ed. 2003a. *Gendered futures in higher education: Critical perspectives for change.* Albany: State University of New York Press.

Ropers-Huilman, B. 2003b. Gender in the future of higher education. In B. Ropers-Huilman, ed., *Gendered futures in higher education: Critical perspectives for change,* 1–12. Albany: State University of New York Press.

Ross, A. 2009. *Nice work if you can get it: Life and labor in precarious times.* New York: New York University Press.

Rothman, B. K. 2005. *Weaving a family: Untangling race and adoption.* Boston: Beacon Press.

Ryan, W. 1976. *Blaming the victim.* New York: Vintage Books.

Safa, H. 1995. *The myth of the male breadwinner: Women and industrialization in the Caribbean.* Boulder: Westview Press.

Salzinger, L. 2003. *Genders in production: Making workers in Mexico's global factories.* Berkeley: University of California Press.

Sandler, B. 1986. *The campus climate revisited: Chilly for women faculty, administrators, and graduate students.* Washington, D.C.: Association of American Colleges. Retrieved from http://www.hws.edu/offices/provost/pdf/campus_climate2.pdf.

Sandoval, A. 1999. Building up our resistance: Chicanas in academia. *Frontiers: A Journal of Women's Studies* 20 (1): 86–92.

Sandoval, C. 2002. *Methodology of the oppressed.* Minneapolis: University of Minnesota Press.

Santa Clara University. 2011. *Department of human resources: Paid family leave.* Santa Clara, Calif.: Santa Clara University. Retrieved from http://www.scu.edu/hr/benefits/leaves.cfm.

Segura, D. 2003. Navigating between two worlds: The labyrinth of Chicana intellectual production in the academy. *Journal of Black Studies* 34 (1): 28–51.

Silva, E. B. 1996. *Good enough mothering? Feminist perspectives on lone motherhood.* New York: Routledge.

Silverthorne, S. 2009. Understanding users of social networks. Harvard Business
School, September 14. Retrieved from http://hbswk.hbs.edu/item/6156.html.

Skandera-Trombley, L. E. 2003. The facts of life for an administrator and a mother.
Chronicle of Higher Education, September 5. Retrieved from http://chronicle.
com/article/The-Facts-of-Life-for-an-Ad/20333.

Smith, G. and J. A. Waltman. 2006. *Designing and implementing family friendly
policies in higher education.* Ann Arbor: Center for the Education of Women,
University of Michigan. Retrieved from www.cew.umich.edu/sites/default/files/
designing06.pdf.

Solorzano, D. G. and D. Delgado Bernal. 2001. Examining transformational resistance through a critical race and LatCrit theory framework: Chicana and Chicano students in an urban context. *Urban Education* 36 (3): 308–342.

Sorcinelli, M. D. and J. P. Near. 1989. Relations between work and life away from
work among university faculty. *Journal of Higher Education* 60 (1): 59–81.

Southwest Breastfeeding Task Force New Mexico. 2009. Southwest New Mexico
Breastfeeding Council update, October 15. Retrieved from http://breastfeeding-
newmexico.org/Local_Chapter_Southwest.html.

Souto-Manning, M. and N. Ray. 2007. Beyond survival in the ivory tower: Black and
brown women's living narratives. *Equity and Education* 40 (4): 280–290.

Spelman, E. 1988. *Inessential woman: Problems of exclusion in feminist thought.* Boston: Beacon.

Springer, K. W., B. C. Parker, and C. Deviten-Reid. 2009. Making space for
graduate student parents: Practice and politics. *Journal of Family Issues*
30:435–457.

Stack, C. B. 1975. *All our kin: Strategies for survival in a black community.* New York:
Harper & Row.

Stanford School of Medicine. 2000. *Faculty Handbook.* Stanford: Stanford School
of Medicine. Retrieved from http://med.stanford.edu/academicaffairs/handbook/
chapt10.html.

Stephen, L. 1997. *Women and social movements in Latin America.* Austin: University
of Texas Press.

Stockdell-Giesler, A. and R. Ingalls. 2007. Faculty mothers. *Academe* 93 (4): 38–40.

Stone, P. 2007a. *Opting out? Why women really quit careers and head home.* Berkeley: University of California Press.

——. 2007b. The rhetoric and reality of "opting out." *Contexts* 6 (4): 14–19.

Stout, P., J. Staiger, and N. Jennings. 2007. Affective stories: Understanding the lack
of progress of women faculty. *NWSA Journal* 19 (3): 124–144.

Swanson, D. H. and D. Johnston. 2003. Mothering in the ivory tower. *Mothering in the academy* 5 (2): 63–75.

Tatonetti, L. 2004. "A kind of queer balance": Cherrie Moraga's Aztlán. *MELUS* 29 (2): 227–247.

Teele, J. E. 2002. *E. Franklin Frazier and black bourgeoisie.* Columbia: University of Missouri Press.

Texas A&M University. n.d. Women's Faculty Network. Retrieved from http://wfn. tamu.edu/general.php.

Thierry, D., E. Viera, P. Diaz, and R. Dunn. 2007. Influence of motherhood on the implicit academic self-concept of female college students: Distinct effects of subtle exposure to cues and directed thinking. *European Journal of Psychology of Education* 22 (3): 371–386.

Timmers, T. M., T. M. Willemsen, and K. G. Tijdens. 2010. Gender diversity policies in universities: A multi-perspective framework of policy measures. *Higher Education* 59:719–735.

Toro-Morn, M. 1995. Gender, class, family, and migration: Puerto Rican women in Chicago. *Gender and Society* 9 (6): 712–726.

——. 2001. Yo era muy arriesgada: A historical overview of the work experiences of Puerto Rican women in Chicago. *Centro Journal* 8 (2): 25–43.

——. 2005. Boricuas en Chicago: Gender and class in the migration and settlement of Puerto Ricans. In C. T. Whalen and V. Vázquez-Hernández, eds., *The Puerto Rican diaspora: Historical perspectives*, 128–150. Philadelphia: Temple University Press.

——. 2008. Beyond gender dichotomies: Toward a new century of gendered scholarship in the Latina/o experience. In H. Rodriguez, R. Saenz, and C. Menjivar, eds., *Latinas/os in the United States: Changing the face of America*, 277–293. New York: Springer.

——. 2010. Migrations through academia: Reflections of a tenured Latina professor. In C. C. Robinson and P. Clardy, eds., *Tedious journeys: Autoethnograpy by women of color in academe*, 63–96. New York: Peter Lang.

Townsley, N. C. and K. J. Broadfoot. 2008. Care, career, and academe: Heeding the calls of a new professoriate. *Women's Studies in Communication* 31 (2): 133–142.

Traina, C. L. H. 2000. Maternal experience and the boundaries of Christian sexual ethics. *Signs: Journal of Women in Culture and Society* 25 (2): 369–405.

Trinidad-Galván, R. 2001. Portraits of *mujeres desjuiciadas*: Womanist pedagogies of the everyday, the mundane, and the ordinary. *International Journal of Qualitative Studies in Education* 14 (5): 161–179.

Tuchman, G. 2009. *Wannabe U: Inside the corporate university.* Chicago: University of Chicago Press.

Tuhiwai Smith, L. 2001. *Decolonizing methodologies: Research and indigenous peoples.* Dunedin, New Zealand: University of Otago Press.

Truitt, F., M. Hanna, L. Martinez, M. del Carmen Salazar, and R. Griffin. 2009. Teaching in the line of fire: Faculty of color in the academy. *Thought and Action* 25 (Fall): 65–74.

Udel, L. 2001. Revision and resistance: The politics of native women's motherwork. *Frontiers* 22:43–62.

United Nations Educational, Scientific, and Cultural Organization (UNESCO). 2002. *Women in management and higher education: A good practice handbook.* Paris: UNESCO.

University of California–Berkeley. 2003. *Leaks in the academic pipeline for women.* Berkeley: University of California. Retrieved from http://ucfamilyedge.berkeley. edu/leaks.html.

University of Colorado–Boulder. 2001. *Faculty recruitment and retention task force report.* Boulder: University of Colorado. Retrieved from http://www.colorado. edu/AcademicAffairs/fac_recruit/index.html.

University of Maine. 2009. *Alternatives-to-teaching duties associated with the birth or adoption of a child.* Orono: University of Maine. Retrieved from http://www. umaine.edu/hr/family/faculty_options_alt_teach.htm.

University of Nebraska–Lincoln. 2009. *Promoting academic excellence at UNL: Faculty resources for work–life integration.* Lincoln: University of Nebraska. Retrieved from http://www.unl.edu/svcaa/faculty/policies/work_life_balance.shtml.

U.S. Congress Joint Economic Committee. 2010. *Women and the economy 2010: Twenty-five years of progress but challenges remain.* Washington, D.C.: U.S. Congress. Retrieved from http://www.dol.gov/wb/media/Women_and_the_ Economy_2010_-25_Years_of_Progress_But_Challenges_Remain%5B1%5D .pdf.

U.S. Department of Labor. 2010. *Women in the labor force in 2010.* Washington, D.C.: U.S. Department of Labor. Retrieved from http://www.dol.gov/wb/fact-sheets/Qf-laborforce-10.htm.

Valenzuela, A. 1999. *Subtractive schooling: U.S.–Mexican youth and the politics of caring.* Albany: State University of New York Press.

——. 2002. Reflections on the subtractive underpinnings of education research and policy. *Journal of Teacher Education* 53 (3): 235–241.

Valverde, L. A. and L. A. Castenell, eds. 1998. *The multicultural campus: Strategies for transforming higher education.* Walnut Creek, Calif.: Altamira Press.

Vancour, M. L. and W. M. Sherman. 2010. Academic life balance for mothers: Pipeline or pipe cream? In A. O'Reilly, ed., *21st century motherhood: Experience, identity, policy, agency,* 234–246. New York: Columbia University Press.

Vanderbilt University. 2009. *Office of the vice chancellor and general counsel: Faculty manual.* Nashville: Vanderbilt University. Retrieved from http://www.vanderbilt. edu/facman/facman_final.pdf.

Van Stone, N., J. R. Nelson, and J. Niemann. 1994. Poor single mother college students' view on the effect of some primary sociological and psychological belief factors on their academic success. *Journal of Higher Education* 65:571–584.

Varallo, S. 2008. Motherwork in academe: Intensive caring for the millennial student. *Women's Studies in Communication* 31 (2): 151–157.

Villenas, S. 2006. Pedagogical moments in the borderland: Latina mothers teaching and learning. In D. Delgado Bernal, C. A. Elenes, F. E. Godinez, and S. Villenas, eds., *Chicana/Latina education in everyday life: Feminista perspectives on pedagogy and epistemology*, 147–159. Albany: State University of New York Press.

Walker, K. 1990. Class, work, and family in women's lives. *Qualitative Sociology* 13 (4): 143–150.

Ward, K. and L. Wolf-Wendel. 2004. Academic motherhood: Managing complex roles in research universities. *Review of Higher Education* 27 (2): 233–257.

Warner, J. 2006. *Perfect madness: Motherhood in the age of anxiety.* New York: Riverhead Books.

Warner, S. 2010. The tender track. In E. C. Mayock and D. Radulescu, eds., *Feminist activism in academia: Essays on personal, political and professional change*, 176–189. Jefferson, N.C.: Farland.

Washington University in St. Louis. 2009. Association of Women Faculty. Retrieved from http://awf.wustl.edu/about.

West, M. and J. Curtis. 2006. Organizing around gender equity. *AAUP faculty gender equity indicators 2006.* Retrieved from http://www.aaup.org/AAUP/pubsres/research/geneq2006toc.htm.

Wiegand, W. 1998. Mom and me: A difference in information values. *American Libraries* 29 (7): 56–59.

Williams, J. C. 2000. How the tenure track discriminates against women. *Chronicle of Higher Education*, October 27. Retrieved from http://chronicle.com/article/How-the-Tenure-Track/46312.

——. 2002. How academe treats mothers. *Chronicle of Higher Education*, June 17. Retrieved from http://chronicle.com/article/How-Academe-Treats-Mothers/46133.

Williams, J. C. and D. L. Norton. 2008. Building academic excellence through gender equity. *American Academic* 4:185–205.

Williams, J. C. and N. Segal. 2003. Beyond the maternal wall: Relief for caregivers who are discriminated against on the job. *Harvard Law Journal of Law and Gender* 26 (Spring): 77–162. Retrieved from http://www.law.harvard.edu/students/orgs/jlg/vol26/williams.pdf.

Williams, M., D. Brewley, R. J. Reed, D. White, and R. Davis-Haley. 2005. Learning to read each other: Black female graduate students share their experiences at a white Research 1 institution. *Urban Review* 37 (3): 181–199.

Wilson, R. 1999. Timing is everything: Academe's annual baby boom. *Chronicle of Higher Education*, June 25. Retrieved from http://chronicle.com/article/Timing-Is-Everything-Acade/2635.

——. 2004a. A journal's special issue on "mothering in the academy." *Chronicle of Higher Education*, April 9. Retrieved from https://chronicle.com/article/Paid-Leave-at-Public-Colleges/19209.

——. 2004b. Where the elite teach, it's still a man's world. *Chronicle of Higher Education*, December 3.

——. 2005. The law of physics: A postdoc's pregnancy derails her career. *Chronicle of Higher Education*, November 11.

——. 2008. More colleges offer part-time options for professors. *Chronicle of Higher Education*, July 18. Retrieved from http://chronicle.com/article/More-Colleges-Are-Adding-Fa/14530.

Wolf-Wendel, L. and K. Ward. 2003. Future prospects for women faculty: Negotiating work and family. In B. Ropers-Huilman, ed., *Gendered futures in higher education: Critical perspectives for change*, 111–134. Albany: State University of New York Press.

——. 2006. Academic life and motherhood: Variations by institutional type. *Higher Education* 52 (3): 487–521.

World Health Organization (WHO). 2007. *Maternal mortality in 2005: Estimates developed by WHO, UNICEF, UNFPA, and the World Bank*. Geneva: WHO.

Yantzi, N. and N. Rosenberg. 2008. The contested meaning of home for women caring for children with long-term care needs in Ontario, Canada. *Gender, Place, and Culture* 15 (3): 301–315.

Yoest, C. C. 2004. *Parental leave in academia*. Charlottesville: University of Virginia. Retrieved from http://faculty.virginia.edu/familyandtenure/institutional%20report.pdf.

Yoest, C. C. and S. E. Rhoads. 2002. What if . . . parenthood wasn't a professional peril on the tenure track? Must academics parent and perish? Paper presented at the annual meeting of the American Association of Public Policy Analysis and Management, Dallas, November 9–11.

Yosso, T. J. 2005. Whose culture has capital? A critical race theory discussion of community cultural wealth. *Race Ethnicity and Education* 8 (1): 69–91.

Zanardo, V., G. Svegliado, F. Cavallin, A. Giustardi, E. Cosmi, P. Litta, and D. Trevisanuto. 2010. Elective cesarean delivery: Does it have a negative effect on breastfeeding? *Birth* 37 (4): 275–279.

Zimmerman, T., J. Aberle, J. Krafchick, and J. Harvey. 2008. Deconstructing the "mommy wars": The battle over the best mom. *Journal of Feminist Family Therapy* 20 (3): 203–219.

CONTRIBUTORS

Vanessa Adel is a doctoral candidate in sociology at the University of Massachusetts–Amherst.

Lisa Baker-Webster is associate professor in the School of Communication at Radford University.

Tamara Mose Brown is assistant professor in the Department of Sociology at Brooklyn College, City University of New York.

Brenda K. Bushouse is associate professor in the Department of Political Science and the Center for Public Policy and Administration at the University of Massachusetts–Amherst.

Devin C. Carey is a doctoral candidate in the Department of Psychology at Loyola University–Chicago.

Mari Castañeda is associate professor in the Department of Communication and the Center for Latin American, Caribbean, and Latino Studies and director of diversity advancement of the College of Social and Behavioral Sciences at the University of Massachusetts–Amherst.

Colleen S. Conley is assistant professor in the Department of Psychology at Loyola University–Chicago.

Summer R. Cunningham is a doctoral candidate and Presidential Fellow in the Department of Communication at the University of South Florida.

Erynn Masi de Casanova is assistant professor in the Department of Sociology at the University of Cincinnati.

Barbara A. W. Eversole is assistant professor in the Department of Human Resource Development and Performance Technologies at Indiana State University.

Sandra L. French is associate professor in the School of Communication at Radford University.

Susana L. Gallardo, Ph.D., is a lecturer in the Department of Interdisciplinary Social Sciences at San Jose State University and a lecturer in Chicana/o studies at Stanford University.

Darlene M. Hantzis is professor in the Department of Communication and the Women's Studies Program at Indiana State University.

Orlee Hauser is assistant professor of sociology and women's studies at the University of Wisconsin–Oshkosh.

Margaret Hostetler is associate professor of English at the University of Wisconsin–Oshkosh.

Kirsten Isgro is assistant professor in the Department of Communication Studies at the State University New York–Plattsburgh.

Michelle Kuhl is associate professor in the Department of History at the University of Wisconsin–Oshkosh.

Virginia L. Lewis is associate professor of German and chair of the Department of Languages, Literature, and Communication Studies at Northern State University.

Irene Mata is assistant professor in the Department of Women's and Gender Studies at Wellesley College.

Allia A. Matta is a faculty member at LaGuardia Community College, City University of New York, and a doctoral candidate in the W. E. B. Du Bois Department of Afro-American Studies at the University of Massachusetts–Amherst.

Larissa M. Mercado-López, Ph.D., is a lecturer in women's studies at the University of Texas–San Antonio.

Michelle Mouton is associate professor in the Department of History at the University of Wisconsin–Oshkosh.

Gilda Baeza Ortego is the university librarian at Western New Mexico University.

Olivia Perlow is assistant professor in the Department of Sociology and faculty in the African and African American Studies Program and the Women's Studies Program at Northeastern Illinois University.

Kim Powell is professor in and head of the Department of Communication Studies and professor in the Department of Women and Gender Studies at Luther College.

Mandy A. Reid is associate professor in the Department of English and the Women's Studies Program at Indiana State University.

Druscilla Scribner is associate professor in the Department of Political Science at the University of Wisconsin–Oshkosh.

Tracy Slagter is assistant professor in the Department of Political Science at the University of Wisconsin–Oshkosh.

Maura I. Toro-Morn is the director of the Latin American and Latino Studies Program and professor of sociology and anthropology at Illinois State University.

J. Estrella Torrez is assistant professor in the Residential College in the Arts and Humanities at Michigan State University.

Wendy K. Wilde is the administrator for the Department of Sociology at the University of Massachusetts–Amherst.

INDEX

absence, power of, 18

academia: Chicanas in, 78, 80, 123–124; children in, 134; commercialization of, 7; and community connections, 131, 132; corporatization of, 65; hierarchy of, 4–5; mat(t)erring, 34–35; men's lifestyles in, 154; patriarchy in, 123, 132; political economy of, 12; role of secretary in, 37–42; from secretary to student in, 42; women in, 2, 113; women in workforce in, 228; women's bodies in, 30, 36; work environment of, 178, 180

academic cultures, need for inclusive, 3–8

academic mothers, 56; in administration, 55; bodily hungers of, 28–29; departmental support for, 166–167, 169; experiences managing of, 161–162; family support of, 223; friendships of, 172; marginalization of, 218; normative narrative of, 164; single, 164; social support networks for, 174–179; stigma of, 161; strategies of, 11; transgressing academic culture, 165–168; transgressing time, 162–165

academic work, 204; flexibility of, 18, 20. *See also* parental leave

Acevedo, Luz, 102

Acker, Joan, 214

Acker, Sandra, 223

Adel, Vanessa, 79

administration, academic: choosing to move to, 53–54; demographics of, 168. *See also* higher education administration

administrative positions, faculty in, 167

adoption: decision making for, 88–89, 90; foster-to-adoption route for, 86; and inclusion, 87; politics of transracial, 85–86

ADVANCE grant program, of NSF, 218

African American children, 86–87, 143

African American families, 139

African Americans, and colleges/ universities, 112

African American women, 112, 146; in academia, 113; contrasted with white women, 115; maternal mortality of, 96. *See also* black women

agency, diminished, 163

Aisemberg, Nadya, 174